40¢

Fiscal Federalism

Fiscal Federalism

WALLACE E. OATES
Princeton University

Under the General Editorship of
William J. Baumol *Princeton University*

HARCOURT BRACE JOVANOVICH, INC.
New York Chicago San Francisco Atlanta

ISBN: 0–15–527452–X

Library of Congress Catalog Card Number: 78–185772

Printed in the United States of America

60,709

Preface

The ever-mounting budgetary difficulties of state and local governments in the United States and, more generally, of decentralized governments in a great number of countries have generated a renewed and serious concern with the problem of intergovernmental fiscal relations. In the United States, President Nixon has called for a "New Federalism" with a supposed heavy reliance on state and local fiscal decisions combined with federal assistance in the form of revenue sharing. Likewise, in another federal country, Canada, a comprehensive re-evaluation of the Dominion-Provincial fiscal structure is under way. This fiscal concern is by no means limited to countries with federal constitutions; for instance, a recent White Paper by the Heath Government in the United Kingdom proposes a redrawing of jurisdictional lines and a new definition of the fiscal responsibilities of different levels of government. Strong pressures for the restructuring of the public sector are evident today in countries with diverse forms of government and at widely differing stages of economic development.

While some of these pressures are primarily political in nature, it seems clear that they also stem, in great measure, from the fact that the existing structure of the public sector has failed to perform its economic functions properly. The progressive deterioration of public services in many of our cities, growing budgetary deficits, and the continually rising levels of state and local taxation have convinced many observers that something is wrong with the alignment of fiscal functions among different levels of government. This has led in some instances to attempts to form new units, such as metropolitan governments, to cope with these problems.

The central issue in this book is what the basic principles of economics have to say about all this. The increasing interest in intergovernmental fiscal problems has led over the past decade to a growing body of economic literature on fiscal federalism. There is yet to appear, however, a comprehensive theoretical and empirical treatment of the economics of federalism—a study that both explores what economic theory implies about the division of fiscal functions among levels of government, and examines the extent to which such a theoretical structure can explain the organization and workings of the public sectors of different countries.

These are the objectives of this book. It attempts first to set forth the economic theory of public finance under a federal system of government. The approach is simply to apply the standard tools of economic analysis and see what they imply about the proper economic structure of the public sector. Second, it begins to explore the extent to which such a theory can provide insights into the actual operation of systems of multi-level finance. The issue here is to determine whether fiscal systems are in fact structured and whether they function as the theory suggests they should. While, as many political scientists have stressed, the fiscal structure of a particular country is no doubt largely the result of the unique political and social history of that nation, it may still be true that certain types of economic incentives have a predictable impact on the structure and operation of the public sector.

The introduction to the book sets forth the underlying framework for the study. It describes briefly the conceptual structure developed by Richard Musgrave for viewing the functions of the public sector as a whole and then presents some preliminary observations on an economist's view of a federal system. This sketch provides a useful point of departure for Chapter One, which examines the relative strengths of highly centralized and decentralized governments in performing the basic economic tasks of the public sector. From this analysis emerges the conclusion that, *in economic terms*, federalism represents the optimal form of government.

This leads in Chapter Two to the central issue of fiscal federalism: the appropriate degree of decentralization of a particular public sector. This problem requires a careful examination of the division of fiscal functions among levels of government. As a point of reference, Chapter Two constructs a highly simplified, essentially normative model of the public sector. In this pure model there is a clear division of functions among levels of government, one that leads to the attainment of a welfare optimum. However, as soon as we relax some of the highly restrictive and unrealistic assumptions of the simple model, matters rapidly become a good deal more complicated. Several of the resultant problems are discussed in Chapter Two, and their resolution, it is argued, suggests the need for certain intergovernmental fiscal programs, particularly for grants-in-aid from the central government to subcentral government units.

Chapter Three is devoted to this issue of intergovernmental grants. It attempts to evaluate the roles of both conditional and unconditional grants in achieving an efficient use of resources and a just distribution of income; the conclusions of the analysis are then compared to the actual use of such grants in federal countries. Next, Chapter Four considers the problems of taxation and debt finance in a multilevel public sector; there we find that the constraints resulting from the openness of local economies imply that the problems of taxation are a good deal more difficult at the local level than at the central level of government. In particular, this suggests that the central government should perhaps play a relatively important role in the collection of revenues, and at the same time employ a system of grants or revenue sharing that permits a substantial retention of expenditure responsibilities by more decentralized levels of government.

Chapter Five shifts the focus to an empirical study of a number of hypotheses suggested by the earlier analysis. More specifically, it attempts to determine the extent to which the theoretical structure developed in this study can explain the structure and operations of actual fiscal systems. The results are frankly somewhat mixed; there is, however, sufficient correspondence between theory and practice on some issues to suggest that the theory does help us understand more about how fiscal systems actually work.

In the concluding chapter, we move away from what has been essentially an exercise in comparative statics to a consideration of the dynamics of federalism. The concern here is the development of fiscal federalism over time, and the chapter offers an evaluation of the hypothesis that federalism is simply a transitional stage in a process of continuing centralization leading to a unitary form of government. The evidence does not seem to support this proposition, although it is clear that some basic changes have occurred (and are occurring) in the organization and functioning of federal fiscal systems.

Throughout the analysis, I have made liberal use of appendices to develop a number of important problems more rigorously and in greater depth. Thus, in some instances, I may state a theorem or the conclusions of an argument in the text, giving only an intuitive justification for the proposition, and then refer the reader who wishes a more thorough treatment to the appendix. I hope that in this way I have made the book accessible to those with a modest background in economic analysis. Accordingly, it should be suitable for use in junior- and senior-level courses in public finance that have as a prerequisite a one-year course in economic principles, with exposure to a text such as Samuelson's *Economics* and to basic regression analysis. On the other hand, some of the theoretical work and much of the empirical analysis is new and will, I hope, be of interest to those engaged in research on fiscal federalism.

Finally, I wish to acknowledge the generous assistance of a number of people in this undertaking. First, I am grateful to Professors Ronald McKinnon, John Gurley, and Edward Shaw of Stanford University who, a number of years ago, helped me with my dissertation; it was my first venture into particular problems in fiscal federalism. Second, for their careful reading of, and most helpful comments on, early drafts of the manuscript, I am deeply indebted to Professors William Baumol and David Bradford of Princeton University. Third, I want to thank several students who provided valuable research assistance along the way: Yukon Huang, Stephen Buser, Robert Plotnick, and Peter Garber. Fourth, I express my appreciation to Carolyn Johnson and Louise Hockett of Harcourt Brace Jovanovich for their excellent editorial help with the manuscript. And fifth, I thank Cathy and Chris for their assistance with the proofs.

Wallace E. Oates

Contents

Introduction

Before beginning the analysis of the division of economic functions among the different levels of government, it is important to explain just what these functions are. The approach adopted in this study is based upon Richard Musgrave's widely used conceptualization of the role of the public sector.[1] Within the framework of modern welfare economics, the effectiveness of an economic system is measured by the degree to which the system provides an equitable distribution of income and an efficient allocation of resources. A genuine state of optimality in this setting requires both that income be distributed justly and that resources be employed in the most efficient manner.

From this perspective, Musgrave has argued that a free-market economy with no government sector is likely to malfunction in three basic ways. First, even if a free-market system were to operate at full employment and were to direct all resources into their most efficient use, there is no particular reason to believe that the distribution of income that emerged from this process would be an equitable one. The distribution

---

[1] *The Theory of Public Finance* (New York: McGraw-Hill, 1959), ch. 1.

of income generated in a competitive system depends upon the ownership of the various resource inputs and upon the whole structure of prices and outputs in the economy, and it is highly unlikely that this particular pattern of income distribution would be regarded by society as the most desirable one. Consequently, it would be only by accident that a no-government economy would lead to a welfare optimum. This, Musgrave argues, implies the need for public policy to attain the socially desired distribution of income among individuals in the economy.

Second, as Keynes taught us, a wholly unregulated economy will not necessarily generate high and stable levels of output and employment. The level of aggregate spending in the private sector will not generally call forth full employment with stable prices. Therefore, such an economy will tend to be characterized by periods of waste caused by idle resources, and at other times by the inefficiencies and inequities generated by excessive spending and the resulting price inflation. Another job of the public sector is, therefore, to employ its tools of fiscal and monetary policy to maintain the economy at high levels of output and employment with reasonable stability in the overall level of prices.

Third, in the absence of a public sector, certain misallocations of resource use among alternative goods and services are likely. The familiar problem of externalities including various types of public goods, decreasing-cost industries, and market imperfections may lead to excessive levels of some activities and insufficient levels of others.[2] As a result, public action in the form of unit taxes or subsidies to induce efficient behavior or, in some instances, actual public provision of certain goods and services will be necessary to ensure an efficient pattern of resource use.

In summary, the public sector has three primary economic problems to resolve if the system is to approach a welfare optimum: the attainment of the most equitable distribution of income (the distribution problem); the maintenance of high employment with stable prices (the stabilization problem); and the establishment of an efficient pattern of resource use (the allocation problem). This last problem, incidentally, in-

---

[2] An excellent study of the sources of allocative inefficiency in a market system is available in Francis Bator, "The Anatomy of Market Failure," *Quarterly Journal of Economics*, vol. 72 (Aug., 1958), pp. 351–79.

cludes ensuring that the economy achieves an efficient allocation of resources through time or, in other words, an efficient rate and pattern of growth.

The conceptual distinction among these three functions of the public sector should not, however, be allowed to obscure their fundamental interdependence. At a purely formal level, the determination of a welfare optimum requires a simultaneous solution for the distribution of income and the allocation of resources. Moreover, at a policy level, practically any public problem will have an impact on the realization of all three of the objectives of public policy. An expenditure on a new public school building, for example, entails a shift in resource allocation to educational services, a redistribution of income in favor of both the owners of those resources used in construction activity and the recipients of the educational services provided by the new school and, finally, an expansion in the level of aggregate demand. This means that, while Musgrave's analytical framework may prove extremely useful for a theoretical study of public finance, one often encounters serious difficulties in the use of this approach to examine actual fiscal institutions and programs; in the area of intergovernmental grants, for example, it is frequently very hard to disentangle the allocative and redistributive objectives and effects contained within a single program.

Nevertheless, Musgrave's conceptual structure does provide a very convenient point of departure for a theoretical study of public finance in a federal system. In particular, the analysis begins by contrasting the strengths and weaknesses, in terms of performing Musgrave's tasks, of a completely centralized fiscal system with those of a highly decentralized public sector. From this analysis a powerful economic case for federalism emerges, because a federal structure of the public sector promises the greatest success in resolving the allocation, distribution, and stabilization problems.

I should stress here that the view of federalism adopted in this study is considerably broader than the one usually employed by political scientists. Kenneth C. Wheare, for example, in his classic study of federalism, was able to identify only four genuinely federal systems of government (and among those four he was willing to grant Canada only "quasi-federal" status).[3] For an economist, however, constitutional and politi-

---

[3] *Federal Government*, 4th ed. (London: Oxford University Press, 1964).

cal structures are of less importance: what is crucial for him is simply that different levels of decision-making do exist, each of which determines levels of provision of particular public services in response largely to the interests of its geographical constituency. By this definition, practically any fiscal system is federal or at least possesses federal elements. And this is not surprising, for decentralized finance has such compelling advantages for some functions that one would not expect to find a total reliance on centralized decision-making on fiscal matters. For this reason, a study of fiscal federalism has relevance for almost all fiscal systems.

*We should also know over which matters
several local tribunals are to have jurisdiction,
and in which authority should be centralized*

Aristotle, POLITICS 4.15

Chapter one
An economic approach to federalism

The federal system was created with the intention of combining the different advantages which result from the magnitude and the littleness of nations

Alexis de Tocqueville, DEMOCRACY IN AMERICA

The functions of the public sector are to ensure an efficient use of resources, to establish an equitable distribution of income, and to maintain the economy at high levels of employment with reasonable price stability. The concern in this chapter is the organization of the public sector that will best allow the government to perform these tasks. In short, the question is, What form of government promises the greatest success in resolving the allocation, distribution, and stabilization problems? To get at this issue, it is useful to consider at a conceptual level two polar or nearly polar forms of government. At one end of the spectrum is complete centralization: a unitary form of government. In this case, the central government, in the absence of other levels of government, assumes full responsibility for the three economic functions of the public sector. As we move in the opposite direction on this spectrum of governmental forms, we approach total decentralization of government. For my purposes, it is useful to stop a bit short of total decentralization, which would presumably represent a state of anarchy. Rather, let us consider as our opposite extreme a highly decentralized system in which the central government is almost completely devoid of economic responsibility. In this instance, a system of small local governments performs virtually all the economic tasks of the public sector. In both cases, however, the society under consideration is understood to be a nation with a single currency and with an absence of restrictions on the movements of goods and services within the system. The sole difference in the two cases is the extent of decentralization of the public sector.

While these cases, especially the latter, are admittedly highly unrealistic (and this in a way is the point), it is instructive to consider briefly the relative economic advantages of the two alternatives. From such an examination, a powerful economic case for federalism emerges.

The economic case for centralized government

An examination of the stabilization problem suggests that a centralized, or unitary, form of government would possess a far greater capability to maintain high levels of employment with stable prices than would a public sector characterized by extreme decentralization. At the outset, it is obvious that there must exist a central agency to control the size of the money supply. If, in contrast, each level of government was able to create and destroy money, there would exist an irresistible incentive to rapid monetary expansion. By simply using a printing press, any local government could create paper with which to purchase real goods and services from neighboring communities. It would clearly be in the interest of each municipality to finance its expenditures by creating money rather than by burdening its own constituents with taxation. The likely outcome would be rampant price inflation; for this reason, some form of centralized monetary control is imperative.

Without access to monetary policy, local governments would have to rely on fiscal policy—that is, expenditure and revenue programs—to stabilize their respective economies. The scope, however, for an efficacious fiscal policy is severely limited. First, small local economies are, in general, highly open economies, as their constituents typically purchase a large portion of the goods and services they consume from other localities.

4

This implies that the leakages from a marginal dollar of private spending are likely to be quite large. As a result, in a simple Keynesian system, the expenditure multiplier (that is, the reciprocal of the sum of the marginal propensity to save and the marginal propensity to import out of income) will tend to be quite small.[1] Much of the expansionary impact of a local tax cut, for example, will be dissipated, since only a relatively small proportion of the new income generated will be spent on locally produced goods and services.

In the appendix to this chapter, local government fiscal policy is analyzed in terms of a local income-and-payments model. In addition to the flows of goods and services included in simple Keynesian systems, this model also allows for the effects of movements of financial assets in response to trade flows; these movements may be of substantial size and importance in small, highly open local economies. In such a system, the constraints on an effective local stabilization policy stand forth very clearly. One finds, for example, that the multiplier effects associated with local government tax and expenditure programs are typically very small, even smaller than those implied by simpler models.

Second, the use of Keynesian deficit-finance policies to stimulate the local economy carries with it a cost to local residents, a cost that is largely absent for such policies at the national level. The cost stems from the nature of local government debt. Within a national economy, there normally exists a high degree of mobility of financial capital; debt issued in one community is generally held to a large extent by residents of other communities. This means, as Alvin Hansen and Harvey Perloff have pointed out, that the use of debt finance by a local government will tend to saddle the community with an external debt.[2] In later years, repayment of principal and interest will necessitate a transfer of real income from the residents of the community to outsiders. In contrast, since the international mobility of capital is normally far less than that which exists

[1] A derivation and discussion of the multiplier effect in an open economy appear in Paul T. Ellsworth, *The International Economy*, third ed. (New York: Macmillan, 1964), ch. 15.
[2] *State and Local Finance in the National Economy* (New York: W. W. Norton, 1944), pp. 194–200. For an alternative view of the relative burden of internal and external debt on later generations, see James Buchanan, *Public Principles of Public Debt: A Defense and Restatement* (Homewood, Ill.: Richard D. Irwin, 1958).

within a nation, interest-bearing debt issued by the central government will take the form primarily of an internal debt. The central government is thus in a position to stimulate the economy without burdening society with the prospect of future income transfers to outsiders.

The logic therefore suggests that, as regards the stabilization problem, a unitary form of government is distinctly superior to a government organization exhibiting an extreme degree of decentralization. A central government is in a position to make good use both of monetary and of fiscal policy in maintaining the economy at high levels of output without excessive inflation. Local governments, in contrast, are seriously constrained in their capacity to regulate the aggregate level of economic activity in their jurisdictions. Moreover, it should be stressed that, among a highly interdependent group of local economies, movements in levels of business activity tend to parallel one another. Contractions or booms in some areas are rapidly communicated to neighboring areas through a contracted or increased demand for exports. This means that cyclical movements in aggregate economic activity are largely national in scope and as such can best be treated by countercyclical policies operating on a nationwide scale.

As in the case of the stabilization problem, the resolution of the distribution problem is a difficult matter in a system characterized by a high degree of decentralization of the public sector. Suppose that the members of society desire a more egalitarian distribution of income than that which emerges from the unfettered operation of the market system.[3] Assume, moreover, that the socially desired distribution of income is one in which the disposable income of each individual or family depends only on the unit's level of income before any redistributive taxes and transfers. The idea here is simply that the desired distribution of income requires the transfer of certain amounts of income from the wealthy to the poor, and the tax paid, or, alternatively, the subsidy received, by a particular individual depends solely on his level of income. In this case, the program required to achieve society's desired pattern of

[3] There is, incidentally, no necessary reason why society should desire the distribution of income to be more (rather than less) equal than that which would come about in the absence of public redistributive activities. This supposition is, rather, based on the observation that explicitly redistributive programs are, almost without exception, at least intended to result in a more equal distribution of income.

6

income distribution is clearly a negative income tax. The existing distribution of income can be translated into the desired one by adopting a certain tax-subsidy schedule by which higher-income units pay taxes that are distributed in the prescribed pattern to lower-income units.[4]

The difficulty is that within the highly decentralized fiscal system, local governments working independently to achieve differing redistributional objectives are likely to run into real trouble. Consider, for example, a community that adopts a strong negative income-tax program designed to achieve a significantly more equalitarian distribution of income than exists in the rest of the nation. Such a program, in view of the relatively high degree of individual mobility that characterizes a national economy, would create strong incentives for the wealthy to move out to neighboring municipalities and for the poor to migrate into the community. A more nearly equal distribution of income might well result, but it would be caused largely by an outflow of the rich and an influx of the poor, with a consequent fall in the level of per-capita income in the community under consideration.[5]

The curious part is that this could happen even if all the members of the community, including the wealthy, genuinely desired to eliminate poverty through an explicitly redistributive policy. Every individual might stand willing to vote for a negative income tax program, and yet, if any one person perceived an avenue through which he could avoid his own con-

[4] The reason for taking some care to make all this explicit is that economists frequently talk about the redistribution of income through lump-sum taxes and transfers. Such redistributive activities presumably have no adverse incentive effects (for example, the introduction of a wedge between the gross and net wage rates). However, if the objective is to effect transfers from those with high incomes to those with low incomes, a tax-subsidy scheme based on income levels—in other words, a negative income tax—is obviously required. If income levels are to be the basis for redistributive programs, there is no way to avoid influencing work-leisure incentives unless one assumes some sort of model in which work effort is fixed or, more generally, in which the individual has no control over the level of income he receives. This points up the further fact that in moving from the existing to the preferred distribution of income, society must take into account the effects the redistributive programs themselves may have on the aggregate level of income.

[5] This constraint on local redistributive activity has been emphasized by George Stigler, "Tenable Range of Functions of Local Government," in Joint Economic Committee, Subcommittee on Fiscal Policy, *Federal Expenditure Policy for Economic Growth and Stability* (Washington, D. C.: 1957), pp. 213–19.

tribution to the program, it might well be in his interest to do so. The point is that the contribution of any single person or family to the general elimination of poverty in a society is likely to be negligible. There is, therefore, a real incentive for so-called free-rider behavior by which an individual would leave to others the burden of financing redistributive programs.[6] For this reason, the migration of relatively wealthy individuals from a locality that adopts an aggressive redistributive program may be perfectly consistent with a general commitment on the part of that society to a policy aimed at reducing or eliminating poverty.

The scope for redistributive programs is thus limited to some extent by the potential mobility of residents, which tends to be greater the smaller the jurisdiction under consideration. This suggests that, since mobility across national boundaries is generally much less than that within a nation, a policy of income redistribution has a much greater promise of success if carried out on the national level. A unitary form of government is therefore likely to be far more effective in achieving the redistributional objectives of the society than is a governmental organization at the opposite end of the spectrum.

Turning last to the allocation problem, one finds again that, for a certain class of goods and services, a highly centralized government is likely to be far more successful in providing appropriate levels of output than is a system of local governments. It is the responsibility of the public sector as a whole either to institute incentives for private production or, alternatively, to provide directly appropriate levels of output of those goods and services not forthcoming in efficient quantities through the operation of free markets. Some of these goods and services may be of such a character that they confer, or could confer, significant benefits on everyone in the nation. Consider, for example, a pure public good [7] whose benefits

[6] For an excellent treatment of the free-rider problem, see James Buchanan, *The Demand and Supply of Public Goods* (Chicago: Rand McNally, 1968), ch. 5.

[7] A pure public good is one that by its very nature is consumed jointly and in the same quantity by all consumers. The point is that for something like clean air, once it becomes available to one individual, it is by implication also available to others. This means that, if the quantity X_i of such a good enters into the ith person's utility function, the same quantity must also enter as an argument in the utility functions of other consumers. See Paul Samuelson, "The Pure Theory of Public Expenditure," *Review of Economics and Statistics*, vol. 36 (Nov., 1954), pp. 387–

extend to the individuals in all communities. The production of X units of the commodity in one community implies that X units are consumed by the residents of all municipalities. A rough approximation to such a commodity might be a missile system established by one community that is bound by an alliance to other communities to regard an attack on one as an attack on all. Under these circumstances, a missile system in any single community would serve as a deterrent to a potential aggressor against any of the others, for the enemy would have to expect missile retaliation should he invade any of the localities. In this case, then, a missile system in one community serves as a substitute for a similar system in a neighboring jurisdiction.

For such a public good, is a system of decentralized decision-making likely to result in the efficient level of output of the commodity? Will the individual communities, each seeking to maximize the welfare of its own constituents, end up providing a missile system such that the cost of a marginal missile is equal to the sum of the values placed on that missile by the residents of all the communities? The answer, as Mancur Olson and Richard Zeckhauser have shown, is generally no.[8] The reason is that each community in determining whether it will or will not produce an additional unit of the good (that is, another missile implacement) considers only the benefits its own residents will receive from the marginal unit. As a result, the full social value of an additional unit of the good is not taken into consideration. As Olson and Zeckhauser explain it, a subefficient output results

> because each ally gets only a fraction of the benefits of any collective good that is provided, but each pays the full cost of any additional amounts of the collective good. This means that individual members of an alliance or international organization have an incentive to stop providing the collective good long before the Pareto optimal [that is, economically efficient] output for the group has been provided. This is particularly true of the smaller members who get smaller shares of the total benefits

89; Richard Musgrave, *The Theory of Public Finance* (New York: McGraw-Hill, 1959), pp. 73–86; and John Head, "Public Goods and Public Policy," *Public Finance*, vol. 17, no. 3 (1962), pp. 197–219.
[8] "An Economic Theory of Alliances," *Review of Economics and Statistics*, vol. 48 (Aug., 1966), pp. 266–79.

accruing from the good, and who find that they have little or no incentive to provide additional amounts of the collective good once the larger members have provided the amounts they want for themselves, with the result that the burdens are shared in a disproportionate way.[9]

The one special case in which an efficient output may be attained is where the various communities have an agreement to share the cost of an additional unit of the good in the same proportion as they share the benefits. In this case, all communities would be willing to support the production of an additional missile site if the value of the marginal missile exceeded its cost. However, in general, one would expect such public goods to be underproduced in a system of decentralized decision-making. In contrast, under a unitary form of government, assuming that public decision-makers seek to maximize the welfare of the entire citizenry, the value of a marginal unit of the public good to members of all the communities would presumably be taken into account. One would therefore expect a central government to provide a better approximation to the efficient level of output of those public goods that benefit the members of all communities than would a system of decentralized decision-making.[10]

The preceding discussion suggests that a unitary form of government has several important advantages over its counterpart at the opposite end of the spectrum. In a system comprising only local governments, the public sector would be seriously handicapped in its capacity to meet its economic responsibilities. Local governments, I have argued, would find it extremely difficult to stabilize their respective economies, to realize the most equitable distribution of income, and to provide efficient levels of output of those public goods that confer benefits on the members of all or several communities. A cen-

[9] *Ibid.*, p. 278.
[10] This is admittedly a simplified view of what is really quite a complicated issue. While an official of the central government is presumably in a better position to take into account the welfare of all members of the society, it doesn't necessarily follow that he will do so. He will have his own set of objectives which might, in some instances for example, lead him purposely to disregard the effects of a particular program on certain uninfluential minorities. A useful approach to and analysis of some of these issues is available in Roland McKean, *Public Spending* (New York: McGraw-Hill, 1968), ch. 2.

tral government, in contrast, is much more capable of performing these tasks satisfactorily. Nonetheless, a system of local governments does possess attractive economic attributes to which we turn next.

The economic case for decentralized government

A basic shortcoming of a unitary form of government is its probable insensitivity to varying preferences among the residents of the different communities. If all public goods are supplied by a central government, one should expect a tendency toward uniformity in public programs across all communities. The problem here is that the level of consumption of a public good almost always involves compromise. Some individuals may prefer an expanded and high-quality program of public services, while others may want less public output and the accompanying reduced level of taxes. For truly national public goods (that is, those goods all individuals consume in identical quantities regardless of their community of residence), such compromise is inevitable. However, for other public goods whose benefits are limited to a specific subset of the population (for example, the members of a single community), there is at least a partial solution in greater decentralization of the public sector.

Consider, for example, a public good whose consumption is limited to the residents of the community in which it is provided. If provided by the central government, the most likely outcome would be similar levels of consumption of the good in all communities. However, such uniform levels of consumption may not be efficient, because they do not take into consideration possible variations in the tastes of residents of differing communities. If, in contrast, each community had its own local government, one might expect variations in the level of provision of this public good across the different localities, variations that would, to some extent at least, reflect the differences in tastes of the constituencies of the communities. The point here is that economic efficiency is attained by providing the mix of output that best reflects the preferences of the individuals who make up society, and if all individuals are compelled to consume the same level of output of a good when

11

variations in individual consumption—or, in this case, variations in consumption among different subsets of the population—are possible, an inefficient allocation of resources is the likely result. A decentralized form of government therefore offers the promise of increasing economic efficiency by providing a range of outputs of certain public goods that corresponds more closely to the differing tastes of groups of consumers.

The possibilities for welfare gains through decentralization are further enhanced by the phenomenon of consumer mobility. As Charles Tiebout has argued, in a system of local government, a consumer can to some extent select as his place of residence a community that provides a fiscal package well suited to his preferences.[11] One can envision a system of local governments where, for example, each community provides a different level of consumption of a local public good and in which the consumer by "voting on foot" selects the community that provides the level of public output that best satisfies his tastes. Through this mechanism, one can get a sort of market solution to the problem of producing efficient levels of output of some public goods. A decentralized form of government thus possesses the advantage of allowing various levels of output of certain public goods, by means of which resources can be employed more efficiently in satisfying the preferences of consumers.

Decentralization may, moreover, result in greater experimentation and innovation in the production of public goods. With a large number of independent producers of a good, one might expect a variety of approaches (for example, varying techniques of instruction in local public schools) that, in the long run, promises greater technical progress in modes of providing these goods and services. Closely connected to this point are the competitive pressures that result from an enlarged number of producers; such pressures will tend to compel the adoption of the most efficient techniques of production. If, for example, public officials in one community have discovered a particularly effective way of providing a certain service, the governments of neighboring jurisdictions will, in all probability, be compelled to adopt similar techniques of production in order to avoid serious criticism from local residents. In

[11] "A Pure Theory of Local Expenditures," *Journal of Political Economy*, vol. 64 (Oct., 1956), pp. 416–24.

contrast, if a single central government provides all public goods with no competitors, one might well expect the forces inducing innovation and efficiency to be less strong. A system of local government may thus promote both static and dynamic efficiency in the provision of public goods and services.

Finally, there is some reason to believe that decentralization may lead to more efficient levels of public output, because expenditure decisions are tied more closely to real resource costs. If a community is required to finance its own public program through local taxation, residents are more likely to weigh the benefits of the program against its actual costs. In the United States, for instance, proposals to improve local school systems are frequently submitted to the local electorate along with a proposed increase in property tax rates to fund the program. In contrast, if funds for local public projects come wholly from a central government, residents of a given community have an incentive to expand levels of local public services as far as possible, since they may bear only a negligible part of the costs of the program. To discourage this tendency, the central government could adopt other fiscal measures; it could, for example, require a community to bear the cost of many of its own programs by varying tax rates among communities or, where possible, by employing user charges. Often, however, this is not an easy matter; the federal government in the United States, for example, is prohibited by the Constitution from levying direct taxes with rates that vary on a geographical basis.

In summary, a decentralized public sector possesses several economically desirable characteristics. First, it provides a means by which the levels of consumption of some public goods can be tailored to the preferences of subsets of the society. In this way, economic efficiency is enhanced by providing an allocation of resources that is more responsive to the tastes of consumers. Second, by promoting increased innovation over time and by providing competitive pressures to induce local governments to adopt the most efficient techniques of production, decentralization may increase both static and dynamic efficiency in the production of public goods. Third, a system of local government may provide an institutional setting that promotes better public decision-making by compelling a more explicit recognition of the costs of public programs.

The optimal form of government: a federal system

The preceding discussion suggests that both a unitary form of government and one characterized by extreme decentralization possess distinct advantages and serious shortcomings in performing the three fundamental economic tasks of the public sector. A central government can best resolve the stabilization and distribution problems, but in the absence of what I have called local governments, serious welfare losses from uniformity in the consumption of public goods and technical waste in their production are quite likely. What is clearly desirable is a form of government that combines the advantages of these two polar forms and avoids the most serious shortcomings of each; a federal organization of government meets this need.

Federalism represents, in one sense, a compromise between unitary government and extreme decentralization. In a federal system there exist both a central government and subcentral government units, each making decisions concerning the provision of certain public services in its respective geographical jurisdiction. From an economic standpoint, the obvious attraction of the federal form of government is that it combines the strengths of unitary government with those of decentralization. Each level of government, rather than attempting to perform all the functions of the public sector, does what it can do best. The central government presumably accepts primary responsibility for stabilizing the economy, for achieving the most equitable distribution of income, and for providing certain public goods that influence significantly the welfare of all members of society. Complementing these operations, subcentral governments can supply those public goods and services that are of primary interest only to the residents of their respective jurisdictions.[12] In this way, a federal form of government offers the best promise of a successful resolution of the problems that constitute the economic *raison d'être*

[12] This particular division of economic functions among levels of government is developed in my "The Theory of Public Finance in a Federal System," *Canadian Journal of Economics*, vol. 1 (Feb., 1968), pp. 37–54. Richard Musgrave has reached similar conclusions in *The Theory of Public Finance*, pp. 181–82, as has Dick Netzer in "Federal, State, and Local Finance in a Metropolitan Context," in Harvey Perloff and Lowdon Wingo, eds., *Issues in Urban Economics* (Baltimore: Johns Hopkins Press, 1968), pp. 435–40.

of the public sector. It is in this sense that federalism may, in economic terms, be described as the optimal form of government.[13]

This chapter is concerned with an overview of fiscal federalism and, pursuing the discussion at a somewhat intuitive level, deliberately ignores a number of complications. In Chapter Two, however, I will set forth more precisely an economic model of a federal system and examine in greater depth the potential of this structure of the public sector for the realization of a welfare optimum.

Before proceeding to this task, however, a closer look at the economic meaning of "federalism" is necessary. The argument presented thus far suggests that a federal structure of the public sector has, at least in economic terms, compelling advantages over alternative forms. If this is true, one would expect to find the federal structure the typical form of government. And yet, political scientist Daniel Elazar's list of federal countries numbers only sixteen nations.[14] Even this list would be considered by some to be overly inclusive; as I have mentioned in the Introduction, Kenneth C. Wheare, writing in the 1940's, was willing to grant federal status to only four nations. This suggests that the economic meaning of federalism differs in some fundamental way from its meaning to most political scientists, which is in fact the case. Therefore, in order to place the analysis in a clearer perspective, it will prove useful

[13] By design, the discussion to this point has been wholly in economic terms. As many writers have argued, however, there are also important political advantages and disadvantages accompanying a highly centralized as opposed to a more decentralized system of government. Increased centralization, for example, may allow a far more effective program of national defense and foreign policy as well as a more efficient use of scarce administrative talent; on the other hand, there are widely recognized dangers in a heavy concentration of power. Moreover, as John Stuart Mill emphasized, decentralized political institutions play an important role in "the public education of the citizens" by allowing more widespread and direct participation in the affairs of government (see Mill's *On Representative Government*). From a political as well as an economic standpoint, a federal form of government thus offers a way to realize the advantages of both centralization and decentralization. In his important study of federalism, Kenneth C. Wheare argues that "federal government . . . stands for multiplicity in unity. It can provide unity where unity is needed, but it can ensure also that there is variety and independence in matters where unity and uniformity is not essential." (From Wheare's *Federal Government*, 4th ed. [London: Oxford University Press, 1964], p. 244.)
[14] "Federalism," in David L. Sills, ed., *International Encyclopedia of the Social Sciences*, vol. 5 (New York: Macmillan, 1968), p. 365.

to examine more closely what an economist means by a federal system.

The economic meaning of federalism

In his pioneering study of federalism, which has provided the basis for much of the later work on federal political institutions, Kenneth C. Wheare defined federalism as ". . . the method of dividing powers so that the general and regional governments are each, within a sphere, co-ordinate and independent." [15] From this definition and from his observations of actual governments (largely that of the United States), Wheare was able to set forth a number of characteristics that a political system must possess in order to qualify as federal; these were primarily constitutional provisions that protected the autonomy of different levels of government. I think it is fair to say that this largely legalistic approach, though not employed in nearly so restrictive a fashion as by Wheare, has characterized much of the later work in political science on this subject.[16]

Such an approach makes a good deal of sense for a political study of federalism. Since a political scientist is interested in the division and use of power, there is real reason to exclude from the federal category a system in which, for example, the power of subcentral governments is exercised solely at the convenience of the central government. A system in which a central government merely delegates certain decision-making functions to regional or local governments will typically have a quite different power structure from one in which the scope of responsibility and independence of each level of government is carefully defined and protected by a written constitution. Related to this, Poul Meyer, among others, has been careful to distinguish between "decentralization," which represents a genuine possession of independent decision-making power by decentralized units, and "deconcentration," which implies only a delegation of administrative control to lower levels in the

---

[15] Wheare, *Federal Government*, p. 10.
[16] See, for example, Geoffrey F. Sawer, *Modern Federalism* (London: C. A. Watts, 1969). For an interesting exception to this, on which I will draw later, see William S. Livingston, "A Note on the Nature of Federalism," *Political Science Quarterly*, vol. 67 (March, 1952), pp. 81–95.

administrative hierarchy.[17] On the basis of such distinctions, political scientists have naturally been willing to recognize as federal countries only the limited number of nations in which, to a significant extent at least, different levels of government each possess an explicitly independent scope of responsibility and authority.

The problem of federalism is, however, quite different for an economist. In particular, the economist's central concerns are the allocation of resources and the distribution of income within an economic system. The structure of government is, for this reason, of interest to him only to the extent that it carries with it implications for patterns of resource use and income distribution. From this perspective, decentralization of the public sector is of importance primarily because it provides a mechanism through which the levels of provision of certain public goods and services can be fashioned according to the preferences of geographical subsets of the population. Therefore, I suggest the following *economic* definition of federalism:

Federal Government: A public sector with both centralized and decentralized levels of decision-making in which choices made at each level concerning the provision of public services are determined largely by the demands for these services of the residents of (and perhaps others who carry on activities in) the respective jurisdiction.

One element of this definition requires special comment. In contrast to the conception of federalism in political science, it makes little difference to the economist whether or not decision-making at a particular level of government is based on delegated or constitutionally guaranteed authority. What matters is simply that decisions regarding levels of provision of specified public services for a particular jurisdiction (be they made by appointed or elected officials, or directly by the people themselves through some form of voting mechanism) reflect to a substantial extent the interests of the constituency of that jurisdiction.

This is not to say, however, that constitutional provisions are wholly irrelevant to the economics of federalism. On the

[17] *Administrative Organization* (Copenhagen: Nyt Nordisk Forlag Arnold Busck, 1957), pp. 56–61.

contrary, constitutional constraints may make it quite difficult or costly in some instances for central government agencies to interfere with local government decisions. To this extent, a formally federal constitutional structure may typically result in a process of public decision-making in which local interests have a relatively major impact on choices affecting primarily the welfare of local residents. Legalistic factors may thus have a real influence on decision-making procedures. Some evidence to support this contention will be presented in Chapter 5. However, it is to be emphasized that it is the extent to which the decisions themselves reflect local interests that matters for the economist, and constitutional structure assumes importance only to the degree that it affects the responsiveness of the provision of local services to local preferences.[18]

This is obviously a far broader view of federalism than that typically employed in political science. In fact, the most useful way for an economist to approach this issue is to treat federalism not in absolute but in relative terms.[19] As suggested earlier, we can envision a spectrum of structures of the public sector along which the difference is essentially one of degree rather than kind. At one end of the spectrum is a unitary form of government with all decisions made by the central authority, and at the opposite pole is a state of anarchy. Aside from the two polar points themselves, the other positions on the spectrum represent federal organizations of the public sector moving from a greater to a lesser degree of centralization of decision-making.

This would imply, however, that *in economic terms* most if not all systems are federal. Aside from an absolute degree of centralization of decision-making—which in practice is almost impossible to imagine—the public sectors of all countries would be federal, with distinctions being made in terms of differing degrees of centralization. I think this is the most useful way to see the issue; and it explains the ease with which I was

---

[18] I am grateful to Roland McKean for emphasizing to me the influence constitutional provisions have on the degree of decentralization in economic decision-making within the public sector.

[19] This is the approach suggested by Livingston, "A Note on the Nature of Federalism." Ursula Hicks similarly contends that "in the modern world, in spite of this basic constitutional difference, the problems of central/local finance in a unitary state and in a federation differ in degree rather than in kind." (*Public Finance*, 2nd ed. [London: James Nisbet, 1955], p. 224.)

able to reach the conclusion that, from an economic perspective, a federal system is the optimal form of organization of the public sector.

Of course, the problem is that within this framework such a conclusion is a vacuous one. If all public sectors are more or less federal in structure, it is obviously tautological to say that federalism is the optimal form of government. The real issue becomes the determination of the appropriate degree of decentralization for a particular government sector. Where along this centralization spectrum should a particular public sector be?[20]

To answer this question requires matching public functions, including the provision of each public service, with appropriate levels of decision-making. This, as I see it, is the central theoretical problem of the subject of fiscal federalism: the determination of the optimal structure of the public sector in terms of the assignment of decision-making responsibility for specified functions to representatives of the interests of the proper geographical subsets of society. This suggests, moreover, that the arguments developed in this chapter, although they may have led initially to a conclusion without great substance, do take us some way into the analysis of the real problem; they indicate, in rough terms at least, a general outline for the appropriate division of fiscal functions between the central and decentralized levels of government. A more careful examination of this issue reveals, however, that the selection of the

---

[20] The discussion up to this point has not been at all precise concerning the meaning of the "degree of centralization" of the public sector. How does one place a given public sector at a particular point on this spectrum? This problem will be confronted more directly in Chapter 5, where, for empirical use, I attempt to develop some operational measures of fiscal centralization. However, some brief comments are in order here. Consider an economic system with a given number of people located in a specified geographical pattern. Limiting this system to a single public good, one could argue that one structure of the public sector is more decentralized than an alternative structure if, under the former, choices concerning levels of provision of the good are made on the basis of smaller geographical subsets of the population than under the latter. With an approach of this type, one could at least develop a ranking of the alternatives. To make this operational, however, and in particular to deal with a public sector that provides a number of public goods, an index of some type must be devised which will lead to a measure of the degree of centralization of the public sector as a whole; to construct such an index, the degree of centralization for each public service will have to be weighted in some manner according to the service's relative importance in the aggregate of public output.

proper level of government to provide a particular public good or service is not an easy problem; there are typically a number of variables that figure in this decision, and in most instances, some form of trade off between welfare gains and losses is involved. It is to the exploration of this problem that we proceed next.

Appendix

Local-government countercyclical policy[1]

This appendix will investigate in some depth the potential for efficacious stabilization policy at highly decentralized, or "local," levels of government. As noted in the text, local governments cannot have access to one of the two basic forms of stabilization policy—namely, monetary authority; the power to create and destroy money must be vested solely in the central government. This implies that, in terms of conventional stabilization measures, local governments must rely wholly on tax and expenditure programs.

A local income and payments model

In order to investigate the potential of fiscal policy at the local government level, it is useful to set forth a simple income and payments model of a local economy. The model embodies several important simplifications. I assume that each of the localities is small and highly open both in the sense that it has a high average and marginal propensity to import out of income and that the demand for its exports depends primarily on national economic conditions and can be taken as exogenously determined.

Within the nation as a whole, financial capital is treated as highly mobile. In fact, it is helpful here to adopt the polar case of "perfect" capital mobility: all securities, irrespective of locality of issue, are assumed to be perfect substitutes for one another and to move without cost among the localities. This assumption implies that interest rate differentials between communities cannot persist. In addition a locality is

[1] The analysis presented here follows closely my treatment of this problem in "The Theory of Public Finance in a Federal System," *Canadian Journal of Economics*, vol. 1 (Feb., 1968), pp. 37–54.

also small in the sense that it can be treated as a price taker in the national securities market; the rate of interest for the community is, therefore, another exogenously determined variable.

The model also includes a simple portfolio-balance argument in terms of financial assets. It must be emphasized that for small, highly open communities it is dangerous to ignore movements of financial assets in response to trade flows. An increase in local income, for example, gives rise to a relatively large increase in imports, which generates an outflow of financial assets from the community. This drain of financial assets must itself come to have a depressive effect on spending and income levels in the community.

The model is summarized in equations 1–3:[2]

(1) $C(Y_d, i_o, A) + G_o + X_o$
$- I(Y_d, i_o, A, G_o) - Y = 0$ commodities market

(2) $L(Y_d, i_o, A) - A = 0$ financial asset market

(3) $X_o - I(Y_d, i_o, A, G_o) = 0$ trade balance

where

Y = real income
Y_d = disposable income
i_o = rate of interest (exogenously determined)
X_o = flow of exports (exogenously determined)
I = flow of imports
G_o = local government expenditure (exogenously determined)
A = real value of the *net* financial asset holdings of the private sector.

The level of income and output, Y, is assumed to be perfectly elastic at the given price level and to adjust in Keynesian fashion to the level of aggregate demand. The demand in both the commodity and financial asset markets depends on disposable income, the rate of interest, and the real value of private, *net* financial asset holdings. In this regard, since local

[2] For a more extensive treatment of the derivation of a similar model, see Ronald McKinnon and Wallace Oates, *The Implications of International Economic Integration for Monetary, Fiscal, and Exchange-Rate Policy*, Princeton Studies in International Finance 16 (Princeton, N.J.: Princeton University, International Finance Section, 1966).

governments have no monetary powers and since the price of bonds in terms of money is fixed by the externally determined rate of interest, it is convenient to aggregate the money and bond markets into a single financial asset market. Private economic units still attempt to establish a portfolio balance between money and bonds, but since this can be done by trading with nonresidents at a fixed price, the model need not take explicit account of this phenomenon.

The trade-balance constraint expressed in equation 3 is a necessary condition for complete stock-and-flow equilibrium in the model. If equation 3 is not satisfied, either an inflow or outflow of financial assets is implied, which changes A and thereby disturbs any existing equilibrium in the commodity and financial asset markets. The system consists of three equations, but only two of them are independent, and they serve to determine the two dependent variables: Y and A. If, for example, equations 1 and 3 are satisfied, it follows from Walras' Law that the financial asset market must be in equilibrium.[3]

To get a feeling for the way in which the model works, consider an exogenous increase in the stock of financial assets, A. Such an injection of assets into the system has a positive wealth effect in the demand functions. As a result the local economy will have an excess demand for commodities and an excess supply of financial assets, in response to which the level of income will tend to rise. But as Y increases imports also rise, which leads to a deficit in the balance of trade. This deficit will drain the excess supply of financial assets from the economy. Note that this drain will continue until the entire increment of financial assets is absorbed, for only then will income and, therefore, imports return to their original equilibrium values and thereby restore a balance-of-payments equi-

---

[3] Walras' Law is formally an additional equation which ensures that, in an interdependent system of n markets, if there exists equilibrium in $(n - 1)$ of the markets, then supply must equal demand in the nth market. In equations 1–3, if 1 and 3 hold, it means that imports equal exports and that the aggregate demand for commodities is equal to their supply; from this it follows, by Walras' Law, that the other market in the system, the financial asset market, must also be in equilibrium. There is, incidentally, a third dependent variable in the system—namely, the level of disposable income, Y_d. This, however, is simply equal to $(Y - T)$, where for our purposes we can take T as an exogenously determined level of taxes. For the sake of simplicity, this additional equation is not included explicitly in the system.

librium. For this reason an injection of financial assets into the system results only in a temporary rise in income, for the additional assets flow out of the economy in response to a deficit in the balance of trade. This result is not surprising, for A and Y are the dependent variables in the system; assuming the model to be stable, a change in either of these variables sets to work forces that restore the initial equilibrium solution.

Local government fiscal policy

Using its fiscal tools in this system, what effect can a local government expect to have on the community's level of output and income? Because of constraints on debt issues, local governments are typically compelled to place much greater reliance on balanced-budget spending than is the central government, which has much greater latitude in the use of deficit financing. We consider first, therefore, the impact of balanced-budget spending in the local income model.

It is convenient, as a point of departure, to adopt one final set of assumptions: a set of symmetry conditions concerning the spending patterns of the public and private sectors. Specifically, I assume at the margin that government expenditures are divided between imports and commodities produced within the community in the same proportion as private expenditures. It is also assumed that the wealth effect results in a similar division of expenditures on commodities. Formally, we have:

(4) $$\partial I / \partial Y_d = \alpha [\partial C / \partial Y_d]$$

(5) $$\partial I / \partial G = \alpha$$

(6) $$\partial I / \partial A = \alpha [\partial C / \partial A]$$

where $0 < \alpha < 1$.

Consider now a balanced-budget increase ($dG = dT$) in local government spending. The immediate impact is to raise the level of spending in the locality, since the government's marginal propensity to spend is unity, while that of the private sector is assumed to be less than one. However, given our symmetry assumptions concerning the pattern of expenditures, a rise in total spending implies an increase in imports. In this way the increase in public expenditures will give rise to a deficit in the balance of trade, and an outflow of financial assets will result. This drain of financial assets from the local economy will tend to depress spending and income until the balance of trade again returns to zero. Given that X_o remains unchanged, the final equilibrium solution must involve an unchanged level of imports, for only then will the outflow of financial assets cease. This means that:

$$(7) \qquad dI = \left(\frac{\partial I}{\partial Y_d}\right) dY_d + \left(\frac{\partial I}{\partial A}\right) dA + \left(\frac{\partial I}{\partial G}\right) dG = 0.$$

Substituting equations 4–6 into 7 gives us:

$$(8) \qquad dI = \alpha \left(\frac{\partial C}{\partial Y_d}\right) dY_d + \alpha \left(\frac{\partial C}{\partial A}\right) dA + \alpha dG$$

$$= \alpha \left[\left(\frac{\partial C}{\partial Y_d}\right) dY_d + \left(\frac{\partial C}{\partial A}\right) dA\right] + \alpha dG$$

$$= \alpha dC + \alpha dG = \alpha(dC + dG) = 0.$$

Therefore,

$$(9) \qquad\qquad\qquad dC = -dG.$$

Private expenditure thus contracts by the full amount of the positive increment in government spending, and the balanced-budget multiplier is zero. If, then, the local government's pattern of spending on locally produced commodities as compared with its spending on imports is the same as that of the private sector, balanced-budget government spending simply supplants an equivalent amount of private expenditure and has no net effect on the equilibrium level of income and output.[4]

The only way the local government can influence the community's equilibrium level of income through balanced-budget

[4] In a simple Keynesian system with no balance-of-trade constraint, the standard proof that the balanced-budget multiplier is unity depends critically on the assumption that the entire increment of government spending is directed to domestically produced goods. In general, the balanced-budget multiplier in an open system is less than one, and it may even be negative. On this point, see William J. Baumol and Maurice H. Preston, "More on the Multiplier Effects of a Balanced Budget," *American Economic Review*, vol. 45 (March, 1955), pp. 140–48. It should also be noted that the above analysis abstracts from possible repercussion effects on the community's level of exports.

spending is through biasing its expenditures in favor of locally produced commodities—that is, by violating the symmetry condition in equation 5. In the limiting case where all government expenditures are directed to commodities produced at "home," the G_o argument drops out of the import demand function completely. It is clear in this case that G_o can be at any level without directly influencing the balance of trade; Y_d need no longer decline when G rises in order to keep imports equal to exports. As a result the levels of Y_d and A are determined independently of G_o. This means that, in this limiting case, the balanced-budget multiplier is unity; the equilibrium level of income rises by the amount of the increase in public expenditure so as to maintain Y_d at its previous equilibrium level.[5]

In the less extreme case, where public expenditures involve some imports but relatively less than in the private sector, the multiplier is positive but less than unity. The rationale for this result is that in such cases government spending has an "import-substitution" effect. By reducing the community's overall (public plus private) propensity to import, a higher level of income and financial asset holdings becomes consistent with any given level of exports and imports. Conversely, should the government's pattern of expenditures entail more imports than that of the private sector, the equilibrium level of income would decline, and the balanced-budget multiplier would become negative. In conclusion, given an unchanged level of exports, local government, in the balanced-budget case, can raise the equilibrium level of income and employment only to the extent that it can reduce the community's propensity to import, and even then, except in the limiting case, the balanced-budget multiplier will be less than unity.

Consider next the case where the increase in local government spending is debt financed. The initial impact of such a

---

[5] As proof that the balanced-budget multiplier is unity where $\partial I/\partial G = 0$, we have: $dT = dG$ *and* $dI = 0$;

$$dI = (\partial I/\partial Y_d)\, dY_d + (\partial I/\partial A)\, dA = 0.$$

Using symmetry assumptions in equations 4 and 6:

$$dI = \alpha dC = 0.$$

Therefore, $dC = 0$.

$$dY = dC + dG = 0 + dG = dG.$$

Thus, $dY/dG = 1$.

program on the demand for commodities is equal to the full increment of public spending, dG, for there is no reduction in disposable income from increased taxes. Income rises, a deficit in the balance of trade results, and financial assets flow out of the local economy. However, at the same time, financial assets are being pumped into the system at a rate equal to dG. A deficit in the trade balance of amount dG can therefore exist without disturbing the state of private financial asset holdings. This implies that, in the case of public deficit-finance, equation 3, the balance-of-trade constraint, must be altered to:

(10) $$(X - I) + D = 0,$$

where $D = $ the deficit in the public budget.

This is clear because if private financial asset holdings, A, are to remain unchanged (which is a necessary condition for equilibrium in the system), the new public securities entering the economy must flow out of the community.[6] The increment in government spending and the inflow of financial assets into the local economy will bid up spending until the deficit in the trade balance becomes equal to the deficit in the public budget, at which point private net financial asset holdings will cease to change further.

Income and financial asset holdings therefore rise to a level consistent with the increased level of imports. If we again adopt the symmetry conditions in equations 4–6, we have, following the argument in equations 7–9:

(11) $$dI = \alpha(dC + dG),$$

but now $dI = dG$.

Therefore,

(12) $$\alpha(dC + dG) = dG,$$

or

[6] This assumes that a resident of the community does not associate a public issue of bonds with an increase in his own liabilities. For a justification of this assumption, see my "Budget Balance and Equilibrium Income: A Comment on the Efficacy of Fiscal and Monetary Policy in an Open Economy," *Journal of Finance*, vol. 21 (Sept., 1966), pp. 491–92.

(13) $$dC = [(1 - \alpha)/\alpha]\, dG.$$

From equation 1 we obtain:

(14) $$dY = dC + dG + dX - dI = dC + dG - dG$$
$$= [(1 - \alpha)/\alpha]\, dG.$$

Therefore,

(15) $$dY/dG = (1 - \alpha)/\alpha.$$

The deficit-spending multiplier thus depends solely on the relative openness of the system; it bears no relationship to the marginal propensity to save. The more open the local economy, the less expansionary the impact of deficit spending on the equilibrium level of income. If the local economy is a highly open one with α in excess of one-half, then the multiplier is less than unity.[7] Therefore, even in the case of deficit-financed expenditures, the multiplier for a highly open local economy is not likely to be very large.[8]

The model also makes clear a most important characteristic of local government debt—namely, that it tends to flow out of the community. The deficit-spending multiplier depends on an unlimited willingness of the local government to alter its net asset position by creating an external debt for the community as a whole. Deficit spending by the central government is generally held by its citizens, but locally issued securities tend to flow outside the jurisdiction. For this reason local governments must treat this debt with considerably greater concern than need the central government, for the eventual repayment of local debt and interest charges will represent a transfer of income to nonresidents. This suggests that local governments have a real incentive for avoiding aggressive deficit-finance programs for stabilization purposes. Not only are the multiplier effects associated with the spending likely

[7] As in the case of balanced-budget spending, the multiplier is larger if the government biases its expenditures in favor of locally produced goods. In the limiting case where $\partial I/\partial G = 0$, the deficit-spending multiplier is equal to $1/\alpha$.
[8] Even in the case of a simple Keynesian system, where no consideration is given to balance-of-payments forces, the deficit-spending multiplier is not very large for a highly open economy. Specifically, the multiplier is equal to the reciprocal of the sum of the marginal propensity to save and the marginal propensity to import. If the latter is in excess of one-half, then the deficit-spending multiplier must be less than two.

to be small, but there is the further disadvantage of burdening the community with a significant external debt.[9]

The model indicates that a local government is likely to be severely constrained in its ability to influence the community's level of output and income. Local government can employ only fiscal stabilization tools, and problems of openness and external indebtedness seriously impair the freedom and effectiveness with which these tools can be used.[10]

A further difficulty regarding local government stabilization policy arises when the compensatory problem is placed in the context of the nation as a whole. The impotence of conventional fiscal measures at the local level implies that local government, if it is to influence significantly the local level of employment, must find other stabilization tools. One method with some promise is to attempt to attract new spending from external sources. In fact, in the United States the bulk of the attack by state and local governments on unemployment has taken the form of inducements to industry to locate in their state or community. To this end, these governments have adopted a wide variety of programs, including such measures as low-interest loans and tax exemptions to incoming business. However, when viewed from the national level these policies are largely of a beggar-thy-neighbor nature; they represent an attempt to attract industry and spending away from other states and localities. Such programs clearly are not suitable to remedy unemployment on a national scale.

[9] George Daly has demonstrated recently that, although local debt may be primarily an external debt, the burden of the debt will not necessarily be shifted to future residents of the community. In the absence of any fiscal illusion, potential entrants into the community will take into consideration the future tax payments implied by any existing public debt of the municipality. As a result the future tax liability may become capitalized in the form of reduced property values. If this takes place, residents of the community at the time the debt is issued will assume the full incidence of the future tax liability associated with the debt issue. See Daly's "The Burden of the Debt and Future Generations in Local Finance," *Southern Economic Journal*, vol. 36 (July, 1969), pp. 44–51.

[10] It is interesting to note that, even if a local government did have access to tools of monetary policy, it could not by these means alter the community's equilibrium level of income. As discussed earlier, an injection of any kind of financial assets into the system results in a balance-of-trade deficit, which drains the entire increment of assets from the economy. Thus, an injection of money into a local economy will not affect the equilibrium level of income. Money is neutral in this model not because changes in the stock of money induce proportional changes in the price level, but because nominal money holdings are restored to their initial equilibrium level through transactions with nonresidents.

The importance of this point is clear when one recognizes that the high degree of interdependence between communities means that movements in real income among the various localities tend to parallel one another. Recessions and booms tend to be national in scope. Under these conditions one can hardly expect that independent local programs, relying largely on beggar-thy-neighbor policies, will be able to produce an effective national stabilization program.[11]

The case for having the central government assume primary responsibility for the stabilization function appears, therefore, to rest on a firm economic foundation. Our local income and payments model suggests that local government cannot use conventional stabilization tools to much effect and must instead rely mainly on beggar-thy-neighbor policies, which from a national standpoint are likely to produce far from the desired results.[12] The central government, on the other hand, is free to adopt monetary policies and fiscal programs involving deficit finance; consequently, the stabilization problem must be resolved primarily at the central government level.[13]

[11] Stanley Engerman reaches a somewhat similar conclusion:

> Thus, as long as stabilization measures are left to particular states, there can be no expectation of an optimal national policy, for there may be either smaller or larger changes in demand than would be considered desirable. In the contemporary situation, given both financial constraints and interstate strategy, the presumption that stabilization measures will be insufficient if they are left to lower-level governments appears most reasonable.

"Regional Aspects of Stabilization Policy," in Richard Musgrave, ed., *Essays in Fiscal Federalism* (Washington, D.C.: Brookings Institution, 1965), pp. 53, 56.

[12] The conclusions reached here apply with less force to a federal system in which the communities are relatively closed, self-sufficient economies.

[13] For an application of some of these ideas to stabilization and exchange-rate policies on an international scale (both under systems of floating and fixed exchange rates), see J. M. Fleming, "Domestic Financial Policies under Fixed and under Floating Exchange Rates," *International Monetary Fund Staff Papers* (Nov., 1962), pp. 369–80; Anne Krueger, "The Impact of Alternative Government Policies under Varying Exchange Systems," *Quarterly Journal of Economics*, vol. 79 (May, 1965), pp. 195–208; Robert Mundell, "Capital Mobility and Stabilization Policy under Fixed and Flexible Exchange Rates," *Canadian Journal of Economics and Political Science*, vol. 29 (Nov., 1963), pp. 475–85; Ronald McKinnon and Wallace Oates, *The Implications of International Economic Integration;* and my "Budget Balance and Equilibrium Income: A Comment on the Efficacy of Fiscal and Monetary Policy in an Open Economy."

Chapter two
The division of functions among levels of government

In great centralized nations the legislator is obliged to give a character of uniformity to the laws, which does not always suit the diversity of customs and of districts
Alexis de Tocqueville, DEMOCRACY IN AMERICA

We turn now to a closer examination of the problem of assigning fiscal tasks to the different levels of government. As we shall see, there exist a number of factors that must be weighed against one another in the determination of the proper level of government to provide a particular public service. Moreover, the importance of some of these factors is likely to vary significantly among societies so that a public good that is best provided centrally in one country may be better provided by decentralized levels of government in another. There is thus good reason to believe that the optimal degree of fiscal decentralization will vary substantially among different societies. The theory developed in this and the preceding chapter isolates some of the determinants of the optimal degree of decentralization, and we shall, in a later chapter, study empirically the ability of these determinants to explain actual variations in the degree of fiscal decentralization among different nations.

As part of the general guidelines in Chapter One, I argued that the central government should assume primary responsibility for resolving the stabilization and distribution problems and for providing efficient outputs of those public goods that significantly affect the welfare of individuals in all jurisdictions. To place these functions at highly decentralized levels of government would in all likelihood result in undesirable levels of these types of programs. The problem in the case of a truly national public good is that decentralized jurisdictions will tend to provide subefficient levels of the good because of the failure to take into account the benefits conferred on residents of other jurisdictions. The obstacle to an efficient allocation of resources in this instance is the inability of decentralized decision-making units to appropriate the social benefits of their programs. And since outputs in other jurisdictions may serve as a substitute for the provision of the good in one's own locality, there is the further incentive to seek a free ride.

The difficulty of appropriating social benefits and the often associated free-rider problem apply to some extent to all three of the functions I have contended should be assigned to the central government.[1] This particular point is usually developed in terms of the allocation of resources to a particular public good (as in the missile example in Chapter One). However, it applies in a way to the stabilization and distribution problems as well. As regards the former, for example, the problem is that no single local government can appropriate the full income and employment benefits of an expansion in local spending; because of the openness of the local economy, the bulk of such benefits accrue to members of other jurisdictions. There is, therefore, a real incentive for any particular locality to avoid extensive countercyclical activity and to rely on whatever stabilization programs are undertaken elsewhere. As a result, one can expect insufficient levels of public countercyclical activities in a highly decentralized system of decision-making.

Similarly, although the analogy is admittedly somewhat more strained in this case, a single jurisdiction may pay a high cost in attempting to redistribute income among indi-

---

[1] John Head, among others, has pointed out that the problems of stabilizing the economy and of attaining an equitable distribution of income (as well as that of providing outputs of certain commodities) involve fundamental elements of the public-goods problem. For all these functions, an individual or business firm is unable to appropriate the full social benefits of its own activities and, at the same time, can benefit from such activities on the part of others. For this reason, Head argues that the resolution of these problems will generally require collective action. See his "Public Goods and Public Policy," *Public Finance*, vol. 17, no. 3 (1962), pp. 197–219.

viduals within its borders. Even though members of all jurisdictions may wish a more egalitarian distribution of income within the society as a whole, it requires concerted action on the part of all subcentral governments to achieve the desired result; any single local government is seriously constrained in its capacity to alter substantially the existing distribution of income. In consequence, one would not expect to find extensive redistributive activity in a highly decentralized public sector.

This does not mean that subcentral governments should totally abandon efforts in these areas. As we move up the scale from local to state to regional governments, the capacity for successful countercyclical and redistributive policies obviously grows, and we would therefore expect the degree of countercyclical and redistributive activity to vary directly with the size of the jurisdiction. The capacity for effective policy to accomplish these two tasks is, however, greatest at the central government level, and as a result it would make sense for the central government to assume primary responsibility for stabilizing the economy and for realizing the most equitable distribution of income.

The problem of assigning the responsibility for providing various public goods (that is, the resolution of Musgrave's allocation problem) is, in contrast, a good deal more complicated, and the bulk of this chapter will be devoted to this issue. In order to keep the analysis tractable, I will assume that the public sector has successfully carried out its job as regards the stabilization and distribution problems so that the economy is operating at full employment with stable prices and with the most equitable distribution of income.

An ideal case: a perfect correspondence

In determining the level of government best suited to provide a particular public service, it is useful to consider first a simple special case. Assume that there exists in the system a finite number, n, of pure public goods. Each of these goods has the Samuelsonian characteristic that all individuals in a specified group consume the good in identical quantities. In other words if X_i of the ith public good is produced, X_i enters into the utility function of all individuals in the group that consumes the good.[2] In addition, the level of consumption of the good is independent of the number of consumers. For my purposes, the crucial characteristic of these goods is that the consumption of each good is defined over a specific geographical subset of the total population. At one extreme we have those public goods that are consumed in equal quantities by all members of the society (that is, a national public good);[3] at the other are those goods consumed by a single individual. In this scheme, then, a private good can be viewed as a public good for which the subset of the population that consumes the good is the individual consumer. I will assume that he is his own government in this case—that he alone, subject to his budgetary constraint, determines his consumption of private goods. For all other goods (that is, those consumed collectively by a group of two consumers or more), I assume for now that the public sector determines the level of output.

Assume further that the geographical distribution of the population is fixed: each individual is confined to his existing geographical location. In this simple case, it can be argued that the optimal form of federal government to provide the set of n public goods would be one in which there exists a level of government for each subset of the population over which the consumption of a public good is defined. This would be sufficient to internalize the benefits from the provision of each good. Such a structure of governments, in which the jurisdiction that determines the level of provision of each public good includes precisely the set of individuals who consume the good, I shall call a case of *perfect correspondence* in the provision of public goods.[4] In the ideal model, each level of gov-

[2] Paul A. Samuelson, "The Pure Theory of Public Expenditure," *Review of Economics and Statistics,* vol. 36 (Nov., 1954), pp. 387–89. Note that this does not imply that all consumers derive the same level of satisfaction from consuming X_i; the level of satisfaction depends on the particular form and parameters of each individual's utility function. All this says is that the same quantity of the public good enters each person's function.
[3] I am assuming here that the national economy is a closed system. However, one can easily extend the argument to include international public goods, which would imply the need for a world government.
[4] Albert Breton has termed a system characterized by this match between the jurisdiction of each governmental unit and the group that collectively consumes the good as a "perfect mapping." See his "A Theory of Government Grants," *The Canadian Journal of Economics and Political Science,* vol. 31 (May, 1965), p. 180. I prefer to avoid this term because the word mapping has a precise and rather different meaning in its usage

ernment, possessing complete knowledge of the tastes of its constituents and seeking to maximize their welfare, would provide the Pareto-efficient level of output—that output for which the sum of the marginal rates of substitution of its constituents equals marginal cost—and would finance this through benefit pricing.[5]

That the allocation of resources resulting from our ideal case of a perfect correspondence is Pareto-efficient is, I think, clear.[6] Nonetheless, it will prove useful to develop one aspect of the argument somewhat more carefully in terms of a proposition I call the Decentralization Theorem.

The Decentralization Theorem: For a public good—the consumption of which is defined over geographical subsets of the total population, and for which the costs of providing each level of output of the good in each jurisdiction are the same for the central or the respective local government—it will always be more efficient (or at least as efficient) for local governments to provide the Pareto-efficient levels of output for their respective jurisdictions than for the central government to provide *any* specified and uniform level of output across all jurisdictions.

Proofs of the theorem and a more extended discussion of its implications appear in the appendix to this chapter. However, the rationale underlying the theorem is quite straightforward.

---

in mathematics. On this issue of internalizing the benefits from a collective good by the establishment of appropriately defined governmental jurisdictions, see also Mancur Olson, "The Principle of 'Fiscal Equivalence': The Division of Responsibilities Among Different Levels of Government," *American Economic Review,* vol. 59 (May, 1969), pp. 479–87; and Vincent Ostrom, Charles Tiebout, and Robert Warren, "The Organization of Government in Metropolitan Areas: A Theoretical Inquiry," *American Political Science Review,* vol. 55 (Dec., 1961), pp. 831–42.

[5] There is a slight complication here. The use of benefit pricing (that is, charging each consumer a price per unit equal to his marginal benefit) still leaves individual consumers with a positive increment to their consumers' surplus on inframarginal units. The distribution of income will consequently not be quite the same after as before the provision of the good, and this may require some adjustments in lump-sum tax and transfer payments to attain the desired distribution of income. The point here is simply that the problems of achieving efficient resource allocation and of establishing the desired distribution of income are not wholly independent.
[6] This assumes that there are no sources of inefficiency in the private sector of the economy.

The assertion is that welfare is maximized if each local government (that is, a government whose jurisdiction coincides precisely with one of the subsets of the population that consumes the same units of output of the public good) provides the Pareto-efficient output for its constituency. Any other level of output of the good in the jurisdiction, one that does not satisfy this condition, will necessarily reduce the level of satisfaction of at least one individual in the locality and probably more.[7] The central government, which we have assumed provides the same level of output across all jurisdictions, cannot therefore provide the Pareto-efficient level of output in each area except in the special case where that level of output is identical across all jurisdictions. It follows, then, that aside from this special case, in which it is a matter of indifference whether the provision of the good is centralized or decentralized, the levels of welfare of the residents of each jurisdiction must be at least as great, and in some areas greater, where local governments cater to local preferences, as compared to the case where the central government provides a single level of output for all localities.[8]

While much of this may belabor the obvious, the theorem does bring into sharp focus two important propositions. First, the theorem contains in it the condition that the costs of providing the good in each jurisdiction are the same for the central government and for the respective local governments. If

[7] I assume here that the residents of each jurisdiction pay for the public goods provided in their locality. I should add that it is not necessarily true that the movement to a state of Pareto efficiency will not make anyone worse off. The implication is rather that no one *need* be made worse off, while at least one person will have an increased level of welfare. The actual pattern of welfare gains and losses among individuals depends on the particular cost-sharing formulas adopted.

[8] Presenting a parallel to this theorem, J. Roland Pennock has shown that, where collective decisions are made by majority rule, a decentralization of political institutions results in fewer (or at least no more) persons casting votes for losing candidates than under a unitary system of government. See his "Federal and Unitary Government: Disharmony and Frustration," *Behavioral Science*, vol. 4 (April, 1959), pp. 147–57. More recently, Yoram Barzel has provided, subject to some restrictive conditions, a proof of a closely related theorem that uses individual demand curves and measurements of consumer surplus. See his "Two Propositions on the Optimum Level of Producing Collective Goods," *Public Choice*, vol. 6 (Spring, 1969), pp. 31–37. Barzel's proof is included in the appendix to this chapter; his approach is particularly useful because it leads to a cardinal measure of the loss in welfare resulting from centralized decision-making.

this is not the case—for example, if the central government can realize important economies of scale in the provision of the good that are not available to the local governments individually—centralization may be desirable in spite of the decentralized character of the consumption of the good. In the absence of such cost-savings from centralization, however, the theorem establishes a presumption in favor of decentralized finance.

Second, the discussion of the theorem, including the special case of indifference between centralized and decentralized provision of the good, suggests that the incentives for decentralization are likely to be greater the more varied the efficient levels of output across jurisdictions; for the more pronounced then will be the divergence of any uniform level of output from the efficient level in most localities. More precisely (and this is demonstrated in the appendix), for a given population size, the welfare gain from the decentralized provision of a particular local public good becomes greater as the diversity in individual demands within the country as a whole increases and as each geographical grouping of consumers becomes more homogeneous in terms of their demands for the good. This proposition suggests, moreover, some testable hypotheses concerning the optimal degree of fiscal centralization, hypotheses that we will examine in Chapter Five.

In this framework, then, we can envision a federal system consisting of a multiplicity of government levels, where each government is responsible for providing the efficient level of output of the public good, or goods, consumed collectively by the individuals in its jurisdiction; and, in our highly purified environment, this would lead to a welfare optimum.[9]

The conceptual framework used to reach this result is, however, extremely restrictive. When we relax some of the conditions assumed in the ideal model, the problem of determining the optimal structure of the public sector becomes consider-

[9] One might argue that, with perfect knowledge of individual tastes, the central government could assume the responsibility for the provision of all public goods and simply ensure that separate Pareto-efficient levels of consumption are provided in all jurisdictions. However, in terms of the economic definition of federalism set down in Chapter One, this is equivalent to the operation of a federal system with a decision-making unit for each jurisdiction; in economic terms, this approach thus represents a federal solution to the problem. It is for this reason that I associate centralized decision-making with a uniform level of consumption of public goods across all jurisdictions.

ably more complex. In particular, if we no longer have a pure public good whose consumption is rigidly defined over precise geographical subsets of the population, the selection of the proper level of government to provide the good involves weighing the potential welfare gains from a greater decentralization of decision-making against the possible gains from increased centralization.

The determination of the optimal-sized jurisdiction

To indicate clearly the nature of the problem, it is useful to retain for the moment the assumptions of a given and geographically fixed population and of costless decision-making. The only changes to the ideal model to be introduced at this point concern the nature of the public goods themselves. More specifically, I want to consider an impure public good whose consumption is not confined by technology to a precise geographical subset of economic units. Protection against certain types of crime, for example, is a good that can be provided in a number of different ways. Individuals may to some extent provide the good for themselves through systems of locks and alarms; groups of residents might jointly purchase the services of police patrols for their areas; or, toward the other extreme, protection from crime might come from a centrally directed national police force. The point is that for this good the number of individuals who jointly consume a particular output is itself a variable.[10]

In this framework the problem becomes that of determining the optimal-sized group to consume the good collectively. There are two sorts of incentives that are important here. First, by consuming the good jointly it may be possible for individuals to get it more cheaply; a given degree of protection may, for

[10] The good envisioned here is admittedly of a complex but not, I think, unrealistic character. While the good may be consumed collectively in groups of different sizes, it is assumed that each group of individuals can exclude others from the consumption of the group's own units of the good (for example, systems of education, fire protection services, etc.). In this sense the good possesses, to some extent at least, what Head has called "jointness of supply" but does not have Head's second characteristic of publicness—namely a high cost of exclusion. See Head, "Public Goods and Public Policy."

example, be provided at less cost *per person* through police patrols in a given area than by individual systems of locks and alarms. As a result there may exist important economies of scale (at least over some range) in the consumption of the good.

For purposes of illustration, the aggregate cost-savings from increasing the number of individuals who jointly consume a particular good are depicted by the curve OC in Figure 2-1. More precisely, OC measures vertically the aggregate in-

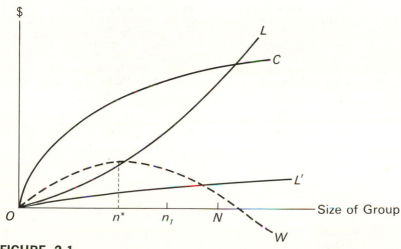

FIGURE 2-1

crease in welfare (that is, the sum of the increases in consumer surplus) that would hypothetically be available to individuals as a result of their being able to purchase units of the good at the reduced price made possible by joint consumption.[11] Starting from the origin, at which point each person

[11] Or, in other words, OC measures vertically the sum over all individuals in the group of what each would be willing to pay for the privilege of consuming his desired quantity of the good at the lower price associated with the collective consumption of the good. Suppose that in Figure 2F-1 private consumption of the good is available to individuals at a unit cost of OP_1. However, through joint consumption in a group of size n_1, a unit of consumption can be provided at a cost of only OP_2 per person. In this case, for the consumer whose demand is depicted in the diagram, the potential gain in welfare from the collective consumption of the good

purchases his own units of the good and consumes them as a private good, we move to the right along the horizontal axis encountering increasingly large groups of consumers until we reach N, at which point all members of society are jointly consuming the same units of output of the good. One might expect that the OC curve would typically rise sharply at first, as the addition of another individual would allow substantial cost-savings within a very small group, but would gradually level off, reflecting the much smaller cost-savings an extra person confers on a larger group.[12]

is the shaded trapezoid MRP_2P_1. A summation of these gains across all individuals would generate the vertical height of the OC curve corresponding to the point n_1 on the horizontal axis in Figure 2-1. I might add that equal cost-sharing of the good among the members of the group is an implicit assumption here. While it is true that the OC curve will in general differ if some other cost-sharing rule is adopted, the reader will note later that the net welfare curve (OW in Figure 2-1) is invariant

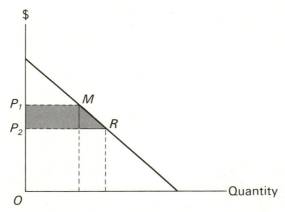

FIGURE 2F-1

with respect to the cost-sharing formula so long as the Pareto-efficient level of the good is provided for the group and so long as there exists over the relevant range a constant marginal utility of income. In this case alterations in the cost-sharing scheme amount solely to a particular redistribution of income among individuals.

[12] In the limiting case of a pure public good, for example, the cost per person of a given output is K/n, where K is total cost and n is the size of the group of consumers. The change in cost per person resulting from the addition of a further individual to the group is approximated by the derivative of this expression with respect to n, or $-K/n^2$. If we multiply this by the size of the group, n, we find that the aggregate

It should be stressed that OC measures only hypothetical increases in economic welfare: the aggregate increase in welfare that could be realized if each consumer were able to purchase the desired number of units at the reduced price per person made possible through joint consumption. There is, however, a price to be paid for joint consumption; the individuals within each group must agree on a single level of consumption of the good. This implies that each individual will not be able to take full advantage of the lower cost per person, because he will in general have to settle for some level of consumption other than that which he would most desire at the prevailing cost to him.

There is, therefore, a welfare cost in terms of the reduction in consumer surplus the individual suffers as a result of what may be for him an other-than-desired level of consumption of the good. There is reason, moreover, to expect that the aggregate welfare loss from the differences between the actual and desired levels of consumption will tend to increase with the magnitude of n. As group size increases, the influence of any particular individual on his own level of consumption of the good diminishes. As a result, with larger groups we generally expect a greater aggregate welfare loss.[13] This loss is represented in Figure 2-1 by the curve OL; like OC, it begins at the origin (at which point the individual alone determines his own level of consumption of the good) and in general exhibits a positive slope.

The nature of the problem is now clear. The determination

cost-savings conferred on the existing membership by the marginal individual is K/n; in other words, the individual's share of the total cost of the jointly consumed units of output. The magnitude of this expression obviously varies inversely with the value of n. In the case of impure public goods, additional members may impose costs of congestion on the existing members (necessitating a greater total expenditure) so that the cost-savings from an enlarged group are not so great. For a more extensive treatment of the issue of group size and the efficient output of public goods for the cases of both pure and impure public goods, see James Litvack and Wallace Oates, "Group Size and the Output of Public Goods: Theory and an Application to State-Local Finance in the United States," *Public Finance*, vol. 25, no. 1 (1970), pp. 42–58.

[13] In the appendix to this chapter it is demonstrated that in the absence of cost-savings from enlarging the size of the group of consumers, it is, aside from one special case, always desirable to provide separate levels of consumption for smaller collections of consumers. In this situation the larger is n, the greater is the aggregate welfare loss from the failure to provide levels of consumption that approximate more closely those desired by individual consumers.

of the optimal-sized group to consume jointly the public good involves a trade off between the increased cost-savings from joint consumption in larger groups versus the greater welfare from more responsive levels of consumption in smaller groups. It may be recalled that the Decentralization Theorem suggests that where cost-savings from centralized decision-making are absent, it is always preferable to provide the good on a decentralized basis. In the limiting case, that of a purely private good, it is clearly better to allow each individual to select the level of consumption that best suits his tastes than to have groups within which all persons must consume the same level of the good. The gains from diverse levels of consumption tailored closely to the demands of individuals in small groups must, therefore, be weighed against whatever savings in costs are available through collective consumption in larger groups.[14]

Such a solution is depicted in Figure 2-1. The curve OW, which represents the *net* increase in welfare from joint consumption for each group size, is derived by the vertical subtraction of OL from OC. OW achieves its maximum value at group size n^*, which, therefore, represents the optimal-sized group to consume the good jointly. It is, incidentally, perfectly possible for the gap between OC and OL to grow continually larger as n rises; such a case is illustrated by OC and OL'. In this instance, OW would possess a positive slope throughout the relevant range, and the optimal-sized group would be N; in other words, society as a whole. Conversely,

[14] This problem is explored in greater depth in the appendix. In particular, the phenomenon of joint consumption enters in formal terms as an additional constraint in the welfare-maximization problem. This constraint will in general prevent the realization of the Pareto-efficiency condition, which would apply in the absence of joint consumption. This implies that there is a welfare cost associated with collective consumption, one that must be offset by cost-savings if, weighing all factors, joint consumption is to increase economic welfare. Useful analyses of this trade-off problem are available in Gordon Tullock, "Social Cost and Government Action," *American Economic Review*, vol. 59 (May, 1969), pp. 189–97; and "Federalism: Problems of Scale," *Public Choice*, vol. 6 (Spring, 1969), pp. 19–29; and in Barzel, "Two Propositions on the Optimum Level of Producing Collective Goods." Also in this connection, John Head and Carl Shoup have argued that the distinction between private and public goods is best made in terms of whether welfare is greater if the good is provided through individual purchases and private consumption or alternatively through collective consumption. See Head and Shoup, "Public Goods, Private Goods, and Ambiguous Goods," *Economic Journal*, vol. 79 (Sept., 1969), pp. 567–72.

if at every point to the right of the origin, OL lies above OC, the good clearly should be consumed privately.

A closer examination of the factors that influence the position of these two curves provides some insight into the determinants of the optimal degree of fiscal decentralization. As regards the OL curve, the potential losses from an increased centralization of decision-making depend primarily on the diversity in individual demands for the good and the extent of geographical groupings of consumers with similar tastes. If, for example, there are wide divergences in individual preferences for the public good and in levels of income within a society that give rise to a wide dispersion of individual demands for the good, and if at the same time people with similar demands tend to reside near to one another geographically, one can expect large differences in desired levels of consumption among various areas in the country. In such cases the potential losses from the collective consumption of the good on a highly centralized basis could be substantial. As demonstrated in the appendix to this chapter (see equation 11), the aggregate welfare loss from the centralized provision of a uniform level of consumption for all individuals, as opposed to more decentralized joint consumption, is proportional to the sum of the squares of the difference between the nationwide uniform level of consumption and the most desired level in each of the subgroups, or jurisdictions. Therefore, the more widely the efficient levels of consumption vary across jurisdictions, the more pronounced is the potential welfare loss from the centralized provision of the good.

If, on the other hand, all individuals possess quite similar preferences for the public good and there is also a high degree of equality in the distribution of income, individual demands for public goods will tend to be very similar, and consequently there will be a much smaller loss in welfare from uniform levels of consumption over large groups of people. Moreover, even if there is considerable diversity in individual demands, the losses from centralization may not be very large, for only if individuals with similar demands are grouped together geographically will there be a substantial divergence in efficient levels of consumption among different areas. What all this implies is that, as there exists a more pronounced diversity in individual demands for the good in association with a geographical proximity of those with similar levels of demand, the OL curve will tend to be higher (at least for relatively large values of n) and, therefore, other things equal, the optimal degree of fiscal centralization will tend to be less.[15]

For the OC curve, the potential cost-savings from collective consumption depend primarily on the technical character of the good itself. In the limiting case of a pure public good that possesses what John Head has called perfect "jointness of supply," an additional person can consume existing units of the good without imposing any costs on the group; the cost-savings from collective consumption will thus tend to be relatively large. More typically, however, the expansion of a group to include more consumers (for example, additional students in a public school system) will increase the total expenditure required to maintain the level of consumption within the group; in these cases the savings in costs from joint consumption in expanded groups will depend on the extent to which further inputs are necessary to accommodate the additional consumers.[16]

[15] The analysis here is developed solely in terms of differences in demand for levels of consumption of the public good. Somewhat more realistically, one might argue that the differences in demand for public goods that are really important involve varying attributes of the good, rather than wide differences in preferred levels of output. It is no doubt the case, for example, that in some countries there is less divergence in desired levels of educational programs than there is in the content of these programs; primarily Catholic areas, for instance, may want a significantly different educational curriculum than that typical of districts populated mainly by Protestants. This suggests that a fruitful approach to the theory of fiscal federalism may exist in the so-called abstract-product concept, which assumes that consumers possess demands for certain "attributes" and that individual commodities provide a vector of these attributes. On this approach see Kelvin Lancaster, "A New Approach to Consumer Theory," *Journal of Political Economy*, vol. 74 (April, 1966), pp. 132–57; and William Baumol, "Calculation of Optimal Product and Retailer Characteristics: The Abstract Product Approach," *Journal of Political Economy*, vol. 75 (Oct., 1967), pp. 674–85.

[16] There is no compelling reason to believe that, for most public goods, the savings from collective consumption increase with continually larger groups in such a way that most services now provided at a local level could be made available more cheaply by the central government. What empirical evidence we have on this matter indicates that, in the United States at least, cost-savings from consolidation for most services are exhausted at a relatively modest community size. In fact, in some instances there may well exist important diseconomies of scale resulting from inefficiencies inherent in bulky administrative units. A useful survey of these cost studies is available in Werner Hirsch, "The Supply

The technological character of some public goods may permit a different type of resolution of this trade-off problem. In some instances the pronounced economies that may exist in the large-scale production of a public good may not be inconsistent with diversification in the consumption of the good. This possibility stems from the distinction between the *provision* and the *production* of a public good. Decentralization implies that local public units determine the level of consumption of the good in their respective jurisdictions, but this does not necessarily mean that the local government must itself produce the units of output. In some cases it may be possible for the local government to purchase the desired number of units of output from a higher level of government (or for that matter from private vendors) whose expanded scale of operation permits the realization of economies of scale in production. This form of organization has in fact been adopted in certain areas in the United States, where relatively small municipalities may contract for the bulk of their public services with the county government.[17] In this way, for some public services, it may be possible to realize the gains both from large-scale production and from decentralized determination of levels of consumption.

The problem of selecting the proper level of government to provide a particular public good has been envisioned in this section as involving a trade off between the cost-savings from collective consumption and the welfare gains from more decentralized levels of provision in accordance with the particular tastes of members of smaller jurisdictions. This, however, is still a greatly oversimplified view, and it will be the purpose of the remainder of this chapter to develop three additional dimensions of the problem: external effects among groups of consumers, the presence of costs of decision-making, and the geographical mobility of individuals among jurisdictions.

---

of Urban Public Services," in Harvey Perloff and Lowdon Wingo, eds., *Issues in Urban Economics* (Baltimore: Johns Hopkins Press, 1968), pp. 477–526.

[17] This is the so-called Lakewood Plan, which has been implemented extensively in Los Angeles County. A municipality in this area can purchase almost any service it wants from the county government. For a more detailed examination of this whole issue, see Ostrom *et al.*, "The Organization of Government in Metropolitan Areas."

The problem of interjurisdictional externalities[18]

An assumption implicit in the analysis in the preceding section was that the spatial pattern of the benefits and costs resulting from the consumption of the good is one that includes only those persons in the jurisdiction or group selecting a particular level of consumption. This, however, is frequently not the case. For example, as Burton Weisbrod has shown, the quality of the educational system in one area may have significant effects on the welfare of individuals in other jurisdictions.[19]

It is generally desirable, as suggested by the condition of perfect correspondence in the ideal model, to internalize, where possible, all the benefits and costs associated with the provision of a particular good. In this way decisions concerning levels of consumption will be more likely to take into account the interests of all those whose welfare they influence. If, however, this principle is adhered to without compromise, it may well imply that consumption levels for the many goods that are mainly of local interest but have some minor external effects must be determined by the central government. This could easily entail substantial losses in welfare from the abandonment of a more decentralized provision of the good.

The point is that the presence and extent of external effects is an additional consideration in the determination of the optimal-sized group to consume a particular public good. The smaller the group, the less the external effects likely to be internalized; for this reason, the expected loss in welfare from such externalities will tend to vary inversely with the size of the jurisdiction. In addition, to the extent that the provision of the good elsewhere can serve as a substitute for local provision (as in the missile example in Chapter One), there will be an incentive to engage in free-rider behavior, which is also likely to be accentuated with a large number of relatively small groups of consumers.[20]

---

[18] The discussion in the next two sections draws heavily on a previously cited paper by Tullock, "Federalism: Problems of Scale."
[19] *External Benefits of Public Education* (Princeton, N.J.: Princeton University, Industrial Relations Section, 1964).
[20] Free-rider behavior stems from the incentive to have others provide

The basic idea here is that the existence of unresolved external effects implies the presence of what are, in effect, potential gains-from-trade; it would thus *be possible* for the various groups of consumers to agree on other levels of provision of the good that could increase the level of welfare of all concerned. In the absence of such agreements, which may be very difficult to reach among a large number of small communities, an increase in the size of the jurisdiction should itself allow the realization of at least some of these potential gains-from-trade through internalizing more of the benefits and costs and, in this way, should result in more efficient levels of provision of the public good.

In regard to Figure 2-1 this means that in addition to the *OC* and *OL* curves, we should include, wherever applicable, a measure of the aggregate welfare gain that results from a given degree of internalization of the benefits and costs associated with the provision of the good. Such a measure of this potential gain appears as the curve *OE* in Figure 2-2; on the whole, we would expect *OE* to have a positive slope, reflecting the increase in welfare as the jurisdictions that provide the good become larger and there is greater internalization of external effects. To determine the optimal-sized group to consume the good collectively, we must now add *OE* to (*OC* − *OL*) to determine *OW*. This will produce a maximum in curve *OW* to the right of the maximum determined on the basis of *OL* and *OC* alone; in other words, the inclusion of external effects in the calculation suggests a larger jurisdiction for provision of the good.

---

or pay for one's consumption of a collective good; if an individual can consume units of a good provided by others (for example, clean air in a given locality), he has reason to try to get others to provide the good so that he can get a "free ride." Within a small group, this may take the form of strategic behavior by which an individual deliberately understates his true preferences in the hope that this will induce others to undertake a larger share of the activity. As the group becomes larger, however, each individual will tend simply to take the existing levels of the activity by others as given and will supplement these to the extent he desires. These types of behavior are also likely among communities that consume a public good jointly; in this case "individual" can be taken to refer to a single community. Excellent treatments of this issue can be found in James Buchanan, "Cooperation and Conflict in Public-Goods Interaction," *Western Economic Journal*, vol. 5 (March, 1967), pp. 109–21; and Mancur Olson, *The Logic of Collective Action* (Cambridge, Mass.: Harvard University Press, 1965).

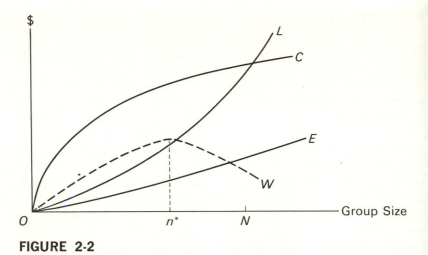

FIGURE 2-2

The costs of collective decision-making

In the ideal model presented in the first section of this chapter, the optimal structure of the public sector was found to be one in which there was a level of government (or a collective decision-making mechanism) for each jurisdiction over which the consumption of a public good could be defined. Under such a perfect correspondence, each government unit provides that level of consumption that equates at the margin the sum of the benefits and costs to its constituency; within the restrictive conditions of the model, this was found to yield a welfare optimum. In subsequent discussion, the size of the jurisdiction in which individuals jointly consumed the good was itself allowed to vary; thus, determining the proper-sized jurisdiction in which to provide the good required a weighing of the welfare gains and losses associated with an increased degree of centralization of decision-making. But even then the implication was that there should exist a level of government corresponding to the optimal group (n^*) for each and every public good.

However, when we take explicit account of the costs of collective decision-making, it becomes clear that, even if it were possible to create a separate level of government to serve each group of the population that jointly consumes a particular public good, there would usually exist strong reasons for not doing so. The formation and operation of a public decision-making organization are themselves costly, and this includes a substantial element of fixed costs. There are, first, the administrative costs (for example, salaries of public officials and other employees, cost of buildings, etc.) and, second, costs to the electorate in the form of the time and effort involved in the election of public officials. If there exist many levels of government, as the preceding analysis would tend to imply, these costs could be quite high; in addition to supporting a large number of independent public agencies, each individual could find it necessary to participate in a huge number of elections. As a result there is a real incentive to reduce the costs of collective decision-making by economizing on the number of levels of government. This is particularly true in the case of more decentralized levels of government, which imply an increased multiplicity of government units.[21]

It seems, then, that there is yet another problem of trade offs in the determination of the optimal structure of the public sector: the gains from establishing an independent unit or level of government to provide a particular public good must be weighed against the increase in costs due to a larger number of public agencies. Where the optimal-sized jurisdiction is roughly the same for a number of public goods (that is, where there is a clustering of the values of n^* for a number of goods), one would think it desirable to establish only a single level of government, which would have the responsibility for providing all of these goods.[22]

Consumer mobility and congestion costs

It remains to examine the implications of removing one additional restriction in the ideal model: the geographical immo-

[21] One may of course defend the desirability of a large number of public decision-making units at decentralized levels on other grounds. John Stuart Mill, for example, stressed the importance of local government as a means of education, in that it provides wider opportunity for direct participation in public affairs. See his *On Representative Government*.
[22] Gordon Tullock has analyzed this trade off in his "Federalism: Problems of Scale," p. 28. He concludes

bility of consumers. The assumption thus far has been that the geographical position of each individual is given and fixed. We shall now relax this restriction and assume that individuals can alter their jurisdiction of residence. Assume, moreover, that, similar to a Tiebout world, the levels of provision of public goods in the various jurisdictions exert some influence on the individual's choice of location. As a result, people with similar demands for public services will tend, to some extent, to locate in the same jurisdiction or in jurisdictions providing much the same menu of public services. We would generally expect such mobility to enhance the gains from decentralized decision-making. As discussed earlier, the welfare gains from the decentralized provisions of public services become larger when individuals with similar tastes locate together geographically; for then it is possible to realize the cost-savings from joint consumption within each group, while at the same time providing a level of consumption that corresponds closely to that desired by most individuals in the group.

Consumer mobility may, however, carry with it some costs as well as gains. Its costs arise where the level of consumption of the collective good is not independent of the number of persons who consume the good; this is the familiar problem of congestion costs. Note that in this case all members of the jurisdiction may still consume the same level of output; this level, however, varies with the number of consumers. As an example, consider an educational system with a given set of inputs and a variable number of pupils. If we assume as fixed the number of classrooms, teachers, etc., the quantity or quality of education provided the pupils in the community will vary with the size of the group that attends the schools. A larger number of pupils means higher pupil-teacher ratios, more crowded facilities, and a generally reduced level of consumption of education for each student. In this case, then, the

---

If I may be permitted to offer a guess, I would imagine that it [the optimal degree of federalization] would end up with each individual being a member of somewhere between five and eight separate government units. These government units would not necessarily bear any particular resemblance to our present governments. It is, for example, quite possible theoretically that we would have two 'national' governments. One of which, let us say, dealt with national defense and the other with all other activities which required nationwide organization.

cost of allowing an additional person to consume the good is not zero as in the case of a pure public good. In formal terms this means that the number of units of the good entering the individual's utility function depends not only on the quantities of inputs and the production function, but also on the number of persons in the jurisdiction.

The congestion problem associated with consumer mobility arises from the free access of individuals to the various jurisdictions; we would expect that, in selecting a location in which to reside, individuals will not consider the impact of their decision on the welfare of others. However, if consumers of a particular impure public good can charge a price (or, alternatively, offer a subsidy) to additional consumers, an efficient solution to the problem can be attained. This can best be seen in terms of Buchanan's example of a privately organized swimming club.[23] The members of the club have, on one hand, an incentive to seek additional members to help share the costs of the construction and operation of the pool. On the other hand, after some point, further expansion of the membership will impose congestion costs on existing members. The optimal club size can thus be determined by accepting additional persons into the club until the marginal gain from further cost-sharing equals the marginal congestion cost to the members. At this point the club would simply cease accepting further applications for membership.

Where the members of a group consuming collectively the output of an impure public good can exclude potential additional entrants, there thus exists a mechanism to realize the optimal size for the group. However, when we turn to the case of a public good provided by government, we find that such a mechanism for controlling the size of the group of consumers is often either totally absent or highly imperfect. In terms of widely held social values, there are strong reasons for allowing the free movement of individuals among jurisdictions; they constitute a persuasive case against regulations that would allow the residents of a particular jurisdiction to exclude systematically further immigration. Interestingly enough, however, the incentives to avoid excessive congestion and to exclude "undesirables" have led to the establishment of

---

[23] "An Economic Theory of Clubs," *Economica*, vol. 32 (Feb., 1965), pp. 1–14.

(often not very subtle) zoning regulations and practices on the part of local realtors seeking some degree of control over the size and composition of the population in a particular jurisdiction.

Where control of group size is absent, inefficiencies are likely to result because a potential entrant to the jurisdiction need not consider the congestion cost he imposes on others.[24] In particular, the relevant consideration for a potential resident is not marginal cost but, rather, average cost: he is concerned with the existing level of congestion in the community, not with the additional costs he imposes on the existing residents of the locality. For example, in the case where marginal congestion cost exceeds the average cost of congestion, the "price" for entry into the community understates the full social cost. The likely result in this instance is excessive congestion, a greater than optimal community size. Consumer mobility in a federal system may thus be to some extent a mixed blessing. On the one hand, it should tend to promote the formation of groups with more homogeneous tastes that can take full advantage of the decentralized provision of public goods in accordance with local demand. On the other hand, however, wholly unobstructed mobility is likely to carry with it a cost in terms of inefficient community size.

To summarize, when we extend the simple ideal model to encompass variability in the size of the group that jointly consumes the good, interjurisdictional externalities, the decision-making costs of public action, and the costs of congestion resulting from the mobility of consumers, the problem of allocating the provision of various public goods among different levels of government is no longer a simple one. In particular, the attempt to maximize the social welfare is likely to involve compromises between the costs and gains of increased decentralization. This suggests that typically the most desirable division of responsibility among the various levels of government for providing public goods will no longer result in a perfect correspondence—a state in which each good is provided by a level of government that encompasses precisely the subset of the population whose level of welfare is influenced

[24] This issue has been treated recently by James Buchanan and Richard Wagner, "An Efficiency Basis for Federal Fiscal Equalization," in Julius Margolis, ed., *The Analysis of Public Output* (New York: Columbia University Press, 1970), pp. 139–58.

by the output of the good. Instead, this division will generally consist of an imperfect correspondence. In some cases, the government that provides a particular public good will not include in its jurisdiction all those who benefit from the good, and in other instances, the jurisdiction may include individuals whose welfare is independent of outputs of the good within that jurisdiction. Both situations are likely to involve some inefficiencies in patterns of resource use.

To enhance the effectiveness of the public sector in a federal system, it would be extremely desirable to find a mechanism to reduce the inefficiencies that arise from an imperfect correspondence in the provision of public goods. There is, in fact, one prominent instrument of policy that appears to have real potential for achieving this goal: intergovernmental grants. Therefore, we shall proceed to a study of grants-in-aid from one level of government to another.

Appendix

The decentralization theorem and the optimal-sized jurisdiction

The Decentralization Theorem provides a useful point of departure for an analysis of the theory of federal finance. The theorem indicates that, in the absence of cost-savings from the centralized provision of a good and of interjurisdictional external effects, the level of welfare will always be at least as high (and typically higher) if Pareto-efficient levels of consumption of the good are provided in each jurisdiction than if *any* single, uniform level of consumption is maintained across all jurisdictions. In this way the theorem establishes, in the absence of other kinds of offsetting benefits from centralized control, a presumption in favor of decentralized finance.

Two proofs of this proposition will be provided. The first shows simply that subject to the conditions mentioned above, some people's position can be improved without reducing the welfare of anyone else if decentralized, rather than centralized, provision of the good takes place. The second approach to the problem, based on papers by Tullock and Barzel, involves the measurement and aggregation of consumer surpluses.[1] While Barzel's proof necessitates some additional assumptions (one of which is rather restrictive), it possesses the advantage of generating a cardinal measure of welfare gains from decentralization. This allows the derivation of some corollaries to the theorem that relate to the determinants of the magnitude of the welfare gains from decentralized finance.

By way of introduction to the problem, it is helpful to con-

---

[1] Gordon Tullock, "Social Cost and Government Action"; and Yoram Barzel, "Two Propositions on the Optimum Level of Producing Collective Goods."

54

sider the special case of a two-person, two-commodity world. Assume that we have two individuals, A and B, each of whom consumes positive quantities of two commodities, X and Y. Commodity X is a pure private good; commodity Y, in contrast, is a more complicated good. A and B can choose to consume Y as a private good (for example, provide for their own protection through individual systems of locks and alarms) or they can consume Y jointly (for example, hire a patrol to cover the area of their residences). Should they consume Y collectively, the one constraint is that they must consume the same quantity of Y.

In the case where A and B choose to consume Y as a private good, we can set up the standard Lagrangian formulation of the welfare maximization problem:

$$(1) \quad L = U_A(X_A, Y_A) - \lambda_1[U_B(X_B, Y_B) - U^o{}_B]$$
$$- \lambda_2(X - X_A - X_B) - \lambda_3(Y - Y_A - Y_B) - \lambda_4[F(X, Y)]$$

where

$$U_A(X_A, Y_A) = \text{ordinal utility function of individual } A,$$
$$U_B(X_B, Y_B) = \text{ordinal utility function of individual } B,$$
$$U^o{}_B = \text{given level of utility of } B,$$
$$F(X, Y) = 0 \text{ is the production constraint for the two commodities, and}$$
$$\lambda\text{'s are the Lagrangian multipliers.}$$

Holding the level of utility of B constant, the maximization of A's welfare leads to the familiar first-order conditions: the marginal rate of substitution of Y for X must be the same for A and B and must in turn equal marginal cost. This implies, among other things, that in terms of the Edgeworth Box diagram, A and B are on their contract curve.

Suppose, however, that A and B consume Y jointly. In this case, we must introduce a further constraint into the Lagrangian expression: $\lambda_5 (Y_A - Y_B)$ to indicate the restriction that A and B must consume the same quantity of Y. Consider first the situation where there are no cost-savings from joint consumption—that is, where the budget constraint for the two individuals is the same under both private and joint consumption of Y. In this instance there is no change in equation 1 aside from the introduction of the additional constraint just cited. It is therefore clear that in this case the level of welfare of A, given that of B, will generally be less than under private consumption, since we have introduced an additional constraint into the maximization problem with no loosening of the other constraints. Only in the special case where the condition embodied in the constraint would have been satisfied even in the absence of the constraint (that is, where A and B would have chosen independently to consume the same quantity of Y) will the collective consumption of Y allow A to reach the same level of utility as with the independent consumption of Y; otherwise, joint consumption implies a decline in welfare.

The character of this loss in welfare from the joint consumption of Y is also apparent from the first-order condition that emerges from the maximization of the Lagrangian function with the inclusion of the joint consumption constraint. If we simply introduce $\lambda_5(Y_A - Y_B)$ into equation 1 and maximize this new expression, the resulting first-order condition is:

$$(2) \qquad MRS_A + MRS_B = 2MC.$$

The sums of the marginal rates of substitution must now equal twice the marginal cost of a unit of output of Y.

A solution that satisfies this condition will not, however, allow person A to achieve, in general, as high a level of welfare, given that of B, as he can where A and B consume Y privately and where their marginal rates of substitution for Y are equal to each other and to marginal cost. In terms of an Edgeworth Box like that in Figure 2A-1, for example, joint consumption implies that the solution must lie on the line YY', which bisects both O_AM and O_BN. Assuming that this is the particular Box in which equation 2 is satisfied, we find that the maximization of A's welfare, if B is on indifference curve B_1, leads to point C. This generates a level of welfare for A indicated by the indifference curve A_1. Person A can clearly do better, however, by consuming Y privately and moving to point D on the contract curve, where he will have increased his level of welfare to A_2.[2]

---

[2] In the one special case where the MRS's of A and B are equal and where, as a result, the point C is itself on the contract curve, it is clearly a matter of indifference whether A and B consume Y jointly or privately.

This simple, two-person case does, I think, make clear the nature of the case for decentralized finance; it is easily seen that in this instance it is never in the interest of A and B to constrain themselves to consume Y jointly unless there are some cost-savings to be realized from collective consumption. Where such cost-savings do exist, the implication is that, by consuming Y jointly, A and B can realize higher levels of con-

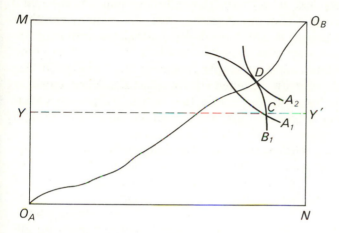

FIGURE 2A-1

sumption of Y without sacrificing any consumption of X. In terms of the Edgeworth Box, this means that for any given output of X (that is, O_AN, the horizontal base of the rectangle), joint consumption allows a higher level of consumption of Y (that is, O_BN, a greater height of the rectangle). In this case the choice between joint and private consumption of Y depends on whether A, given B's utility, can reach a preferred position (a higher indifference curve) on a contract curve in the smaller Box or off the contract curve in a larger Box.[3]

---

[3] In a system with many economic units, this type of approach may also be appropriate for the problem of two individuals considering the creation of a monopsony, or, more simply, agreeing to purchase the same item so that they can obtain a quantity discount. In such cases the concerned parties must decide whether or not the constraints imposed on them in terms of the nature of their purchases are more than offset by the reduced price for which they can buy the desired items.

The case involving separate groupings of many individuals can be treated in essentially the same manner as the two-person situation. In this instance, an association of the groups to consume collectively the same units of output is equivalent to a constraint that everyone must have the same level of consumption of the good. A more decentralized provision of the good, which allows separate groups of the total population to determine their own levels of consumption, will generally permit an increase in welfare. The point is that the separate groups can always choose the same level of consumption that would be forthcoming under a wholly centralized provision of the good, and decentralized provision enlarges the set of combinations of levels of consumption among individuals in the system. Assuming an absence of cost-savings from consolidation, this will generally permit (as in the two-person case) the realization of a superior pattern of consumption of the good.

From this it follows that, if consolidating groups of consumers for purposes of joint consumption does not allow a reduction in costs per unit of consumption per person, it is in general undesirable. Welfare will be maximized by allowing each of the separate groups to provide the Pareto-efficient level of consumption for its members. Even if there exists a single level of consumption across all groups (which generally will imply an other than Pareto-efficient level in at least some groups), we can clearly make at least one person better off, without reducing the welfare of anyone else, by moving to separate groups. Therefore, in the absence of cost-savings from increasing the size of the group of consumers, it is always preferable to provide Pareto-efficient levels of consumption for subsets of a group than for the group as a whole.[4]

In addition, to the extent that further subdivisions of the group are possible without any loss of economies of scale in consumption, the preceding argument implies that it is desirable to do so. In the limiting case (that of a pure private good), it is obviously best to allow each individual to select the level of consumption of the good that independently maximizes his own welfare (subject to his own budget constraint).

<hr>

[4] Again, the one qualification to this statement is the special case where the Pareto-efficient levels of provision of the good are the same for all jurisdictions, in which instance it makes no difference whether the good is provided centrally or at decentralized levels of decision-making.

Joint consumption within larger groups is, therefore, potentially desirable only where it allows members of the expanded group to obtain units of consumption more cheaply than otherwise; and in this case, the potential cost-savings must be weighed against the welfare loss from joint consumption within a larger group to determine if enlargement of the group is, on net, beneficial.

This comparison of potential gains and losses in welfare is facilitated by an approach that allows the measurement of their magnitudes. In their papers on this subject, Tullock and Barzel have set out to measure the loss in consumer surplus resulting from joint, as contrasted with individual, consumption of the good.[5] Consider the provision of a pure public good in a jurisdiction with a fixed population. If we assume, for simplicity, that the cost of additional units of the good is constant and that individual demand curves are linear over the relevant range, we can represent the situation of a single individual in Figure 2A-2. If P_o is the price per unit to each

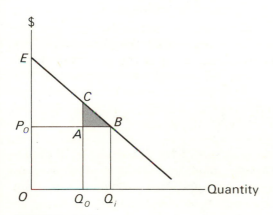

FIGURE 2A-2

person (that is, his share of the cost per unit of the good), Figure 2A-2 indicates that individual i's desired level of consumption would be Q_i. Assume, however, that instead of Q_i, the government provides a level of Q_o. We can generate a measure of the welfare loss to i resulting from this divergence of the actual from his desired level of consumption by com-

[5] The presentation here closely follows Barzel's argument.

puting the difference in the consumer surplus accruing to i at Q_i and Q_o.[6] This is equal to EBP_o minus $ECAP_o$, which is the shaded triangle ABC. If i's demand curve is equal to

$$(3) \qquad Q_i = a_i + b_iP,$$

we can express this loss in welfare as:

$$(4) \quad \Delta W_i = -\left[\frac{1}{2}(Q_i - Q_o)\cdot-\frac{1}{b_i}(Q_i - Q_o)\right] = \left(\frac{1}{2b_i}\right)(Q_i - Q_o)^2.$$

If we assume further that the value of a marginal dollar of income is the same for all individuals, we can then aggregate the loss in consumer surplus over all individuals in the group consuming the good. Thus, for the group of n persons as a whole, the sum of the welfare losses from each person having a level of consumption of the good other than that he most desires equals:

$$(5) \qquad \Delta W_g = \sum_{i=1}^{n}\left(\frac{1}{2b_i}\right)(Q_i - Q_o)^2.$$

To simplify matters further, assume that the slope of the demand curve, b_i, over the relevant range is the same for all individuals, so that:

$$(6) \qquad \Delta W_g = \sum_{i=1}^{n}\frac{1}{2b}(Q_i - Q_o)^2 = \frac{1}{2b}\sum_{i=1}^{n}(Q_i - Q_o)^2.$$

In order to maximize the welfare of its constituency, the government of this jurisdiction must provide that level of consumption, Q^*, that minimizes equation 6. The minimization procedure, which generates in this case the least square estimate, leads to a Q^* equal to the arithmetic mean of the Q_i. Thus, the optimum level is:

$$(7) \qquad Q^* = \frac{\Sigma Q_i}{n}.$$

It is not immediately clear that Q^* is the Pareto-efficient level of output, for the derivation has assumed that all indi-

[6] This assumes that over the range under consideration, the marginal utility of income to the individual is constant.

60

viduals are confronted by the same price, P_o, while the Pareto-efficient level of output of a pure public good generally involves differential pricing according to individual marginal rates of substitution. Subject to the assumption that the slopes of all individual demand curves are the same, it is the case, however, that Q^* is Pareto-efficient. This is easily shown by summing the prices individuals would be willing to pay for a marginal unit at output Q^*, which turns out to be equal to marginal cost.[7]

With this as background we can quickly establish the validity of the Decentralization Theorem. Suppose that instead of each local government providing Q^* for its own constituency, the central government provided a single level of consumption across all localities. Following the preceding line of reasoning, the central government would maximize economic welfare by providing the level (Q') that represented the arithmetic mean of the quantities demanded by all m individuals in the nation:

$$(8) \qquad Q' = \frac{\Sigma \, Q_i}{m}.$$

If we sum the welfare losses to each individual resulting from the divergence of Q' from his most desired level of consumption, we have:

$$(9) \qquad \Delta W_c = \frac{1}{2b} \sum_{i=1}^{m} (Q_i - Q')^2.$$

[7] The sum of the prices that each consumer would pay for a marginal unit of the good at output Q^* is:

$$(a) \qquad S = \Sigma \frac{1}{b} (Q^* - a_i).$$

Noting that $Q^* = \Sigma Q_i / n$, we have:

$$(b) \qquad Q^* = \frac{\Sigma (a_i + bP_o)}{n}.$$

Substituting equation b for Q^* in equation a and then simplifying yields:

$$(c) \qquad S = \frac{1}{b} \Sigma \, bP_o = nP_o = \text{marginal cost}.$$

The sum of the marginal benefits therefore equals marginal cost, which is the first-order condition for the Pareto-efficient level of output of a public good.

However, invoking the identity of the sum of squares (familiar from the analysis of variance), we have, where there are k localities:[8]

$$(10) \quad \sum_{i=1}^{m} (Q_i - Q')^2 \equiv \sum_{j=1}^{k} \left[\sum_{i=1}^{n_j} (Q_i - Q_j^*)^2 \right] + \sum_{j=1}^{k} (Q_j^* - Q')^2.$$

If we multiply both sides of equation 10 by $(1/2b)$, we recognize that the left side of the equation is equal to the welfare loss, ΔW_c, from a national output of Q', while the aggregate loss, $\Sigma \Delta W_g$, from a pattern of outputs of Q_i^* (the Pareto-efficient output for each locality) is expressed by the first term on the right side of equation 10. The welfare loss from Q' therefore exceeds that from the Q_j^* by the amount:

$$(11) \quad \frac{1}{2b} \sum_{j=1}^{k} (Q_j^* - Q')^2.$$

The expression in equation 11 thus constitutes a measure of the potential welfare gain from decentralized finance. Only in the special case where $Q_1^* = Q_2^* = \ldots = Q_k^* = Q'$ will there be no loss from a nationally determined uniform level of output.

From equation 10 we can see further that the gains from decentralization expressed by equation 11 depend both on the degree of diversity in individual demands for the public good in the nation as a whole and in the individual localities themselves. If there exists considerable heterogeneity in individual demands in the nation as a whole and if, at the same time, individuals are divided geographically into groups with relatively similar demands, the potential gains from decentralized finance are enhanced (that is, there will exist sizeable differences between some of the Q_j^* and Q'). The latter part of this proposition suggests in addition the desirability of consumer mobility in accordance with tastes for local public goods as

[8] If we have n observations of a variable, which are divided into k groups, the sum-of-squares identity tells us that the total variance of the n observations about their mean can be expressed as the sum of the variances in each of the k groups about their respective group means plus the variance of the k group means about the mean of the whole set of observations. On this, see, for example, John E. Freund, *Modern Elementary Statistics*, 3rd ed. (Englewood Cliffs, N.J.: Prentice-Hall, 1967), ch. 12.

envisioned in the Tiebout model, for this leads to a greater homogeneity of individual demands within each locality. Conversely, if nearly all persons have roughly similar demands for the public good and if what diversity there exists is spread fairly equally across all jurisdictions, there will be in our simple model little increase in welfare from the independent local provision of the public good (that is, the Q_j^* will differ little from Q'). These corollaries of the Decentralization Theorem are of particular interest, because they can be used to generate testable hypotheses concerning variations in the optimal degree of decentralization of the public sector; we will consider some of these hypotheses in Chapter Five.

Chapter three
The theory and use of intergovernmental grants

There is and can be no final solution to the allocation
of financial resources in a federal system. There can
only be adjustments and re-allocations in the light of
changing conditions. What a federal government needs,
therefore, is machinery adequate to make these adjustments

Kenneth C. Wheare, FEDERAL GOVERNMENT

A prominent feature of fiscal institutions in countries with federal governments is the use of intergovernmental grants. In these countries one finds that governments encompassing relatively large jurisdictions, especially central governments, frequently supplement the revenues of public units at more decentralized levels with grants of funds. These grants are of two basic types: conditional and unconditional. In the case of the former, the grantor defines, to some extent at least, the purposes for which the recipient is to use the funds. Where the grants are unconditional, there are, in contrast, no such specifications, so that the recipient government can employ the grants according to its own set of priorities. Within the category of conditional grants, there exists a variety of possible forms. One popular type, for example, is the matching grant, where, according to a specified formula, the recipient government is required to match each grant-dollar it accepts with a certain number of dollars from its own revenues.

Federal organization of the public sector thus opens up an important problem in the theory of public finance: the issue of government grants not to individual, private economic units, but to other levels of government. The purpose of this chapter is to investigate, primarily in terms of the conceptual framework developed in the first two chapters, the rationale for intergovernmental grants and to examine the suitability of different types of grants for achieving particular objectives. However, before turning explicitly to the subject of grants among units of government, it will prove useful to consider briefly the current state of the debate concerning subsidies and taxes to individual economic units.

External effects and unit subsidies or taxes

In the case where an activity of an individual decision-maker (for example, his level of consumption of a particular commodity) influences the welfare of other persons outside the scope of the market system, there exists the presumption that the individual, ignoring the spillover benefits or costs he generates, will engage in inefficient levels of the activity. The traditional prescription for curing this malady has been developed by A. C. Pigou: in the case of external benefits, the economic unit generating the spillover should receive a unit subsidy equal to the value at the margin of the spillover benefits it creates.[1] In this way the decision-maker will have an incentive to take into account the external effects of his behavior. This is easily seen in Figure 3-1. Consider an individual who in his consumption of good X generates spillover benefits for other persons. The curve MPB reflects the marginal private benefits from the consumption of the good. Considering only the benefits he himself realizes, the individual will extend his consumption of X to OA, at which point the benefits from a marginal unit of X equal the price (which in a competitive system equals marginal cost) he must pay for a unit of X. OA, however, here represents a less than efficient level of consumption of X. The curve MSB (marginal social

[1] *The Economics of Welfare*, 4th ed. (London: Macmillan, 1932), part 2.

benefits), which includes both the benefits to the individual consumer and the spillover benefits to others, lies above the *MPB* curve. The efficient level of consumption of X by the individual is, therefore, OB, at which point the gains to the whole of society from the consumption of an additional unit of X equal marginal cost. To induce the individual to purchase the additional quantity of X, the Pigovian theory argues that the individual should receive a unit subsidy of CD.[2] This subsidy will reduce the effective price of X from P_1 to P_2, and, assuming individual maximizing behavior, will thereby induce the individual to expand his purchases of X to the efficient level OB. The traditional Pigovian theory thus suggests that individual economic units that generate spillover benefits should receive a unit subsidy equal to the value at the margin of the external benefit created.

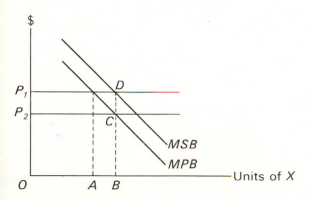

FIGURE 3-1

The Pigovian theory of grants has, however, been the subject of some formidable assaults in recent years. In particular, Ronald Coase has argued that in some circumstances such grants will be quite inappropriate, because the potential inefficiency will be resolved through voluntary collective action

[2] In the case where the spillovers are costs rather than benefits (where *MSB* lies below *MPB* in Figure 3-1), a unit tax instead of a subsidy is the appropriate policy. The analytic treatment of the problem of spillover costs parallels precisely the case of external benefits; for this reason, I will for the most part consider only the latter.

among the interested parties.[3] As mentioned earlier, the existence of externalities implies the presence of potential gains-from-trade, and these gains provide an incentive for mutually advantageous agreements to reach a state of Pareto efficiency. If the activity of one economic unit confers benefits at the margin on another, it is in the latter's interest to encourage (perhaps by a formal contract involving payment) an increase in the level of the activity by the generator of the externality. Coase demonstrates that, in the absence of decision-making costs and strategic behavior, maximizing behavior will lead to joint action to establish an efficient allocation of resources. (This is necessarily true, because any other state of resource allocation would imply the existence of yet-unrealized mutual gains from joint decisions.) The presence of spillover effects will not, therefore, necessarily result in inefficiencies in the use of resources.

Moreover, in cases where such collective action occurs, the introduction of government grants will induce inefficient rather than efficient behavior. If we assume that all inefficiencies have been removed through bargains struck among the concerned economic units, the introduction of a program of government grants would provide incentives for yet further modifications in behavior, which would imply a movement away from an efficient pattern of resource use.[4]

The implication of the Coase argument is that Pigovian grants should not be instituted where there is reason to expect that joint action will develop to prevent serious inefficiencies arising from spillover effects. This raises the question of under what circumstances such joint action will be likely and when unlikely. Since the validity of the Coase conclusion depends on an absence both of decision-making costs and strategic behavior, it is useful to consider when these assumptions will represent a reasonable approximation to actual conditions. Probably the most important factor is the size of the group.

Where the externality involves only a few decision-making units, particularly if they are in close proximity, the difficulties or costs of reaching a satisfactory agreement *may* be relatively

---

[3] "The Problem of Social Cost," *Journal of Law and Economics*, vol. 3 (Oct., 1960), pp. 1–44.
[4] For an intensive and more formal treatment of these points, see James Buchanan and William Stubblebine, "Externality," *Economica*, vol. 29 (Nov., 1962), pp. 371–84.

small; also, each decision-maker is likely to realize that his behavior may have a significant impact on the actions of the others and hence on the aggregate level of the activity. For these reasons, the small group case offers promise of joint action to reduce the distortions in resource allocation resulting from external effects.[5] This suggests, for example, that in instances where a few neighboring jurisdictions provide a good with significant spillover benefits (for example, air purification programs), a higher-level government may do better to encourage joint planning and decision-making in this area than to provide grants to each locality as an incentive to increase its individual level of the activity.

In contrast, where the externality involves large numbers of decision-making units, the difficulties of effective coordinated action are likely to be much greater. In particular, there is good reason to expect widespread free-rider behavior. Since each decision-maker is only one of many, he can anticipate that his own behavior will have only a negligible effect on the aggregate level of the activity. Consequently, each individual has an incentive to ignore the external effects of his own choices and, where possible, to reduce his own provision of the good in favor of consuming units of output provided by others.[6] In the large group case, it is therefore much less likely that joint action will solve the problem; individual maximizing behavior, where the individual decision-maker takes the behavior of others as given and disregards any external effects of his own activities, is to be expected.[7] The example cited earlier of

[5] Even in the case of small groups, however, certain types of strategic behavior (for example, an understatement of one's true preferences in order to get others to pay a larger share of the cost of the good) can easily lead to inefficient outcomes.
[6] A classic case of the free-rider phenomenon is the individual consumer and the provision of national defense. Since any person in a given country consumes whatever national defense is provided and since his own contribution in terms of resources has only a negligible effect on the level of output, it is in his interest, in the absence of collective action, to abstain from supporting the provision of this service with a portion of his own income; the rational consumer will seek a free ride. Government provision of national defense (involving coercive payments in the form of taxes) thus becomes essential if anything like the efficient level of output is to be provided.
[7] There is no universal magic number by which we can call a group small or large for purposes of this analysis; in any particular instance much depends on the make-up of the group and probably also on the commodity involved. The point is rather that, as a given group becomes larger, it will tend to become progressively more in the interest of an

the national spillover benefits generated in the local provision of public education is probably relevant here. In such cases, the Pigovian prescription may still be the proper one: unit subsidies or taxes that induce individual units to take notice of external effects may still be needed to generate efficient patterns of resource use. Where the group of decision-makers is small, however, and where joint decision-making to resolve inefficiencies is feasible, the role of the national government should generally be to facilitate this process of collective planning, not to provide Pigovian grants.[8]

A second difficulty with the Pigovian theory is its partial equilibrium character, a problem that comes into sharp focus in the presence of "reciprocal externalities." Where they exist, not only does the level of activity of individual A provide benefits to (and perhaps serve as a partial substitute for the same activity on the part of) person B, but B's level of this activity has at the same time spillover effects on A. In terms of the Buchanan-Kafoglis examples, inoculations against a communicable disease on the part of some persons reduce the possibility of others contracting the disease and thereby lessen the need for the latters' inoculation.[9] In this case there is an obvious problem of interdependence, and one must consider the process of interaction in the provision of the good. Therefore, in the case of reciprocal externalities where individual decision-makers react to the levels of the activity of other economic units in determining their own, the question is whether simple Pigovian subsidies will still lead to an efficient pattern in the levels of the activity.

The answer to this question is a qualified yes; at least for a broad class of interaction situations, it is possible to determine a set of Pigovian unit subsidies that will induce efficient levels

---

individual decision-maker to ignore the impact of his behavior on others. An excellent treatment of this whole issue is available in James Buchanan, "Cooperation and Conflict in Public-Goods Interaction," *Western Economic Journal*, vol. 5 (March, 1967), pp. 109–21.

[8] William Baumol has also pointed out that, where externalities are present, there is reason to expect with some frequency the violation of second-order conditions and the presence of corner solutions and multiple maxima, any of which can invalidate the simple Pigovian formula; my treatment of the Pigovian analysis is subject to this reservation. See Baumol's "External Economies and Second Order Optimality Conditions," *American Economic Review*, vol. 54 (June, 1964), pp. 358–72.

[9] James Buchanan and Milton Kafoglis, "A Note on Public Goods Supply," *American Economic Review*, vol. 53 (June, 1963), pp. 403–14.

of the activity on the part of all economic units. For this class of cases, each decision-maker will undertake the efficient level of the activity if he is the recipient of a unit subsidy equal to the value of the marginal benefits he confers on others. A proof of this Pigovian proposition appears in Appendix A to this chapter. I might mention here that the determination of the efficient set of subsidies becomes quite complicated in the case of reciprocal externalities because the subsidy to one economic unit depends on the subsidies provided for others. The problem thus requires the solution of a set of simultaneous equations, and the expression for the efficient subsidy to any one economic unit must include as arguments the ability of all other relevant units to generate spillover benefits. This raises serious questions as to whether in practice it is possible to determine the desired set of subsidies with any precision. Nevertheless, the Pigovian prescription does represent at least a conceptual solution to the problem. And even this does point to one important, if obvious, principle in determining the level of grants—namely, that the size of the unit subsidy to a particular economic unit should be greater the larger the value of the marginal spillover benefits generated by that individual.

Imperfect correspondence and intergovernmental grants

As suggested in the preceding chapter, the pattern of provision of public goods in a federal system will not usually constitute a perfect correspondence—that is, a situation in which each public good is provided by a government unit whose jurisdiction coincides precisely with the group whose welfare depends on the unit's output. Rather, since various compromises are necessary in determining the optimal pattern of production of public goods, we would generally expect an imperfect correspondence between outputs of public goods and groups of consumers. This implies that we would anticipate the presence of some interjurisdictional external effects: the levels of consumption of certain public goods in at least some jurisdictions will influence the level of welfare of persons residing elsewhere. In this case, for the reasons suggested earlier, some inefficiencies in the levels (and in the pattern of output among jurisdictions) are likely.

While the Pigovian theory of unit subsidies and taxes is typically treated in terms of the behavior of individual consumers or producers, it can easily be extended in principle to the case where public economic activity in one jurisdiction generates spillover benefits or costs for residents of other localities. We need only reinterpret the marginal private benefits curve (*MPB*) in Figure 3-1 to represent now the sum of the marginal benefits to the residents of the locality. Assuming that the local government extends the provision of the good to the point where the sum of these marginal benefits equals the marginal cost *to the local treasury*, a Pigovian subsidy equal to the value of the spillover benefits conferred at the margin on outsiders will (as depicted in Figure 3-1) induce the locality to provide the efficient level of output.

To prevent any misunderstandings from diverse terminology, it should be noted here that Pigovian unit subsidies are equivalent to matching grants. If, for example, the cost per unit of the public good is one hundred dollars and the spillover benefits per unit of output are worth forty dollars, the efficient subsidy to the jurisdiction providing the good is forty dollars per unit; this implies that the effective unit cost of the good to the grant recipient will be sixty dollars. Note that this subsidy is precisely equivalent to an open-end matching grant in which the contributions of the grantor and the recipient are two-fifths and three-fifths, respectively, or, in other words, to a grant program with a forty–sixty matching formula.[10]

While this extension of Pigovian prescriptions to intergovernmental grants is in principle perfectly legitimate, there are reasons to be more uneasy about the likely efficacy of such subsidies in the case where the recipients are government units rather than individual private units. The analysis throughout the first two chapters has assumed first that local governments know the preferences of the individuals who make up their constituencies, and second that these governments act to maximize the economic welfare of their respective residents. These are, however, somewhat tenuous assumptions. In the first

---

[10] If marginal cost is not constant, as assumed in this example, a given unit subsidy is clearly no longer equivalent to a *uniform* matching-grant program; maintaining this equivalence would then necessitate a *variable* matching formula, one in which the shares of the grantor and recipient varied with the level of the subsidized activity.

place, while the private sector can register the preferences of consumers directly in their buying and selling of goods and services, governments must seek other means, such as voting systems, to determine the preferences of their constituents. These mechanisms typically exhibit certain imperfections; for example, incentives for strategic behavior may lead individuals to misrepresent their true tastes, or perhaps not even to vote at all.[11] Moreover, even if all preferences are known with perfect accuracy, the government may well seek to achieve objectives other than the maximization of the welfare of its constituency. Anthony Downs, for example, has explored the implications of government behavior directed toward the objective of maximizing the number of votes received at the polls and has shown that it will typically result in some misallocation of resources.[12]

The Pigovian theory of grants is, however, based on the assumption that economic units act in accordance with their true preferences and seek to maximize their economic welfare. In the absence of such behavior, there is no presumption that these grants will induce economically efficient behavior. Where individual consumers and producers are concerned, there is a strong presumption that behavior is, for the most part, of this kind; but for the reasons suggested above, this assumption is more suspect in the area of public decision-making. As a result one must adopt a somewhat more skeptical stance on the likely efficacy of intergovernmental grants as a remedy for spillover effects.

The limited applicability of its basic assumptions suggests that the Pigovian theory of unit subsidies and taxes is itself subject to some important qualifications and, further, that one must have reservations about extending even the properly qualified theory to the use of intergovernmental grants. While some may feel that these objections are sufficient to warrant a complete dismissal of Pigovian prescriptions for grants to correct for spillovers among governmental units, I am inclined to stop short of such a rejection. As discussed earlier, one must recognize that there are cases where Pigovian grants or taxes are clearly inappropriate: where joint planning and decision-making by the concerned governments promise to

[11] See, for example, Richard Musgrave, *The Theory of Public Finance* (New York: McGraw-Hill, 1959), chs. 4 and 6.
[12] *An Economic Theory of Democracy* (New York: Harper & Row, 1957).

resolve inefficiencies, these processes should be encouraged by higher-level public authorities in lieu of any program of unit subsidies or taxes to the individual units. However, where it is evident that such cooperation will not be forthcoming, I believe a real case for Pigovian grants still remains. While all governments are far from perfectly responsive to the wishes of their constituents, there is in a democratic system at least a presumption that government decisions will typically promote the welfare of the residents of the relevant jurisdiction; public officials who consistently ignore the preferences of their electorates usually find themselves out of a job.[13] For this reason, where interjurisdictional cooperation is absent, we can expect local provision of public goods to reflect primarily local preferences with little consideration given any existing external effects. And there exists a strong presumption that the failure to consider, for example, significant external benefits will result in distorted patterns of resource use involving less than efficient levels of consumption of the good.

There is, therefore, good reason in such instances to adopt programs that provide incentives for expanded levels of activity; intergovernmental grants represent a policy tool capable of creating just such incentives. There are admittedly real obstacles to determining the precise set of grants necessary to induce efficient behavior, but there is at least a presumption that the effects of such programs are in the proper direction. Moreover, as the analysis has shown, Pigovian grants can provide, subject to certain conditions, a theoretical solution to the externalities problem. This is somewhat encouraging, for in conceptual terms it suggests that there is a way of eliminating or at least reducing one of the major costs associated with an increased decentralization of activity in the public sector.

However, there remains a great need for a theory of intergovernmental grants in terms of an explicit framework of collective choice. As emphasized above, the effects of intergovernmental grants, both on the allocation of resources and on the distribution of income, depend fundamentally on the

---

[13] For a provocative treatment of the types of incentives and constraints operative in public decision-making, see Roland McKean, *Public Spending* (New York: McGraw-Hill, 1968), ch. 2. Viewing public officials as utility maximizers, McKean argues that a type of "unseen hand" is at work in government in the form of various bargaining mechanisms. And this may to some extent provide incentives to public officials that encourage decisions favorable to an efficient use of resources.

political process by which the recipients of the grant make their collective fiscal decisions. An attempt to develop such a theoretical framework appears in Appendix B to this chapter. More precisely, this appendix presents a theoretical structure into which collective decision rules can be introduced and the allocative and distributive effects of various types of intergovernmental grants analyzed. It is noteworthy that, at least for some simple rules of collective choice, the comparative effects of various types of grants are the same in qualitative terms as in the standard model of individual choice. It is shown in Appendix B, for example, that, if the collectivity makes its fiscal decisions by simple majority rule under a system of given tax shares, a matching grant will always induce a larger expenditure toward the public good than will an unconditional grant of the same sum.

Conditional and unconditional grants and resource allocation

The preceding analysis indicates that the appropriate form of intergovernmental grant to correct for interjurisdictional externalities is an open-end, matching grant, not a lump-sum conditional or an unconditional grant. In view of the widespread use of all three of these forms of intergovernmental grants, it is of some importance that we examine carefully the likely effects of each on the allocation of resources.

The need for a matching grant to deal with the problem of external effects can be seen in terms of Figure 3-2. Assume (subject to all their acknowledged shortcomings) that I, II, and III represent community indifference curves between a public good X and all other goods.[14] Each curve identifies alternative combinations of outputs of the public good and all

---

[14] This analysis of the effects of different types of intergovernmental grants draws heavily on the work of James Wilde, "The Expenditure Effects of Grant-in-Aid Programs," *National Tax Journal*, vol. 21 (Sept., 1968), pp. 340–48. Wilde's analysis is essentially positive in nature, for he is interested in predicting the effects of grants on the expenditure levels of recipients; thus he treats the indifference curves in Figure 3-2 as simply representing the preference map of the decision-maker receiving the grant. Inasmuch as the analysis here is also meant to have normative implications, I need a framework within which to make statements concerning levels of social welfare; hence the use of community indifference curves.

other goods that would yield the same level of welfare to the members of the community, with successively higher curves indicating increased levels of welfare. In the absence of any subsidies and with a budget constraint *MN*, the community depicted in Figure 3-2 would choose a level of consumption of *X* equal to *OA*. If, however, an efficient unit subsidy were

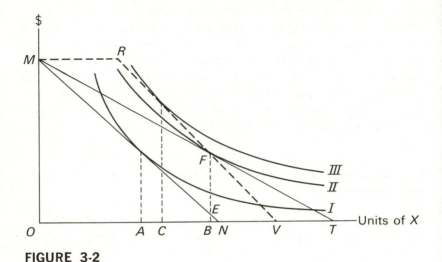

FIGURE 3-2

provided the community—a subsidy that would, in effect, reduce the price of *X* to the community and thereby pivot the budget constraint to *MT*—the consumption of *X* would rise to the socially desired level *OB*. In this case the total grant (that is, the sum of the unit subsidies going to the community) would equal the vertical distance *EF*. Suppose, however, that instead of this unit subsidy, the community were given a lump-sum grant of *EF*, with the proviso that these funds were to be used in the provision of *X*. How would this influence the community's provision of *X*? Such a grant would alter the budget line from *MN* to *MRV*. Note that although this second grant requires that a sum of at least *EF* be spent to provide a minimum output of *X* of *MR*, it does not change the effective price per unit of the public good for units in excess of this minimum, so that the slope of *RV* is the same as the slope of the community's original budget constraint. As a result the provision of X would rise to OC, which would be less than the efficient level.

The problem is that, subject to one qualification, the lump-sum, conditional grant has only an income effect: the output of X rises simply because the grant has enriched the community. The interesting point is that there really is no difference in this case between a conditional, lump-sum grant and an unconditional grant. In each case the community that receives the grant is free to select the combination of goods that best satisfies its preferences under the existing structure of prices. Unlike the matching grant, the lump-sum, conditional grant does not alter the terms of choice between the public good and other commodities; the community is free simply to redirect its own income (exclusive of the grant) into the purchase of other goods. The one qualification to this argument is the case where the community uses none of its own income to provide the public good. In this instance, since it is necessary to spend at least the grant funds on the public good, there can be no leakage of the grant into the provision of other goods. Aside from this special case, however, there would appear to be no real role for conditional, lump-sum grants in achieving efficient levels of output of public goods.[15] To correct for distortions stemming from externalities in the provision of public goods, the matching grant is the proper instrument of policy.[16]

The analysis to this point has proceeded in terms of a

---

[15] Conditional, lump-sum grants may, however, be used to induce recipient governments to adopt certain desired practices. The grantor might, for example, make the availability of funds dependent on the introduction of certain budgetary and planning procedures. In this way the grant may serve to encourage public officials to adopt more effective techniques of fiscal management.

[16] It would of course be possible to induce the recipient government to provide output OB in Figure 3-2 by increasing the conditional or unconditional grant to the point either where the income effects induce this level of provision or where, under the conditional lump-sum grant, this output is financed wholly by grant funds. However, this will always be more expensive for the grantor than inducing this level of provision through a program of matching grants (see Wilde, "The Expenditure Effects of Grant-in-Aid Programs"). Moreover, when one recognizes that grants must be financed by taxes, it becomes clear that the income effects from nonmatching grant programs may be largely or even wholly offset by the negative income effects of the necessary tax programs.

specified unit subsidy for outputs of public goods exhibiting spillover benefits. The issue becomes somewhat more complicated if we allow for the likely possibility that the spillover benefits generated vary with the level of provision of the public good. Assume, for example, that the spillover benefits from a community air purification program are very high for an initial minimal program but gradually decline as the degree of air pollution is reduced. In terms of Figure 3-1, this would imply that the vertical distance between *MSB* and *MPB* diminishes as *X* rises. The policy implication of this situation is straightforward: to provide the proper set of cost signals to the community producing the good, the unit subsidy to the local government should be relatively large for the minimal program and should gradually decline for additional units of output. More specifically, the subsidy for a particular unit of output should equal the spillover benefits accruing from that specific unit—that is (*MSB — MPB*) for that unit. Since (*MSB — MPB*) falls as *X* expands, the subsidy per unit of output should be reduced accordingly for additional units. In the case, then, where the external benefits vary with the level of output of the goods, a "variable" matching grant program is appropriate.

Unconditional intergovernmental grants and the redistribution of income

The argument throughout this chapter has contained as an implicit assumption the existence of an equitable distribution of income. As was stressed in Chapter One, one cannot make much of a case on grounds of economic welfare for an allocation of resources in accordance with consumer preferences if there is not a just distribution of this output among the individuals in the society. A welfare optimum requires both allocative efficiency and an equitable distribution of income.

The issue in this section is whether or not intergovernmental grants have a role to play in achieving the just distribution of income. One finds in Australia and Canada, for example, that the central government makes substantial unconditional grants to subcentral governments and that these grants contain significant equalizing elements: poorer jurisdictions get more funds per capita. In addition, the United States is now considering the adoption of unconditional grants in the form of revenue sharing with state governments, which may also contain a modest equalizing effect. In this last case, some equalization would occur because the equal per-capita grants proposed to all states would be financed primarily through the progressive federal individual income tax. As a result, wealthier jurisdictions, although receiving the same per-capita grant as poorer states, would presumably have paid in a larger sum per capita to support the grant program.

The obvious problem in employing intergovernmental grants for redistributive purposes is that these are grants from one group of people to another. The just distribution of income, in contrast, involves a distribution among individuals. As a result, it may not be possible to achieve the desired income distribution through intergovernmental grants. Consider, for example, the following simplified case. The nation, we assume, is composed of two communities each with two individuals. The actual income of each individual is indicated in column 3 of Table 3-1, while that corresponding to the socially desired

---

Table 3-1

(1) INDIVIDUAL	(2) COMMUNITY	(3) ACTUAL	(4) DESIRED	(5) REQUIRED
1	A	$100	$90	$−10
2	A	60	65	+5
3	B	80	75	−5
4	B	40	50	+10

---

distribution of income appears in column 4. To reach the desired distribution of income requires a transfer of $10 from individual 1 to 4 and a transfer of $5 from 3 to 2. Assuming no effects on gross income earned, the necessary redistribution could easily be accomplished at the national level through a properly designed negative income-tax program. The central government, employing a personal income tax with a progressive rate structure, would collect $10 from individual 1 and $5 from 3 and would make payments of $10 to individual 4 and $5 to 2.

Could the central government also realize the just distribution of income through the use of a non-negative national income tax and intergovernmental grants? The answer is yes, *provided* the central government can employ differing sets of income-tax rates among the various jurisdictions. Assume, for example, that the unconditional grants to each community are used by the recipient governments to reduce equally the tax payments of their two residents. In this case, if the central government collected $15, 0, $15, 0 from individuals 1 through 4, respectively, and accompanied this with a grant of $10 to community A and $20 to community B, the desired distribution of income would be attained. But note that this particular solution requires that individuals 1 and 3 with different incomes pay the same tax to the central government. If we further constrain the central government (for example, as the Constitution of the United States does) by not allowing geographical differentials in income-tax rates, it will generally be impossible to reach the desired distribution of income.[17]

[17] The set of intergovernmental grants and tax bills in the example is not unique. A vector of tax payments, $T = \{20,5,20,5\}$, and grants to communities A and B of $G = \{20,30\}$ will also produce the socially desired distribution of income. There is, in fact, an infinite number of combinations of such vectors that will do the trick. The point is that for any number of communities greater than one, the number of unknowns exceeds the number of equations so that in general the value of some of the unknowns can be set arbitrarily. More precisely, to determine the set of intergovernmental grants and income-tax bills needed to attain the socially desired distribution of income, we must solve a set of simultaneous equations:

(a) $$t_{ij} + (1/n_j)G_j = a_{ij} \quad \text{for all } (i,j),$$

(b) $$\Sigma\Sigma\, t_{ij} = \Sigma\, G_j.$$

In these equations, t_{ij} is the tax payment of the ith person in the jth community, n_j is the number of persons in community j, G_j is the grant to the jth community, and a_{ij} is the given *net* transfer for individual (i,j) needed to establish the desired distribution of income. This formulation assumes, as in the text, that the grant to each community is divided equally among its respective residents, although other assumptions could be made without altering the substance of the argument. There will be one equation of type a for each of the (i,j) persons in the nation plus equation b, which will clearly be less than the number of unknowns (the t_{ij} and G_j) whenever $j > 1$. In the case where geographical differences in income-tax rates are not allowed, there will exist constraints on the t_{ij} (that is, constraints indicating that people with higher incomes must pay higher taxes and that persons with the same income pay the same tax). This will typically cause the number of equations to exceed the number of unknowns so that a solution will not generally exist.

Moreover, even if it were both legally and politically feasible to adopt geographically discriminatory rates for a national income tax, the determination of the set of rates and the accompanying grant for each jurisdiction would be a very complicated matter. When we recognize further that, in most countries, differing sets of tax rates across jurisdictions are for one reason or another not a realistic possibility, it is clear that equalizing-intergovernmental grants are not a satisfactory substitute for a national negative income-tax program. Typically, some of the redistributive effects of equalizing-intergovernmental grants will be perverse. Suppose, for example, that, using a single national set of income-tax rates, the central government decides to try to achieve a more equal distribution of income through relatively generous grants to the governments of poorer jurisdictions. The problem is that even relatively poor communities usually contain some wealthy persons, and, similarly, rich jurisdictions often have some poor residents. As a result, in some cases, the intergovernmental grants may well tend to exaggerate rather than reduce the existing degree of inequality in the distribution of income; some income will tend to move from persons of lower incomes to relatively wealthy individuals. In terms of the example in Table 3-1, intergovernmental taxes and grants that redistributed income from wealthy community A to poor community B would imply a transfer of income from individual 2 to 3, even though 3 already has a higher level of income than 2.

This is not to say that this type of grant program is completely useless. Political constraints may in some cases render this the only reasonably effective redistributive policy available, and as such it might, on balance, be preferable to the absence of any redistributive program. We should, nevertheless, recognize its shortcomings. To achieve a just distribution of income among the individuals in a nation, a national program that redistributes income among individuals, not among jurisdictions, is the preferred alternative.

Unconditional grants and the problem of horizontal equity

While intergovernmental grants may be a highly imperfect means of redistributing income, equity considerations do provide a case for unconditional grants to poorer jurisdictions. This case is based on an extension of the principle of horizontal equity (that is, the equal treatment of equals) to a system of federal finance; moreover, from this viewpoint, such grants can be seen as a means to maintain an equivalence between the distribution of nominal income and its purchasing power in terms of goods and services both private and public.

As Musgrave has argued, "Perhaps the most widely accepted principle of equity in taxation is that people in equal positions should be treated equally."[18] However, as Buchanan has shown, this dictum is likely to be violated in a federal system.[19] Even if the central government treats equals equally in fiscal terms and each subcentral government unit does the same, the impact of all the public budgets combined will generally be such that individuals with equal incomes are treated unequally. The problem is that, if we consider two communities with an identical output of public goods and services, the wealthier of the two communities will, other things equal, be able to meet its revenue requirements with lower tax rates. Raising a given amount of revenue per resident requires lower tax rates the higher the level of per-capita income. As a result, for a specified amount of local public services, an individual in a wealthier community will have a smaller tax bill than his equal in a poorer locality. Therefore, from the standpoint of the system as a whole, equals tend not to be treated equally.[20]

This can, moreover, introduce unwanted distortions in the overall distribution of income. Suppose, for example, that the

[18] Musgrave, *The Theory of Public Finance*, p. 160.
[19] "Federalism and Fiscal Equity," *American Economic Review*, vol. 40 (Sept., 1950), pp. 583–99; reprinted by American Economic Association in *Readings in the Economics of Taxation* (Homewood, Ill.: Richard D. Irwin, 1959), pp. 93–109.
[20] As Musgrave points out, this problem does not arise where local taxation is on a benefit basis.

> If state taxes, imposed to finance public services, are allocated on a benefit basis, all citizens of the federation will be taxed on a benefit basis by their respective states. In this case, no central equalization is needed since the requirement of horizontal equity is met by the very condition of universal taxation according to benefits received.

See his "Approaches to a Fiscal Theory of Political Federalism," in National Bureau of Economic Research, *Public Finances: Needs, Sources, and Utilization* (Princeton, N.J.: Princeton University Press, 1961), p. 119.

government has established the socially desired distribution of nominal income. The violation of the horizontal equity criterion muddies the correspondence between this distribution of income and what is presumably of greater importance—namely, the distribution of purchasing power or the command over flows of real goods and services. An individual in a relatively poor locality will, in effect, pay a higher price for public goods and services than he would in a wealthier jurisdiction. Consequently, the distribution of real goods and services will not correspond accurately to the distribution of nominal income.

Such differentials can, in addition to generating inequities, introduce inefficiencies into the economic system. An individual will, other things equal, have an incentive to locate in a jurisdiction with relatively wealthy residents where he can consume public outputs for a small tax payment. In this way, varying levels of income between communities create inducements for relocation that do not reflect differences in real costs or other considerations relevant to efficient resource utilization. This means that there will be a tendency toward a distortion in the allocation of resources in the form of overmigration into relatively wealthy communities.[21]

There are two possible approaches to establishing horizontal equity in a federal system. The first is the adoption of geographically discriminating income-tax rates by the central government. By levying higher rates on residents of relatively wealthy localities, the central government could, in effect, equalize the cost of public goods to all individuals with a given

---

[21] The problem of fiscal differentials and efficient location under a federal system has been the subject of a series of papers. See the James Buchanan-Anthony Scott exchange: "Federal Grants and Resource Allocation," *Journal of Political Economy*, vol. 60 (June, 1952), pp. 208–17 and (Dec., 1952), pp. 534–36 and 536–38; Scott, "A Note on Grants in Federal Countries," *Economica*, vol. 17 (Nov., 1950), pp. 416–22 and "The Economic Goals of Federal Finance," *Public Finance*, vol. 19, no. 3 (1964), pp. 241–88; Charles Tiebout, "An Economic Theory of Fiscal Decentralization," in National Bureau of Economic Research, *Public Finances: Needs, Sources, and Utilization* (Princeton, N.J.: Princeton University Press, 1961), pp. 93–94; Richard Musgrave, "Approaches to a Fiscal Theory of Political Federalism," pp. 120–22, with Buchanan's comment on pp. 122–29 and Musgrave's reply on pp. 132–33; and James Buchanan and Richard Wagner, "An Efficiency Basis for Federal Fiscal Equalization," in Julius Margolis, ed., *The Analysis of Public Output*, National Bureau of Economic Research Conference (New York: Columbia University Press, 1970) pp. 139–58.

income, regardless of locality. Individuals in poorer jurisdictions would be compensated for their higher local tax bills by reduced income-tax payments to the central government. Alternatively, the central government could seek to equalize the fiscal capacity of all jurisdictions by instituting a program of unconditional grants to poorer localities. In this way, a given set of tax rates could raise the same sum, including grant funds, in a poor community as in a wealthy one. Either of these measures would result in equal treatment of equals.[22] Since there typically exist constitutional or other political obstacles to the adoption of geographically discriminatory tax rates, a program of unconditional grants, where the grant per capita varies inversely with the level of per-capita income in the jurisdiction, would appear to be the more feasible solution to the problem. Unconditional government grants may, therefore, have a role in federal finance in terms of ensuring an equal treatment of equals.

While the Buchanan case for equalizing-grants is, in principle, a compelling one, two sorts of objections to such intergovernmental grants have been raised. First, Anthony Scott has argued that within a federal system equal treatment of equals by the central government and independently by each local government may be sufficient: "Complete over-all horizontal equity is not achieved, chiefly because its achievement is not a prime goal in a federation." [23] We could, therefore, simply choose to ignore the issue of overall horizontal equity. This raises the whole problem of fiscal objectives within a federal system of government—a problem we will examine in the last section of this chapter.

A second line of criticism has been a more pragmatic one. Musgrave contends that Buchanan's treatment, as regards its relevance to the United States, is "a much too simplified view of the problem." [24] In particular, complications stemming from the interjurisdictional shifting of tax burdens, the levying of many state and local taxes on firms instead of directly on

---

[22] In his treatment of this problem, Buchanan considers explicitly the expenditure side of the budget by dealing with the "fiscal residuum" (the individual's tax bill minus his expenditure benefits). In these terms, overall horizontal equity requires that the fiscal residua for equals be equal regardless of community of residence.
[23] Scott, "The Economic Goals of Federal Finance," p. 251.
[24] Musgrave, "Approaches to a Fiscal Theory of Political Federalism," p. 121.

individuals, and differing cost functions for local public services render Buchanan's argument of dubious practical importance. The point is that differing levels of income across jurisdictions is only one of the many sources of horizontal inequity in a federal system, and not necessarily the most important one. Such inequities (and, as noted earlier, some accompanying inefficiencies), so long as they are not allowed to become too serious, can simply be regarded as part of the price of a decentralized fiscal system. While this may be true, it is nevertheless the case that poorer jurisdictions can and frequently do have significantly higher tax rates than wealthier areas but yet have inferior programs of public services; this hardly seems fair to those living in these jurisdictions. This issue is of particular interest when viewed in the perspective of the actual intergovernmental grant programs adopted in federal countries.

Some reflections on the theory and use of intergovernmental grants

The theory of intergovernmental grants developed in this chapter suggests that matching grants may sometimes be needed to reduce inefficiencies resulting from interjurisdictional spillover effects, and that unconditional grants may serve to maintain horizontal equity and to prevent undesired distortions in the distribution of real income within a federal system. Turning to the actual use of intergovernmental grants in federal countries, one finds that the basic structures of existing grant programs can be understood to some extent in terms of this analytic framework. Most federal countries have made extensive use of both conditional and unconditional grants to more decentralized levels of government.[25] The former are typically used to encourage spending on such items as education and roads, which involve significant interjurisdictional external effects, or in some cases to support explicitly redistributive programs for which the central government

[25] The U.S. federal government has been an exception to this proposition, for it has relied exclusively on conditional grants. There is, however, considerable pressure for the adoption of a modest revenue-sharing program consisting of unconditional grants to the states, with provisions for the passing on of some of the funds to local governments.

usually must assume a primary responsibility. Moreover, one finds that these grant programs frequently involve equalizing provisions so that poorer jurisdictions receive more generous support. In fact many of these programs incorporate explicit provisions to account for the particular expenditure requirements, or "need," of each jurisdiction in addition to its "fiscal capacity" to meet that need. These considerations are evident in the following statements by various federal governments on their philosophy of intergovernmental grants:

AUSTRALIA:

Special grants are justified when a State through financial stress from any cause is unable to discharge its functions as a member of the federation and should be determined by the amount of help found necessary to make it possible for that State by reasonable effort to function at a standard not appreciably below that of other States.

Commonwealth Grants Commission,
Third Report, 1936, p. 75

CANADA:

The issue is not the liability of the Dominion to a province for the adverse effects of federal policy, but the ability of the province to perform its functions under the federal system. The measure of assistance which should be forthcoming from the Dominion is not, therefore, the net damages from federal policies, but the fiscal need of the province arising from any cause.

Rowell-Sirois Commission, *Report, Book II*, p. 233

SWITZERLAND:

The Confederation encourages financial equalization among the cantons. In particular, when federal subventions are granted, the financial capacity of the cantons and the situation of the mountainous regions must be considered in an appropriate fashion.

Article 42 of the Constitution

A Federal law requiring the consent of the Bundesrat shall ensure a reasonable financial equalization between financially strong Lander and financially weak Lander, due account being taken of the financial capacity and requirements of communes. . . .

Article 107 (2) of the Basic Law

In the United States, as in most other federal countries, equalization has come to be regarded as an essential element in many intergovernmental grant programs. In particular, the major conditional grant programs in the United States have been designed with two primary objectives: (1) the achievement of national minimum levels of certain basic public services; and (2) an equalization across jurisdictions of the "fiscal effort" required to provide these minimum program levels.[26] To meet these objectives, the grant formulas for many programs in the United States, as elsewhere, contain terms to reflect both need and fiscal capacity (where the latter is typically measured by the level of per-capita income). The matching share of the federal government (or in some instances the amount of funds authorized for a certain jurisdiction) varies directly in these cases with some measure of need and, inversely, with per-capita income. The goal is that every jurisdiction provide at least a specified minimum level of the most important public services and be able to support these services with a set of tax rates that is essentially the same as in other areas. As Selma Mushkin points out:

> Because the variations in [taxable] capacity among the states often led to widely divergent program performance, it became necessary to incorporate a measure of relative capacity as well as relative need in grant allocations. Accordingly, a number of post-World War II grant programs have been designed so that they are more effective than earlier grants in recognizing state capacity differentials. Formulas in these newer programs have moved closer toward achievement of the twin objectives of equalization—a uniform minimum nation-

[26] See the Advisory Commission on Intergovernmental Relations, *The Role of Equalization in Federal Grants* (Washington, D.C.: 1964), p. 4.

87

wide program level and uniform fiscal effort from state to state to support such a minimum program. It is intended that state and local governments will build upon these minimum standards in response to local variations in services needed and desired.[27]

These two objectives do seem, to some extent at least, to be consistent with the theory of intergovernmental grants. The goal of ensuring an adequate level of basic public services, including, for example, education and health, can be justified, in part, on the grounds of external effects. It is simply in the interest of everyone in a society to have satisfactory levels of key public services available in all jurisdictions. As Burton Weisbrod has emphasized, this is particularly true in view of the growing mobility across jurisdictions, which implies that any given individual is likely at various times to consume public services in different localities, and, consequently, that each jurisdiction will have to provide services for a changing composition of residents.[28]

Moreover, by varying grants with need and fiscal capacity, the central government is presumably able to eliminate or at least reduce any differences in the taxes a given individual would have to pay in different jurisdictions for the same level of public services. There does seem to be something here that is very close to the economist's notion of horizontal equity. Proponents of grant programs are quick to point out that their purpose is not to redistribute income among individuals; Howard Schaller, in discussing the objectives of federal grants in the United States, stresses that they are not "directed specifically toward the reduction of per capita income differences among the 48 states."[29] The idea is rather to ensure that every individual has access to a sound program of public services within his chosen locality at a cost in line with what he would pay elsewhere.

From a broad perspective the economic theory of intergovernmental grants seems to provide some insight into the actual structure of grant programs in federal countries. On closer

[27] "Federal Grants and Federal Expenditures," *National Tax Journal*, vol. 10 (Sept., 1957), p. 194.
[28] *External Benefits of Public Education* (Princeton, N.J.: Princeton University, Industrial Relations Section, 1964).
[29] "Federal Grants-in-Aid and Differences in State Per Capita Incomes, 1929, 1939, and 1949," *National Tax Journal*, vol. 8 (Sept., 1955), p. 287.

examination, however, we often find that grant provisions do not square as well with the theory as one might suppose. To develop some of the anomalies, it is useful to consider in some depth an actual system of intergovernmental grants.

As noted earlier the federal government in the United States has relied almost solely on conditional grants. These grants have, moreover, grown extremely rapidly in recent years from a level of $2.3 billion in 1950 to 24.4 billion by 1970.[30] The trend has been to adopt matching grants (over 80 percent of grant funds require matching), a substantial portion of them in the form of variable matching grants under which poorer jurisdictions have a smaller matching share than do more wealthy states or localities.

A number of these grant programs (those for education, highways, etc.) can clearly be justified on the grounds of external effects; in these cases one would expect to find open-end, matching grants. Nearly all these grant programs are, however, closed-end (that is, federal matching ceases at some, typically modest, level of expenditure). It may well be that efficient, open-end grants would exhibit a declining share for the grantor at higher levels of the activity to reflect declining spillover benefits, but it requires rather peculiar preference functions to justify closed-end grants for allocative purposes. In particular, closed-end matching implies that, at a certain level of provision of the public service, spillover benefits suddenly become zero.[31]

In addition, while the equalization provisions in these grant programs appear consistent with the case for horizontal equity, the question arises as to why such equalization is limited to those programs receiving support under conditional grants. Complete equalization implies that a jurisdiction should be able to provide a full range of public services at tax rates in line with those elsewhere. This condition is clearly not satisfied where equalizing funds are limited to the provision of a

[30] *Economic Report of the President*, U.S. Government Printing Office (Feb., 1971), p. 280.
[31] Indeed, as Wilde points out, in "The Expenditure Effects of Grant-in-Aid Programs," closed-end grants will in some cases be no more effective in stimulating spending than conditional, nonmatching grants. Once the recipient exceeds the level of the activity for which external support is provided, the grant has nothing but an income effect, since it no longer influences the marginal cost of the program to the recipient. See also George Break, *Intergovernmental Fiscal Relations in the United States* (Washington, D.C.: Brookings Institution, 1967), ch. 3.

select group of services. In fact it has been a frequent complaint in the United States that in poorer areas the bulk of locally generated revenues are directed into matching-grant programs with little remaining for the support of other state and local services.[32]

It seems to me that one can react to these apparent inconsistencies in two ways. First, one can argue that the program of intergovernmental grants in the United States is somewhat ill-designed to meet the goals of economic efficiency and equity. In particular, the problem appears to be one of trying to realize too many goals with too few instruments of policy.[33] Full equalization suggests the need for unconditional grant programs, and adjusting for spillovers requires matching grants. To achieve both goals thus requires two sets of grant programs.

Second, one may take the position that the normative framework adopted in this study is unnecessarily narrow. In addition to efficient resource allocation and an equitable distribution of income among individuals, one can contend that in a federal system there typically exist additional objectives relating to the relative well-being of residents of different jurisdictions. There is certainly considerable support for this position. In their studies of federalism, political scientists continually stress the interplay of governments: the interests local governments have with one another and with the central government.[34] Musgrave has, moreover, provided a catalogue of possible objectives within a federal system and has developed the fiscal implications of each.[35] We could argue, then,

---

[32] See Alvin Hansen and Harvey Perloff, *State and Local Finance in the National Economy* (New York: W. W. Norton, 1944), pp. 127–28; and James Maxwell, *Financing State and Local Governments* (Washington, D.C.: Brookings Institution, 1965), pp. 58–59.

[33] To achieve simultaneously a given number of policy objectives requires in general at least as many policy instruments as there are objectives. See Jan Tinbergen, *On the Theory of Economic Policy* (Amsterdam: North-Holland, 1952). Lester Thurow has applied this principle to the problem of intergovernmental grants to show that both conditional and unconditional grants are needed to achieve simultaneously allocative and redistributive goals. See his "The Theory of Grants-in-Aid," *National Tax Journal*, vol. 19 (Dec., 1966), pp. 373–77.

[34] See, for example, the seminal study of Kenneth C. Wheare, *Federal Government*, 4th ed. (London: Oxford University Press, 1963); and R. J. May, *Federalism and Fiscal Adjustment* (Oxford, England: Clarendon Press, 1969).

[35] Musgrave, "Approaches to a Fiscal Theory of Political Federalism."

that the objective of minimum program levels of basic public services in all jurisdictions financed by an equal fiscal effort constitutes in itself an attractive goal of federal finance and that although it may require some sacrifice in terms of efficient resource allocation and an equitable distribution of income among all individuals in the nation, it is legitimate in its own right.

Even this, however, does not wholly remove a fundamental anomaly in the structure of conditional grants in the United States. One of the two primary objectives of these programs is ensuring the provision of national minimum levels of key public services. In the words of the Advisory Commission on Intergovernmental Relations, the purpose is to "achieve a national minimum level of program operations by varying the Federal grant offer to the States directly in proportion to their program needs and inversely with their fiscal capacities." [36] Matching grants, however, do not ensure that the minimum service level envisioned in the program will in fact be attained. Federal monies will probably be substituted to some extent for the funds of the recipient; it is therefore a matter of some conjecture as to precisely how much a given matching-grant program is likely to expand total expenditures on the service in question.[37] The point is that under matching-grant pro-

---

[36] *The Role of Equalization in Federal Grants*, p. 4.
[37] What evidence there is on this issue is far from consistent. A few studies in the United States have attempted to determine the impact state school aid to localities has on the local level of expenditures on education. Two of these studies suggest that the stimulative effects of such grants are very modest, that the state aid is primarily substituted for local funds. See Jerry Miner, *Social and Economic Factors in Spending for Public Education* (Syracuse, N.Y.: Syracuse University Press, 1963), ch. 5; and Edward F. Renshaw, "A Note on the Expenditure Policy of State Aid to Education," *Journal of Political Economy*, vol. 68 (April, 1960), pp. 170–74. However, a more recent study of state school aid in New England indicated that an extra dollar of state aid was associated with a 40- to 80-cent increase in total local expenditure per pupil. See George Bishop, "Stimulative versus Substitutive Effects of State School Aid in New England," *National Tax Journal*, vol. 17 (June, 1964), pp. 133–43. Studies of the influence of federal government grants on state and local spending have generally found substantial stimulative effects. Examples here are Seymour Sacks and Robert Harris, "The Determinants of State and Local Government Expenditures and Intergovernmental Flows of Funds," *National Tax Journal*, vol. 17 (March, 1964), pp. 75–85; and Jack Osman, "The Dual Impact of Federal Aid on State and Local Government Expenditures," *National Tax Journal*, vol. 19 (Dec., 1966), pp. 362–72. There is some reason, however, to believe that the econometric techniques used in these studies result in biases

grams the final determination of the level of provision of the service is in the hands of the recipient of the grant. As a result, the realization of the minimum program level cannot be assured. Matching grants, whether variable or not, therefore appear to be a rather imperfect policy tool for achieving national minimum levels of output of local public goods. If such minimums are in fact desired, the certain way to reach this goal is for the central government to finance these minimum levels completely; lump-sum conditional grants sufficient to finance the desired level of output would ensure success.

However, one can make some sense of the use of matching grants to achieve minimum program levels. Consider a situation where the central government has a number of high-priority grant programs for which minimum national levels of services are regarded as highly desirable. The central government is, however, normally subject to some form of budgetary constraint and, as a result, may not be able to implement the full range of programs on the agenda; it must settle for using its limited grant funds to induce minimum levels of provision for as many of these programs as possible. As pointed out earlier, to ensure that all jurisdictions achieve the desired minimum level of operation for a specific program, it is generally sufficient for the central government to provide all the funds. If, however, the central government finances all the costs of realizing the prescribed program level in all jurisdictions, it is possible that the central authorities will exhaust their available funds on a few programs. This could well mean the failure of the central government to stimulate spending on a large number of other important public goods. From this vantage point, it may make more sense to attempt to ascertain just how big a central government share is necessary to induce recipients to provide the desired program level. If, for example, a 50-percent central share is sufficient to meet this goal, then the remaining 50 percent of the funds becomes available for use in other programs. For this reason matching grants may be an effective instrument for allocating scarce central government funds.[38]

that are likely to overstate the effects of these grants on the spending levels of recipients. On this, see my "The Dual Impact of Federal Aid on State and Local Government Expenditures: A Comment," *National Tax Journal*, vol. 21 (June, 1968), pp. 220–23.

[38] As has been pointed out to me by one observer in Washington, there is a sense in which the federal government in the United States treats

There is reason to believe, moreover, that variable matching, where the grantor's share is larger for poorer jurisdictions, is likely to be more effective than uniform matching grants in conserving central government funds. In general, one can expect that poorer areas will require more assistance in attaining a specified program level than will relatively wealthy areas; rich jurisdictions simply tend, in the absence of assistance, to provide higher levels of public services than do poorer ones. Where a 30-percent central government share may be sufficient to induce wealthy localities to reach the desired level of provision, it may require, for example, 50–50 matching to pull up the levels of services in poorer areas; in the interest of conserving its own scarce funds, it would make sense in this case for the central government to employ a variable-matching formula in which the grantor's share is 30 percent for rich jurisdictions and 50 percent for poorer localities. Variable-matching grants may in this way allow the central government to get the maximum stimulative effect from a given amount of grant funds. Thus, variable matching has a real attraction in terms of realizing minimum activity levels for a number of programs.[39]

---

state and local dollars as "free." The goal of federal authorities, as envisioned here, is to stretch federal grant funds as far as possible in stimulating state and local expenditures on certain programs. The substitution of a state dollar for a federal dollar on one of these programs releases the federal dollar to induce yet further state and local expenditures on such programs. The point is that state funds expended on these programs do not reduce the amount of federal monies available for grants. It may be stretching matters a bit, however, for the federal government to regard such state and local expenditures as wholly "free," since a state dollar expended on one grant program may result in reduced state spending on another grant-supported program.

[39] A variable-matching formula of the type discussed here may also make some sense in terms of our discussion of interjurisdictional spillover effects. Suppose, for example, that the marginal value of the spillover benefits from the provision of a local public service declines as the level of the activity increases. In this case the subsidy for marginal units should presumably decline with the level of the provision of the good. Since, however, poorer jurisdictions typically provide lower levels of consumption of most public goods for their residents than do wealthier communities, it follows that the unit subsidy, or grantor's share, should generally be larger for a marginal unit in a poor locality than in a rich one. The most direct way to deal with this problem is, of course, for the government providing the grant to allow its share to decline with the recipient's level of activity, but a grant formula under which this share varies inversely with the level of per-

The conclusion that emerges from all this is that a theoretical view of intergovernmental grants, which suggests the need for matching grants to compensate for external effects and the use of unconditional grants for equity purposes, can take us some distance toward understanding systems of grants in most federal countries. However, when one looks more closely at the structure of particular systems of grants, practices inconsistent with the theory are evident. Undoubtedly these are to some extent the result of political processes and various pragmatic considerations, which lead to imperfect programs. But to some degree they may also reflect the presence in many federal systems of objectives that are not wholly consistent with a narrow view of economic efficiency and equity.

---

capita income in the recipient jurisdiction will at least tend to work in the same general direction.

Appendix A

Reciprocal externalities and intergovernmental grants

This appendix examines the problem of reciprocal externalities in the provision of local public goods and discusses its implications for a program of intergovernmental grants or taxes designed to achieve an efficient allocation of resources. I will seek first to derive the Pareto-efficiency conditions for the case of reciprocal externalities. Since individual maximizing behavior will not generally satisfy these conditions, we proceed to the issue of the subsidy or tax policy required to correct these inefficiencies. Anticipating the results, we find that in the model the introduction of reciprocal externalities does not alter the substance of the Pigovian prescription; grants (or, where appropriate, taxes) to individual economic units that internalize existing spillovers still lead to Pareto efficiency. The determination of the efficient set of subsidies or taxes in the presence of reciprocal externalities is, however, quite complex, since the efficient subsidy or tax for one economic unit depends on the spillover-generating capabilities of all units.

It will simplify matters to consider initially the case of a reciprocal interdependency in the utility functions of two individuals in a world of only two commodities; the solution reached is easily generalized to a system of many persons and commodities. (It will be shown later in the discussion that the solution can be applied to the case of intercommunity externalities and intergovernmental grants.) Assume that the first of the two commodities, X, is a standard private good whose consumption involves no externalities. The other, Y, we assume to be an impure public good. More specifically, when one individual increases his consumption of Y through the purchase of an additional unit, the other person's consumption of Y rises also, although not generally to the full extent of the expansion in consumption by the first person. The model is summarized in equations 1 through 3:

(1) $$U_1 = U_1(X_1, Y_1 + \alpha Y_2)$$

(2) $$U_2 = U_2(X_2, \beta Y_1 + Y_2)$$

(3) $$F(X_1 + X_2, Y_1 + Y_2) = 0$$

where $0 < \alpha, \beta < 1$.

Equations 1 and 2 are the utility functions of the two persons, where X_1, Y_1, represent the purchases of X and Y by the first person; X_2, Y_2, the purchases of the second, and equation 3 is an overall constraint on output that defines the production-possibilities frontier. Note that there does not exist a simple one-to-one relationship between quantities produced or purchased and quantities consumed. This is of real importance, and the failure to make this distinction has resulted in considerable confusion in some of the literature on the problem of externalities.[1] The point is that the aggregate level of consumption of Y by individuals 1 and 2 depends not only on their total purchases of Y, but also on the distribution of these purchases between the two individuals. This is significant, because in the general case, where α is not equal to β, the two persons are not equally effective in generating spillover benefits. In the case where $\alpha > \beta$, for example, the purchase of a unit of Y by person 2 results in a greater aggregate consumption of Y than if individual 1 were to buy the extra unit.

The efficiency conditions

The first problem is to determine the conditions that will characterize an efficient allocation of resources in this system. Adopting the criterion of Pareto efficiency, we must maximize

[1] James Buchanan and Milton Kafoglis show the significance of this characteristic of public goods in their "A Note on Public Goods Supply," *American Economic Review*, vol. 53 (June, 1963), pp. 403–14.

the utility of one individual while holding constant that of the other. Including the production constraint, we must maximize the expression:

$$(4) \quad L = U_1(X_1, Y_1 + \alpha Y_2) + \lambda_1[U_2(X_2, \beta Y_1 + Y_2) - U^0{}_2] \\ + \lambda_2[F(X_1 + X_2, Y_1 + Y_2)]$$

where λ_1 and λ_2 are Lagrangian multipliers and $U^0{}_2$ is individual 2's given level of utility. This procedure produces the following first-order efficiency conditions:

$$(5) \quad\quad MRT = MRS_1 + \beta MRS_2 \\ = \alpha MRS_1 + MRS_2.$$

Equations 5 say that the marginal rate of transformation, MRT, of X for Y must equal both of the expressions to the right involving the marginal rates of substitution, MRS, of the two consumers. In the special case where $\alpha = \beta = 0$, the case where Y, like X, is a private good, equations 5 reduce to the standard conditions that the MRS of both consumers must be equal and must in turn equal the MRT. In the opposite polar case, where $\alpha = \beta = 1$, Y is a pure Samuelsonian public good, and we have the familiar result that the MRT equals the sum of the individual MRS's. The intermediate cases are also subject to straightforward interpretation. The equality to the right says, in effect, that the joint benefit from the purchase of an additional unit of Y must be the same regardless of which consumer purchases the marginal unit. If this condition were not satisfied, it would be possible to increase welfare by shifting more Y to that person whose purchases of Y generate a greater joint gain. Finally, the equality to the left indicates that the opportunity cost of an extra unit of Y in terms of X must equal the joint benefit measured in terms of the amount of X individuals 1 and 2 would be willing to give up for an additional unit of Y. In short, the sum of the benefits of an extra unit of Y must equal its marginal cost.

Assuming that the second-order conditions are satisfied and that we have an interior solution, these, then, are the conditions that must be satisfied to realize a Pareto-efficient allocation of resources. The next question is whether or not competitive maximizing behavior will satisfy these efficiency conditions, and the answer is, in general, no. Each individual, setting out to maximize his own welfare, will purchase units of Y up to the point where his own MRS equals MRT. This result is, except for one special case, unaltered by the fact that he is receiving "spillin" effects from the consumption of Y by the other person. This is perhaps best seen in terms of Figure 3A-1, which maps the preferences of individual 1 along with

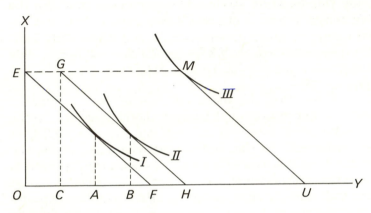

FIGURE 3A-1

his budget constraint EF. If individual 2 consumes none of Y, person 1, with no spillin benefits, will consume OA of Y. Assume now that 2 consumes Y_2, a nonzero amount of Y. Person 1 will now experience an increase in his own consumption of Y equal to $OC = \alpha Y_2$, and as a result his new budget line becomes EGH. However, so long as 1 continues to purchase any positive amount of Y (that is, so long as his entire consumption of Y is not in the form of spillins from 2), it is still the case that at the margin his $MRS = MRT$. The point is that the spillin benefits have, in this case, only an income effect. The solution is identical to that which would result from an increase in 1's income of EG in terms of Y.[2] Only where the spillovers account for all of 1's consumption of Y (for example, a point like M) will this condition not be satisfied. It is therefore clear that, in the absence of collective action, competitive be-

---

[2] The analysis here is precisely analogous to the treatment of conditional, nonmatching grants in the main body of the chapter.

havior will not, in general, produce an efficient allocation of resources.[3]

An efficient set of grants

What set of grants to individuals 1 and 2 will induce a pattern of efficient behavior in a competitive system? It is useful in answering this question to consider first the case where the spillover benefit is just a one-way affair rather than of a reciprocal nature. Assume in equations 1 and 2 that only individual 1 generates external benefits. In formal terms, this means that $\alpha = 0$ while β is positive. Equations 5 in this case reduce to:

$$(6) \qquad MRT = MRS_1 + \beta MRS_2 = MRS_2.$$

With competitive behavior, each individual will consume Y such that the $MRT = MRS_1 = MRS_2$. Since $MRS_2 = MRT$, the efficient subsidy is, in this case, clear: individual 1 should receive a unit subsidy equal to βMRT. If, for example, there exists over the relevant range constant costs in the production of both of the commodities and the competitive market price and marginal cost of Y is \$5, we know that the value individual 2 will place on a marginal unit of Y is \$5. If $\beta = 1/2$ (that is, the purchase of an extra unit of Y by 1 increases 2's consumption by 1/2 unit), individual 1 should be paid a subsidy of \$2.50 (that is, charged a price per additional unit of Y of \$2.50). In this way, maximizing behavior will lead person 1 to expand his purchases of Y to the point where the value he himself places on an extra unit of Y is \$2.50. Therefore the value of the marginal unit to 1 plus the value of the spillover benefit to 2 equals MC. In this case, then, the simple Pigovian prescription remains valid: the individual who generates the external benefit should receive a unit subsidy equal to the value at the margin of the spillovers he creates.

The determination of the efficient set of subsidies is, however, somewhat more complex in the case of reciprocal externalities,

---

[3] As mentioned earlier, it is certainly possible that collective action will in some cases be undertaken voluntarily by the concerned parties. Where the inefficiency is resolved in this manner, there is obviously no need for grants.

because it is no longer true that the *MRS* of the recipient of the spillin benefit (since he himself is being subsidized) will equal the *MRT*. Returning to equations 5, we have as our efficiency condition:

(5)
$$MRT = MRS_1 + \beta MRS_2$$
$$= \alpha MRS_1 + MRS_2.$$

In this case both individuals require subsidies, and, as a result, each of their *MRS*'s will diverge from the *MRT*. To find the efficient set of subsidies requires the solution of a set of simultaneous equations. Specifically we have:

(7)
$$MRS_1 = MRT - s_1$$

(8)
$$MRS_2 = MRT - s_2$$

(9)
$$MRT = MRS_1 + \beta MRS_2$$

(10)
$$MRT = \alpha MRS_1 + MRS_2.$$

where s_1, s_2 equal the unit subsidies in terms of X given, respectively, to persons 1 and 2. Equations 7 and 8 indicate the outcome of individual maximizing behavior: each individual will extend his purchases of Y to the point where the value he places on a marginal unit (*MRS*) is equal to the unit price he must pay ($MRT - s_i$). The problem is to select a set of subsidies s_1 and s_2 such that the pattern of maximizing behavior will lead to a satisfaction of our efficiency conditions, which appear as equations 9 and 10. Substituting equations 9 and 10 into 7 and 8 immediately suggests that the solution is in the Pigovian spirit:

(11)
$$s_1 = \beta MRS_2$$

(12)
$$s_2 = \alpha MRS_1.$$

The efficient subsidy to each individual is equal to the value at the margin of the additional consumption of Y that he confers on the other. Further manipulation of equations 7 through 10 yields:

(13)
$$s_1 = \left[\frac{\beta(1 - \alpha)}{(1 - \alpha\beta)}\right] MRT$$

100

$$(14) \qquad s_2 = \left[\frac{\alpha(1 - \beta)}{(1 - \alpha\beta)}\right] MRT.$$

Each of the efficient subsidies thus depends on the spillover-generating capability of both persons. Assuming constant costs of X and Y over the relevant range of production, which implies a constant MRT, equations 13 and 14 have some interesting implications. Given α, a higher β implies in 13 that individual 1 should receive a larger subsidy; likewise, a larger α, given β, means a bigger unit subsidy for 2. This means that, given the other individual's propensity to produce spillovers, an individual's subsidy should vary directly with his own capacity to generate spillover benefits. In addition, if we divide equation 13 by 14, we can, in terms of the resulting equation 15, say something about the relative size of the subsidies to the two individuals:

$$(15) \qquad \frac{s_1}{s_2} = \frac{\beta(1 - \alpha)}{\alpha(1 - \beta)}.$$

Given α, a larger β implies a larger subsidy to 1 relative to the subsidy given person 2, and vice versa. This means that as the relative ability of one individual to confer spillover benefits on the other grows, he should receive a subsidy that is larger relative to that of the other person. This suggests, as Mancur Olson and Richard Zeckhauser have argued recently, that there is a problem here of comparative advantage.[4] The individual who, in relative terms, can generate the larger joint consumption of Y through the purchase of a unit of the good, should receive an incentive to expand his own purchases of Y relative to those of the other person. In this sense the person who has a comparative advantage in the generation of consumable units of Y should, to some extent, specialize in purchases of Y relative to the other.

While the set of subsidies required to achieve an efficient allocation of resources in the case of reciprocal externalities is clearly of a Pigovian kind, the analysis does suggest that the determination of the precise set of subsidies is quite complex. In the case of more than two persons, for example, the expressions for the efficient subsidy to each individual would include

[4] "The Efficient Production of External Economies," *American Economic Review*, vol. 60 (June, 1970), pp. 512–17.

terms reflecting the ability of all the individuals in the group to generate spillover benefits. Moreover, it is also possible that α and β might not be constants; the spillovers produced may themselves vary with the level of activity of each individual. All this suggests that in a more general case the specification of the efficient set of subsidies could become a monstrously complicated problem although still conceptually soluble.[5]

Some further considerations

There remains the further problem of the taxes needed to finance the grants. If the subsidies are funded through the levying of truly neutral lump-sum taxes, the previous results stand unaltered. The only direct effect of such taxes will be income effects: each (or at least one individual) will suffer a loss of disposable income. While a reduction in income will tend to alter the bundle of goods purchased by each individual, it will not affect the efficient set of subsidies; as shown in the preceding section, the desired set of subsidies, assuming constant costs over the relevant range, depends only on α and β, which we have assumed constant for the relevant levels of consumption of Y.[6] Therefore, so long as the taxes adopted do not introduce inefficiencies of their own, the set of subsidies derived above will lead to a state of Pareto efficiency.

It by no means follows from this that the adoption of the efficient set of subsidies in conjunction with an arbitrary set of lump-sum taxes will increase social welfare; such programs may well make some individuals worse off. The problem is that the *movement* to a state of Pareto efficiency may not itself be

[5] If the functions assume what Otto Davis and Andrew Whinston have termed a "non-separable" form, there is the real possibility of the non-existence of a solution. Moreover, in a game-theoretic framework, the authors show that nonseparability implies the absence of dominance. As a result it becomes difficult for one participant (in our case a local government) to anticipate how other jurisdictions will react to its own choice of level of output, a reaction that in part determines this choice. See Davis and Whinston, "Externalities, Welfare, and the Theory of Games," *Journal of Political Economy*, vol. 70 (June, 1962), pp. 241–62.

[6] If α and β vary with Y_2 and Y_1, respectively, the efficient set of subsidies will obviously change as individuals 1 and 2 adapt their levels of purchases of Y to a reduced level of disposable income. The efficient set of subsidies will in this case also depend on the system of taxation adopted to finance the subsidies.

Pareto efficient. In our two-person case, a move from a point inside the utility-possibilities frontier to a position on the frontier may reduce the welfare of one individual. What is true, however, is that there is at least one set of lump-sum taxes that, combined with the efficient subsidies, will increase the welfare of both persons. Starting from the purely competitive position, we can therefore find a set of lump-sum taxes to accompany our subsidies that will both achieve a state of Pareto efficiency and increase the welfare of both persons.

Finally, I want to show that this analysis is also applicable to the case of reciprocal externalities among communities in the provision of public goods. Assuming that the consumption of each individual in a given community is enhanced by an identical amount by these external effects (that is, α or β is the same for all residents of a particular locality), the maximization procedure followed earlier now yields the following efficiency conditions:

$$(16) \qquad MRT = \sum_{i=1}^{n} MRS_i + \beta \sum_{j=1}^{m} MRS_j$$

$$= \alpha \sum_{i=1}^{n} MRS_i + \sum_{j=1}^{m} MRS_j$$

where the first summation is over the n persons in community I and the second includes the m individuals in community II. If each community acts independently to maximize the welfare of its own residents by setting $MRT = \Sigma MRS$ of its own constituents, the situation is precisely analogous to our case of two individuals; such independent behavior will, in the absence of further incentives, typically lead to a less than efficient level of aggregate consumption of the good.[7] Solving the set of

[7] While independent maximizing behavior will in general lead to aggregate underconsumption of the public good, it may well result at the same time in a greater than efficient *output* of the good. The inefficiency manifests itself in part in terms of a distorted pattern of provision of the good such that jurisdictions that generate relatively little in the way of spillover benefits will provide too large a quantity of the good. As a result a higher number of units of the good may actually provide a reduced level of aggregate consumption. See Buchanan and Kafoglis, "A Note on Public Goods Supply." Alan Williams has in this connection argued that it is possible for the independent provision of local public goods to lead to overconsumption rather than underconsumption. See his "The Optimal Provision of Public Goods in a System of Local Government," *Journal of Political Economy*, vol. 74 (Feb., 1966), pp. 18–33. However, William Brainard and F. Trenery Dolbear have shown that Wil-

simultaneous equations corresponding to equations 7 through 10 yields an efficient set of subsidies identical to those in the two-person case. To achieve an efficient allocation of resources, the central government should, therefore, adopt the set of matching grants for the local governments of each community implied by the subsidies in equations 13 and 14.

---

liams' result stems from an alteration in the intercommunity distribution of income; if this distribution of income is kept constant, independent decision-making results in a less than efficient level of aggregate consumption of the public good. See their "The Possibility of Oversupply of Local 'Public' Goods: A Critical Note," *Journal of Political Economy*, vol. 75 (Feb., 1967), pp. 86–90.

Appendix B

Intergovernmental grants in a model of collective choice

There exists at the present time a serious deficiency in the theory of intergovernmental grants. One either treats the effects of intergovernmental matching and lump-sum grants in terms of the standard theory of individual choice, in which the grant recipient is viewed as an individual decision-maker with preferences defined over public and private goods, or one must fall back on the use of community indifference curves, whose validity and usefulness are open to serious question.

The central point is that intergovernmental grants are not grants to individuals. They are grants to groups of people, and, as such, their allocative and distributive effects depend on the political process by which the group makes its collective fiscal decisions. To predict and describe the effects of various types of intergovernmental grants on both the allocation of resources and the distribution of income, it is clear that we need a theoretical framework in which we can treat explicitly the political process (that is, the collective decision-making procedures) by which the community makes its public budgetary choices.

This appendix presents an analytic framework for collective budget determination within which we can study the effects of different types of intergovernmental grants. After developing the theoretical framework itself, I shall illustrate its application by exploring the properties of lump-sum and matching grants where the group makes its fiscal choices by a specific and reasonably realistic decision rule: simple-majority voting.[8]

[8] The analysis in this appendix is based upon my recent work with David Bradford. In particular, see our "The Analysis of Revenue-Sharing in

Intergovernmental grants in a model
of individual choice

Before proceeding to a theoretical structure of collective choice, we review briefly the standard model of individual choice and establish one proposition concerning the stimulative impact a matching grant has on public expenditure relative to a lump-sum grant of equal size. This proposition proves to be of some value for the case of collective choice as well.

In this approach the recipient of the grant is typically assumed to be an individual decision-maker with convex preferences defined over quantities of a private good and a public good as in Figure 3A-2. To simplify the analysis, assume that

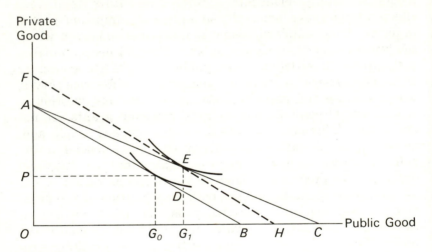

FIGURE 3A-2

units of both goods are chosen such that the price of the public good in terms of the private good is unity. Subject to a pre-grant budget constraint of AB, the community selects an output of the public good of OG_o, which leaves OP to be consumed in the form of the private good. Assume next that the community is the recipient of a matching-grant program; the central gov-

a New Approach to Collective Fiscal Decisions," *Quarterly Journal of Economics*, vol. 85 (Aug., 1971), pp. 416–39; and "Towards a Predictive Theory of Intergovernmental Grants," *American Economic Review*, vol. 61 (May, 1971), pp. 440–48.

ernment, for example, might agree to share the cost of providing the local public good by funding a specified percentage of the community's expenditure on the good. In terms of Figure 3A-2, such a grant pivots the community's budget constraint outward about the point A, reflecting what is now, in effect, a lower unit price of the public good to the local community. As a result, provision of the public good in Figure 3A-2 rises to OG_1, and the community receives a grant of DE.

Suppose, however, that instead of a matching grant of DE, the grantor chose to give the community a lump-sum grant of the same amount. Such a grant would shift the community's budget constraint outward to FH but would not alter the relative prices of the private and public goods. Moreover, it is clear from Figure 3A-2 that the lump-sum grant would induce a smaller increase in spending on the public good than would the matching grant; since FH passes through E but is steeper than AC, it follows, given normal convexity properties of the preference map, that the tangency of FH with an indifference curve must lie to the left of E. Or, in economic terms, the matching grant induces more expenditure on the public good because it not only enriches the community (that is, has an income effect), but also reduces the price of the public good to the recipient (that is, has a substitution effect). In the individual model, a matching grant thus possesses a greater stimulating effect on public spending than does a lump-sum grant of the same amount. We now turn to a reconsideration of the properties of these grants in a framework with explicit collective decision-making.

An analytic structure for collective budget determination

For simplicity I will continue to use a model in which there is a single pure public good, a single private good, and a given and constant price of each where the units of these goods are defined such that the price of the public good in terms of the private good is unity. We need next to describe in conceptual terms the local community and its political process. Briefly, let us represent what I will call the *state of the community* by a vector $[Y_1, Y_2, \ldots Y_n, g]$, whose first n components indicate the disposable incomes (or claims to the private good) of each of the n members of the community and whose last component, g, is the number of units of the public good. The set of *feasible states* of the collectivity represents the community's budget constraint; for each total quantity of the private good available for distribution among the members of the community, the boundary of this set indicates the maximum level of provision of the public good attainable.

Not all feasible states for the community, however, will be political equilibria. For example, a state in which all the community's resources were used for provision of the public good would probably generate political pressures that would lead to a state in which members of the community would consume a positive quantity of the private good. In this framework, we can view the *political process* (or the rule for collective decision-making) as the mechanism through which one feasible state is transformed into another (possibly itself). *For a given set of feasible states,* a political process thus defines for each initial feasible state, the resulting equilibrium state; it is a mapping that indicates how the political process transforms each state of the community into an equilibrium state. Note in particular that, starting from a given feasible state, the political process simultaneously determines both the level of output of the public good and the disposable income of each member of the community.

From this perspective, we can characterize a grant to the community as a disturbance to the existing equilibrium state and a change in the feasible set. One could think of the grant as initially taking the form of an increment to the level of provision of the public good. However, this new state, which is itself a member of an enlarged set of feasible states, will generally not represent a political equilibrium. Typically it will itself be transformed by the political process into a new equilibrium state.

It is extremely useful for analytic purposes to explore one particular question relating to the response of the community to a grant program. Specifically, in the case of each grant to the community as a whole, we will ask *whether there is some way the grantor might have distributed the grant funds directly to the individual members of the community such that precisely the same equilibrium state of the community would result.* If this is the case, we can show that a particular intergovernmental grant is precisely equivalent, both in terms of its ultimate impact on the provision of the public good and on the disposable income of each member of the community, to a set of grants made directly to the individuals themselves. For example, in the case of a lump-sum grant to a collectivity, if this equivalence holds, it is clear that the lump-sum grant to the community (as might take place under a program of revenue-sharing) is precisely equivalent in terms of its allocative and distributive effects to a particular set of grants or tax rebates to the individual members of the community. Or, in short, revenue-sharing, say by the central government with local governments, is in this case exactly equivalent to a particular pattern of federal tax cuts to individuals.

To illustrate how the analytic framework can be used to explore the allocative and distributive effects of intergovernmental grants, the next section will consider a case of a particular collective-decision rule.

Intergovernmental grants and simple-majority rule

An important case in which we can employ the analytic framework to examine in some detail the effects of different programs of intergovernmental grants is where the community makes its collective fiscal decisions by simple-majority rule. More specifically, I will take as the model a community in which each individual's tax share is known and fixed and in which the level of provision of the public good is determined by a simple-majority voting rule. By this I mean that the community votes on alternative pairs of provision of the public good until one is found that at least $\left(\dfrac{n}{2} + 1\right)$ of the n members of the community prefer to any other. This model could represent, for example, a local school district that finances its expenditures through a local property tax and employs majority voting to determine the annual school budget. In this instance, each individual's tax share is defined by the assessed value of his property divided by the total assessed value of taxable property within the district. His tax bill is then determined by the product of his tax share and the size of the school budget selected by the electorate.

Figure 3A-3 indicates the position of any individual, say the

i^{th}, member of the community. Since by construction the price per unit of the public good in terms of the private good is unity, the slope of his budget constraint, AB, is equal to his tax share, h_i (that is, the "tax-price" to him of a unit of the public good). Assuming that each person's preference map exhibits indifference curves of the usual shape, it follows that the preferences of each member of the community for the public good will be single-peaked. In terms of Figure 3A-3, where OG_i is the individual's most preferred level of provision of the public good,

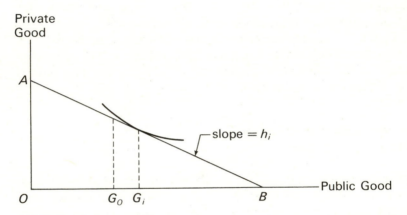

FIGURE 3A-3

this means that, between any two levels of the public good greater than OG_i, he prefers the smaller of the two (that is, the one closer to OG_i). Similarly, for any two budgets less than OG_i, he prefers the larger. With preferences that satisfy this property of single-peakedness, Black's theorem states that, under simple-majority rule, the equilibrium budget is the median peak, or, in other words, the median of the most preferred levels of provision of the public good.[9] This means that, aside from the individual who possesses the median peak, the equilibrium public budget will not be the budget most preferred by any given member of the community. In Figure 3A-3, for

[9] Duncan Black, "On the Rationale of Group Decision-Making," *Journal of Political Economy*, vol. 56 (Feb., 1948), pp. 23–34. Black shows that the budget preferred by the median voter is the only budget that will get at least $\left(\dfrac{n}{2} + 1\right)$ votes when paired against *any* other budget.

example, the equilibrium budget, say OG_o, will generally differ from the individual's most preferred budget, OG_i.

Let us now disturb the political equilibrium represented in Figure 3A-3 by introducing an intergovernmental grant program. Consider first the case of a lump-sum grant to the collectivity; assume that the central government provides the community with an unconditional grant of a specified sum. In Figure 3A-4, if the grant were $EH = BD$, this would imply that, if each member of the community were to maintain his

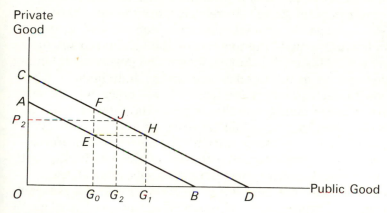

FIGURE 3A-4

level of consumption of the private good at its previous equilibrium level, the output of the public good could increase to OG_1, or by the full amount of the grant. The full range, however, of alternative bundles of private and public goods available to the ith individual is indicated by the new budget constraint, CD, and it is unlikely that the point H will represent a new political equilibrium. Suppose instead that, using majority-rule, the community decides to increase the public budget to OG_2 so as to increase consumption of the private good also. In Figure 3A-4, point J by assumption thus indicates the new equilibrium provision of the public good and the level of private consumption, OP_2, of individual i.

We now ask if, instead of using an intergovernmental grant, the grantor could have generated the identical equilibrium state of the community by parcelling out the grant funds directly to the individual members of the community. The answer is yes. If, for example, the central government had given person i in Figure 3A-4 a lump-sum grant of EF, this individual would have had precisely the same new budget constraint, CD, as in the case of the grant of EH to the collectivity. With the same budget constraint and a given preference map, his array of preferences for public budgets and hence his voting pattern would be exactly the same in the two cases.

Note next that $EF = h_i$ (EH); the grant to each individual, which from his position is equivalent to the grant to the collectivity, is equal to the product of his tax share and the intergovernmental grant. Moreover, since the tax shares (the h_i) sum to one, it follows that the sum of the grants to the individuals equals the amount of the original grant to the collectivity. This means that, if the central government simply divides up the grant monies among the individuals in proportion to each person's *local* tax share, precisely the same state of the community results as when the total of the grant funds is given to the public treasury of the community. A lump-sum grant to a community in this model is, therefore, an implicit set of grants to the members of the community with each individual's grant proportional to his local tax share.

Consider next the case of a matching grant to the community. In Figure 3A-5, with AB again possessing slope h_i

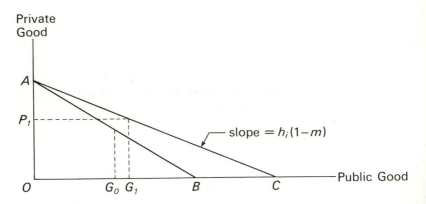

FIGURE 3A-5

and representing the individual's pre-grant budget constraint and with G_o the original equilibrium public budget, the grant pivots the individual's budget line about point A to AC. Note that the slope of AC is $h_i(1-m)$, where m is the fraction of the unit cost of the public good funded by the grantor. If, for example, the grantor adopted a 1:1 matching grant, this would imply that $m = \dfrac{1}{2}$, or that the effective tax price to the individual is now $h_i(1-m) = h_i(1-\dfrac{1}{2}) = \dfrac{1}{2}h_i$. A matching grant to the community thus reduces the tax price per unit to each taxpayer by the fraction m. As a result of the grant the community will, by majority rule, select a new level of provision of the public good, which we indicate by G_1 in Figure 3A-5. In this particular case, the ith person ends up consuming OG_1 of the public good and OP_1 of the private good.

It is easy in this case to see how the central government could generate this same equilibrium state of the community by dealing directly with the individual residents rather than by issuing a matching intergovernmental grant. For instance, the central government could refund directly to each individual the fraction m of his local tax payment. Or, perhaps more realistically, the central government might allow the ith individual a credit of mT_i against his tax bill from the central government, where T_i is the ith person's local tax bill. In either case, the effect on each individual in the community would be identical to that resulting from an intergovernmental matching grant where the central government funded the fraction m of the local budget. In all these cases the resulting budget constraint for each individual, and hence his voting pattern, would be the same. It is thus clear that the median peak of preferred budgets would be OG_1 in Figure 3A-5 for all these alternatives. Within the model of simple-majority voting with fixed tax shares, an intergovernmental matching grant in which the grantor pays x percent of the local expenditure on the public good is therefore precisely equivalent, in terms of its effect both on the public budget and on the disposable income of each person in the community, to a refund to each individual of x percent of his local tax bill.

On the basis of the preceding analysis, we are now in a position to compare the effects matching and lump-sum grants of equal size have on the level of the public budget. Consider first in Figure 3A-6 the effects on the ith person of a matching-grant program to the community where the fraction m again represents the grantor's share of local public expenditures and results in an increase in public spending from OG_o to OG_1. In this case the implicit grant to the ith individual (that is, the rebate on his local taxes he would have received from the central government under a program equivalent to the matching grant) is the distance EF. The grant to the community would thus equal $\Sigma(EF_i)$, which as indicated earlier is the distance EK.

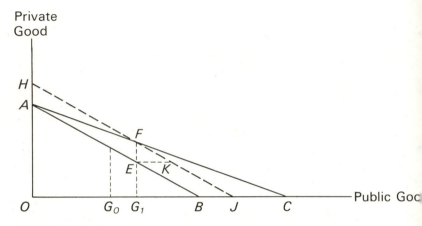

FIGURE 3A-6

Suppose next that, instead of a matching grant to the community, the central government chose to make a lump-sum intergovernmental grant of this same sum, EK. From the earlier analysis it is clear that this would be precisely equivalent to a set of lump-sum grants directly to the individuals in the community such that the size of each person's grant is proportional to his local tax share; in Figure 3A-6, for example, the ith individual would receive a lump-sum grant of EF. This would shift the individual's budget line up by the distance EF to the new budget line HJ. It is now clear that in this model, lump-sum and matching intergovernmental grants of the same total sum have precisely the same implicit pattern as grants to the individual members of the community: they both imply a distribution of the grant funds among individuals in proportion to each individual's local tax share. The difference is that the matching grant has a price effect as well as an income effect, whereas the lump-sum grant results only in an income effect.

114

With this result, it can now be proved that under simple-majority rule with fixed tax shares, a matching intergovernmental grant will always produce a larger expenditure on the public good than will a lump-sum grant of the same amount. On first glance, it might appear that we could simply invoke the analysis of grants in the model of individual choice and argue that, because the matching grant has a favorable price effect in addition to an income effect, the ith individual will always prefer a larger public budget under the intergovernmental matching grant than under a lump-sum grant of the same size; and that therefore, since all persons prefer a larger public budget, the median of the most preferred budgets will obviously also be larger. This, however, is not quite true.

This argument is indeed valid for the median voter. The equilibrium local budget is his most preferred budget so that, under the matching grant in Figure 3A-6, he would have an indifference curve tangent to AC at point F. The argument from the model of individual choice clearly is applicable in this instance; a lump-sum grant to him of EF (or, equivalently, an intergovernmental lump-sum grant of EK) would lead him to a most preferred provision of the public good, which is smaller than that under the matching-grant program.

Consider next, however, the case in Figure 3A-7, where an individual's most preferred budget under the matching grant is indicated by point M, a budget that is less than that of the median voter. In this instance it is possible that this person could prefer a larger budget (for example, that indicated by point N) if the community received a lump-sum grant of EK than under the matching-grant program. This can occur because the individual's implied grant, EF, under the lump-sum intergovernmental grant exceeds the implicit sum he would receive under his most preferred budget under the matching grant. In this case the added income effect of the larger implicit lump-sum grant may be stronger than the substitution effect of the hypothetical matching grant. Note, however, and this is crucial to the argument, that although such a person's most preferred budget may be larger under the lump-sum intergovernmental grant, it will never be as large as the equilibrium budget under the matching grant. It is clear from the geometry in Figure 3A-7 that the tangency of an indifference curve with a budget line under the lump-sum grant must always occur on a curve that is higher than that which passes through *M*, and this means that the point *N* must always lie to the left of *F*.

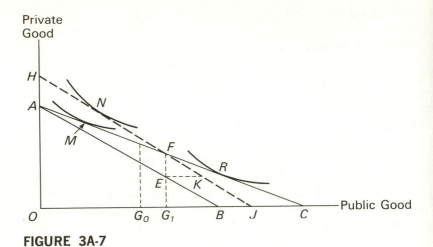

FIGURE 3A-7

We have shown, therefore, that all voters with most preferred public budgets less than the median under the matching grant will continue to vote for budgets under the lump-sum grant that are smaller than the equilibrium budget under the original matching grant. Since the model of individual choice shows that the median voter under the matching grant will himself most prefer a smaller budget under the lump-sum grant, it follows that the median of the most preferred public budgets will be smaller under a lump-sum intergovernmental grant than with a matching-grant program of the same amount. It is, incidentally, easy to see that people who prefer relatively large budgets under the matching grant (for example, like point *R* in Figure 3A-7) will generally prefer smaller budgets under the lump-sum grant. For these individuals, the most preferred budget under the matching grant implies a larger income effect than the lump-sum grant, as well as the price effect.[10]

[10] In his comments on this analysis, Charles Goetz has shown that this proposition can be proved in a slightly different manner using a revealed-preference approach, which eliminates the need for assuming the convexity of individual preferences. See his presentation in "Economics of Political Decentralization: Discussion," *American Economic Review*, vol. 61 (May, 1971), p. 463. In addition, Goetz and Charles McKnew

On generalizing these results

In the preceding section, an analysis of intergovernmental grants in terms of a theoretical framework of collective choice yielded a number of specific conclusions concerning the allocative and distributive effects of both matching and unconditional grants. However, the analysis was conducted within a rather restrictive model in which there was a single public good, convexity of preferences, and in which decisions were made by simple-majority rule with fixed tax shares.

This raises the important issue of the generality of these results. In our paper on revenue-sharing, David Bradford and I were able to demonstrate the basic theorem of the existence of a set of individual lump-sum grants, which is equivalent to a lump-sum grant to the collectivity as a whole for a fairly broad class of collective-decision processes in which there are any number of collective goods and in which there are virtually no restrictions on the properties of individual preferences. The same formal analysis implies that, for this same broad class of political processes, there exists a set of tax credits to individuals and lump-sum redistributive payments within the community that would duplicate the allocative and distributive effects of any particular intergovernmental matching-grant program.

While we have been able to demonstrate this equivalence theorem for a fairly general class of collective-decision processes, we have found it more difficult to generalize the result that is true for the simple models of majority rule and also for the Lindahl model: that the grant to the individual member of the community, which is identical in its effects to the grant to the collectivity, is equal to the individual's tax share times the total grant to the group. This difficulty arises because the concept of a tax share is not at all well defined in more general

---

have shown that in one particular model of collective choice in which the collectivity makes separate decisions on the aggregate level of public spending and the mix of public programs, it is conceivable that under simple-majority voting, if individual preferences bear a particular kind of relation to one another, a lump-sum grant could lead to greater public expenditure than would a matching grant of the same sum. See their "Paradoxical Results in a Public Choice Model of Alternative Government Grant Forms," in James Buchanan and R. S. Tollison, eds., *The Theory of Public Choice: Essays in Application* (Ann Arbor: University of Michigan Press, forthcoming).

models. The problem of determining the precise set of equivalent grants to individuals has thus far proved possible only within the context of a few specific collective-decision rules.

These propositions concern political choices within a given set of alternative states. The theorem comparing the stimulative effects of lump-sum and matching grants presents additional difficulties because the two grants imply different sets of feasible states. Bradford and I have been able to prove the greater stimulative impact of matching grants for the Lindahl method of budget determination, as well as for the case of simple-majority rule presented here. Goetz, moreover, has shown that by the use of a revealed-preference approach and with the Hicks composite-good theorem, the proof can be generalized to a case of many public goods and no longer requires the assumption of convexity of preferences.[11]

All this seems to suggest that this is a promising approach to the problem of developing both theoretical and empirical measures of the effects of intergovernmental grants on both the distribution of income and the allocation of resources, but this is obviously just a beginning.

[11] Goetz, "Economics of Political Decentralization: Discussion."

Chapter four
Taxation and debt finance in a federal system

This [the power of taxation], *I contend, is manifestly*
a concurrent and coequal authority in the United
States and in the individual States

Alexander Hamilton, THE FEDERALIST

To simplify the analysis, we have generally assumed that governments employ only benefit pricing.[1] Following Musgrave, the presumption has been that, within the context of the just distribution of income, consumers finance the cost of public goods by payments in accordance with benefits received. In fact, however, strict benefit pricing typically characterizes the provision of only a few public goods in most societies. Far greater reliance is generally placed on other forms of taxation often based on the ability-to-pay doctrine.[2] The point is that for pedagogical purposes it is often very useful to assume the existence of a central agency that operates behind the scenes with lump-sum taxes and transfers to maintain the socially desired distribution of real income. However, when we treat the problem of taxation explicitly, it becomes necessary to drop

[1] It did prove convenient in a few instances in Chapters Two and Three to consider cases of nonbenefit taxation. This was necessary, for example, to develop the case for unconditional grants to maintain horizontal equity in a federal system.
[2] An excellent treatment of the ability-to-pay principle of taxation is available in Richard Musgrave, *The Theory of Public Finance* (New York: McGraw-Hill, 1959), ch. 5.

119

this abstraction. The difficulty of determining the allocation of benefits from public programs means that benefit taxes are frequently impractical, and, more important, the absence of the central agency mentioned above implies that we must be concerned with the distributional implications of the taxes adopted to finance the public budget. In fact, the incidence of a tax, whether real or imagined, is frequently the most important characteristic of the tax for determining its political acceptability. Incidence, the question of who pays the tax, is quite naturally a matter of real concern to the taxpayer. For these reasons, it becomes necessary to move a step closer to reality by considering the range of taxes available to the government in terms of their implications both for economic efficiency and for the distribution of income.

Here we find again that the existence of a federal system of government creates an additional set of problems for the theory of public finance. Economists are familiar, for example, with the sorts of inefficiencies an income or a sales tax introduces into a closed system; these inefficiencies stem from the wedge the tax creates between the price paid and revenue received for the taxed good or service. In a system characterized by a substantial decentralization of finance, however, one must confront not only these problems but also the effects of these taxes on interjurisdictional flows of commodities and factors of production. Indeed, one finds that some taxes stack up very well on the standard efficiency and equity criteria when adopted by the central government but are often far less satisfactory at more decentralized levels of government.

There are many important technical questions in the actual design of a system of taxation under decentralized government, such as the treatment under a local corporation income tax of income earned from sales and other operations outside the taxing locality, or the application of a local sales tax to purchases in nearby jurisdictions. My intent here, however, is not to treat these technical problems of a tax structure but rather to determine some general theoretical principles to serve as guides in the construction of a system of taxation under a federal form of government. As a first step, it will be useful to review the standards for the evaluation of a revenue system. We will then use these standards to study the problems of multilevel taxation.

Criteria for the evaluation
of a tax system

When we move away from our ideal world into one in which tastes for public goods are not known with any great degree of precision and in which there exist scattered inefficiencies throughout the system, the problem of specifying an effective tax system becomes extremely complicated. We will, in all likelihood, be operating at something less than a welfare optimum, and this means that we have entered the world of the second best. In this world, as Richard Lipsey and Kelvin Lancaster have shown, it is very difficult to make definitive statements as to the relative desirability of different public programs.[3] A policy, including perhaps a tax or expenditure program, that increases social welfare under one set of circumstances may be undesirable in other situations. More precisely, the principle of the second best states that a program resulting in the satisfaction of a Pareto-efficiency condition may worsen *on efficiency grounds alone* rather than improve the state of the system unless all other efficiency conditions are realized simultaneously. This means that the attempt to set forth the characteristics of a desirable tax system is, to some extent, an act of faith: we cannot derive these attributes in a rigorous way. Nevertheless, most economists would agree, I think, that we can at least establish a realistic presumption in favor of certain general characteristics of a revenue system. These will provide us with a set of criteria with which to examine the problem of taxation in a federal system of government.

Let us assume that we must adopt a system of taxes to divert needed resources into the public sector. What sorts of attributes would we want this set of taxes to possess? One characteristic, long stressed by economists but often ignored by public officials, concerns the avoidance of *excess burden*. What we want is a set of taxes that extracts the needed revenues but has no undesirable side effects on the operation of the economic system. A tax system that introduces distortions into the functioning of the economy typically imposes a loss of welfare on consumers over and above that resulting from the tax pay-

---

[3] "The General Theory of Second Best," *Review of Economic Studies*, vol. 24, no. 1 (1956), pp. 11–32.

ments themselves; this extra welfare loss is the excess burden of the tax.[4]

This efficiency criterion establishes a presumption in favor of "neutral" taxes. A neutral tax is one that does not *directly* alter the terms on which individuals choose among alternative commodities, inputs, or other activities. In terms of price theory, a neutral tax has only an income effect, no direct substitution effects. This implies that any neutral tax can be duplicated in terms of its effects by an appropriately selected set of lump-sum taxes. This does not mean, however, that a neutral tax leaves equilibrium prices and quantities unchanged: to the extent that moving from one form of tax to another redistributes income among individuals with differing preferences, it will alter expenditure patterns and thereby change the equilibrium structure of relative prices and quantities in the marketplace.

The attraction of a neutral tax is that it does not interfere with the operation of the price system. Such a tax simply extracts the needed resources from the system and then, subject only to the reduced disposable income of the individuals in the society, allows the market system to reestablish equilibrium prices and quantities in the various markets without further interference. There is, therefore, no way for an individual to escape the burden of the tax by adjusting his behavior, and this is what is wanted, because it is precisely these alterations in behavior to avoid payment of the tax that result in an excess burden. What we desire is a tax that stays put: individuals pay the tax and react simply to the reduction in their disposable income.[5] There will be a need for unit taxes on certain types of activity to correct for externalities, but, aside from these taxes, the first criterion is that the system of taxation should be as neutral as possible; it should generate the desired level

---

[4] For an illuminating study of both the meaning and measurement of excess burden, see Arnold Harberger, "Taxation, Resource Allocation, and Welfare," in Conference Report of the National Bureau of Economic Research and the Brookings Institution, *The Role of Direct and Indirect Taxes in the Federal Revenue System* (Princeton, N.J.: Princeton University Press, 1964), pp. 25–80.

[5] Some examples of neutral taxes are a head tax or a tax on a commodity for which either the demand, over the relevant range, or the supply is completely fixed. In these instances, the taxpayer does not alter his behavior to escape the tax; he simply adjusts his pattern of purchases and sales to his reduced level of disposable income.

of revenues but should not, as far as is possible, introduce distortions into the operation of the market system.

Related to this traditional principle of minimizing excess burden is the problem of developing a tax system conducive to effective collective decision-making. The revenue system may itself influence the level and composition of public expenditures, and it is therefore important that the system of taxes be one that encourages the right sorts of decisions on potential expenditure programs.[6] Ideally, what one would want is a tax-expenditure system that makes clear to each individual the benefits and costs of each program. In this way each citizen would be in the best position to decide whether he should support or oppose the proposed public project. What this suggests, as James Buchanan has stressed, is that it is desirable where possible to adopt earmarked taxes (that is, taxes whose revenues are directed to a specified program) and taxes for which the individual can easily determine his tax liability.[7] Where these conditions are satisfied, the individual in his role as a member of the electorate will presumably be able to make more intelligent decisions regarding the fiscal operations of the public sector.

Buchanan points out further that those taxes that rank high on our preceding efficiency criterion (that is, those taxes nearly neutral) will typically also get good marks on this second scale.[8] Neutral taxes normally have a relatively clear and certain pattern of incidence, since economic units are, by definition, unable to avoid the burden of the tax by altering behavior. In contrast, nonneutral taxes (which frequently generate the least opposition because those on whom they are levied realize that they can escape them) often have a highly uncertain pattern of incidence. The costs community members bear for a program to improve the local school system, for example, are usually much clearer if the program is financed through a local property tax rather than by a local corporation income tax. Consequently, it may be quite difficult in the case of highly nonneutral taxes for an individual to assess with any precision the likely cost to him of a particular public program.

---

[6] This is one of James Buchanan's central themes in *Public Finance in Democratic Process* (Chapel Hill, N.C.: University of North Carolina Press, 1967).
[7] *Ibid.*, ch. 6.
[8] *Ibid.*, pp. 43–44.

Neutrality, while generally a desirable characteristic of a tax system both in terms of our first and second criteria, by no means assures that the tax system will encourage proper collective decision-making. In addition to neutrality, the tax should have a pattern of incidence that corresponds roughly to the distribution of benefits. In this case, projects that promise an excess of benefits over costs will typically receive general support, and the opposite is also true. In contrast, if the incidence of the tax varies radically from the pattern of benefits, some persons will strongly support the program while others may just as forcefully oppose it. The outcome is, then, likely to depend on the political power of the two groups rather than on the expected costs and benefits of the program. This suggests that to establish a fiscal system that promotes efficient collective decisions, we require a set of taxes with an explicit, recognized pattern of incidence that corresponds approximately to the distribution of benefits from public spending.

This second criterion also implies that it is generally desirable, at least at the margin, to have decentralized levels of government finance programs with their own revenues rather than with funds from external sources. If revenues are not raised locally, the explicit link between the benefits and real costs of the programs is broken. If, for instance, the central government finances a local project by supplying funds to local public officials, the local officials have an incentive to expand the project as far as possible, since the locality will bear only a negligible part of the cost. To match benefits with costs in order to promote a more effective selection of worthwhile programs implies, therefore, the desirability of having each group explicitly finance the programs that significantly affect its welfare.

The third criterion—that the tax system should have an equitable pattern of incidence—has not been a problem up to this point, for we have assumed that a central agency is quietly working with lump-sum taxes and transfers to maintain the just distribution of income. However, without this perfect system of lump-sum transfers, we must consider explicitly the effect of both public expenditure and revenue programs on the distribution of income. Incidence in its complete meaning refers to the full effects of budgetary policy on the level of satisfaction of each individual in the system. This implies that the determination of the incidence of a particular budgetary program requires a general equilibrium analysis. To know the incidence of such a program necessitates complete information concerning the new general equilibrium solution: the benefits conferred by the public services, the loss of welfare stemming from any tax payments, and the complex of effects resulting from any alterations in the structure of relative prices.[9] I stress especially the importance of considering the effects both of the expenditure and revenue sides of the public budget, for this becomes of central importance in a system with local government finance where it is the relationship between the benefits and tax costs of public goods that partially determines the individual's choice of a community of residence.

One possible inconsistency among our criteria for an effective tax system now becomes apparent. The preceding discussion suggests the desirability of closely matching the incidence of the tax system to the pattern of benefits from the expenditure side of the budget. Benefit taxes may not, however, correspond at all closely to the incidence desired on equity grounds. The society may feel, for example, that, in view of the existing distribution of income, it is just that a wealthy man pay a significantly larger sum in taxes than a poorer man. This does not necessarily mean that the tax system will diverge radically from a benefit system of taxes, since one may expect that the benefits from public goods (measured in terms of the amount an individual is willing to pay for these goods) will typically be significantly greater for the rich man than for the poor man. There is, however, little reason to expect a very close correspondence between a tax system designed on benefit principles and one constructed to achieve an ethically desirable pattern of incidence; the problem of resolving this potential conflict between efficiency and equity criteria in a federal system will be of central interest in the later discussion.

Finally, a good system of taxes is characterized by low costs of administration and compliance. Neither public officials nor those paying the taxes should have to incur significant costs in order to ensure the proper remission of revenues. In summary,

[9] Two of the best general treatments of the problem of incidence, both of which stress the general equilibrium character of the problem, are Musgrave, *The Theory of Public Finance*, ch. 10; and Peter Mieszkowski, "On the Theory of Tax Incidence," *Journal of Political Economy*, vol. 75 (June, 1967), pp. 250–62.

then, an ideal tax system is one that introduces no undesired distortions in the functioning of the pricing system; promotes effective public decision-making; has, in conjunction with expenditure programs, an equitable pattern of incidence; and imposes only minimal costs of administration on tax officials and of compliance on taxpayers.

Local spending and taxation: an analytic framework

The general principles of efficiency and equity are relatively well understood for taxes in a closed economy. When, however, we move into an open system (one characterized both by inflows and outflows of commodities and individuals), the problem of constructing an effective system of taxation becomes more intricate. We must concern ourselves not only with the effects budgetary programs have on patterns of production and consumption within a locality, but also with the implications of these programs for intercommunity movements of commodities and persons.

For the sharpest contrast between the problems of centralized and decentralized finance, it is useful to consider a Tiebout world, in which consumers select their community of residence according to their tastes for public goods.[10] Assume, for simplicity, that we have in the system two pure, Samuelsonian public goods. The first is a national public good that the central government provides; the other is a local public good. Each local government provides a certain amount of this latter public good, which is equally available to all residents of the community but not to members of other communities. As in the case of a perfect correspondence in Chapter Two, we assume that the benefits from the local public good are exhausted within the locality under consideration.

[10] Charles Tiebout, "A Pure Theory of Local Expenditure," *Journal of Political Economy*, vol. 64 (Oct., 1956), pp. 416–24. Since the distinctive character of the problem of taxation at decentralized levels of government stems from the interjurisdictional mobility of economic units (including consumers, factors of production, and units of output), it will be useful in this chapter to adopt a model in which such mobility plays a central role. This is in contrast to the "ideal" model in Chapter Two, where an individual's location was taken as fixed and where consumer mobility was introduced later as a complication to the model.

Since all persons in the nation consume whatever units of output of the national public good the central government provides, there is obviously no range of choice for the individual consumer; he consumes the existing output and in exchange remits his prescribed tax payment to the central treasury. At the local level, in contrast, the individual has some choice among levels of consumption; he selects a community of residence that provides the public good at a level well suited to his preferences in return for which he pays local taxes. What is interesting about this distinction between central and decentralized finance is that in the latter case only, the individual's tax payment becomes, in effect, the price he voluntarily chooses to pay to consume a particular level of the public good. The consumer thus finds himself in something analogous to a market situation; he is confronted by an array of communities offering differing levels of consumption of public goods at varying prices, and he selects the community whose fiscal package best corresponds to his own tastes.

In this model of consumer mobility, therefore, finance problems at the local level are quite different from those of the central government. We can envision a process of production and consumption of local public goods that bears a substantial resemblance to the operation of the private market. Specifically, we can conceive of a system in which the individual can choose higher levels of consumption of public goods with a correspondingly higher local tax bill or, alternatively, a lesser level of consumption and reduced taxes. The attraction of such a system is that it gets us around the difficult problem of inducing individuals to reveal their preferences for public goods. The central government has no direct way, aside from various imperfect voting mechanisms, to determine the level of demand for national public goods. In consequence, decisions concerning efficient levels of output of these goods must be undertaken in an atmosphere of considerable uncertainty. In a Tiebout world of local finance, however, consumers reveal their tastes in their selection of a community and in so doing may promote an efficient allocation of resources. Therefore, at this level of argument, the case for placing the responsibility both for the provision and for the financing of public goods on decentralized levels of government is a strong one.

The treatment to this point, however, has been highly intuitive; I have not, for example, specified with any care the type of pricing policy (that is, the tax system) to be adopted by local governments. When we attempt to be more precise about the nature of this model, we find that matters are a good deal more complicated than the preceding discussion would suggest. Moreover, the sorts of complications that arise suggest it may, in some cases, be desirable for the central government to take a more active role in the collection of revenues on behalf of more decentralized levels of government.

A model of efficient local finance

In the preceding section, we outlined a system of local finance in which a multitude of municipal governments offer consumers various levels of output of a pure public good whose consumption is limited to the residents of the municipality. Consumers in this simple model choose as a community of residence the locality that provides the most attractive level of output at the cheapest price. Now we turn to the pricing policy, or tax system, of the local government. Assume for simplicity that each local government charges to each of the residents of the community the same fee, which is just sufficient to enable the municipal government to cover the costs of providing the public good. In other words each individual in the community receives a tax bill equal to the total public expenditures in the locality divided by the number of residents. Hence, if we compared communities of different sizes offering the same output of the public good, we would find that residents of larger communities pay smaller tax bills for the same quantity of public goods. Since the localities, by assumption, provide a pure public good, the level of consumption of any individual is independent of the size of the population of the community. The more people the better, since this means that there will be more persons to share the cost of the public output.

This model implies that it will typically be in an individual's interest to leave a small community and seek a more heavily populated locality where he can consume more public output for a smaller tax payment. In fact, it is quite possible that this simple model might degenerate into a single community system. If one community can serve everyone, it may well be a waste of resources to have other communities provide the same good.

In the real world people have not congregated into a single or a few municipalities for at least one obvious reason: congestion costs. In fact, when one considers the goods and services typically provided by local government, including such things as roads, education, sanitation, police, and fire protection, it is clear that they are not pure public goods. As discussed in Chapter Two, the level of educational services per pupil provided by a given number of inputs into an educational system varies with the number of pupils; more students mean fewer teachers per pupil. The goods and services provided by decentralized governments are for the most part highly impure public goods. To obtain a model that more closely approximates the real world and yields more plausible results, it is thus necessary to incorporate congestion costs into the model.

Let us assume, then, that local governments provide impure public goods; more specifically, assume that, while the level of consumption is equal for all members of the community, the quantity consumed per capita depends both on the level of output of the good *and* on the population of the community. A larger population, given the output of the good, means less consumption for everyone. In formal terms, the argument in each individual's utility function for the level of consumption of the local public good is itself a function both of the output provided and the number of residents in the community.[11]

To simplify matters further, I will assume that all communities possess identical production functions for the local public good and that they produce this good under conditions of constant costs. By this latter provision I mean, for example, that the level of law enforcement services provided for one hundred people can be maintained for two hundred people by simply doubling the expenditure for the police force. Finally, let us assume at the outset that each community is committed to maintaining a specified level of consumption of the local public good; the level of consumption will vary across communities but remain unchanged within any given community. For example, a community might provide a level of law enforcement

[11] For a formal treatment of the problem of group size and the efficient output of both pure and impure public goods accompanied by an empirical study of the degree of decentralization in United States state-local finance, see James Litvack and Wallace Oates, "Group Size and the Output of Public Goods: Theory and an Application to State-Local Finance in the United States," *Public Finance*, vol. 25, no. 1 (1970), pp. 42–58.

services that requires an expenditure per resident of fifty dollars per annum; when an additional resident enters the community, a further expenditure of fifty dollars on law enforcement services becomes necessary in order to maintain the specified level of consumption.

It is interesting in this setting to reconsider the various pricing policies of local governments. Assume first, as we did earlier, that the municipal government simply charges a fee per resident adequate to cover its expenditures; accordingly, each resident might be billed fifty dollars annually to provide for law enforcement services. Residents would, in effect, purchase local public goods much as they purchase private goods in a competitive system: they would pay a price equal to marginal cost. Marginal cost here refers to the additional public expenditure undertaken to provide for the marginal person at the community's prescribed level of consumption. A head tax of this type has real appeal in this model, because it implies that individual decisions concerning the consumption of local public goods would be based, as in competitive markets, on real opportunity costs. Individuals with a relatively high demand for public goods would live together in communities that provide a high level of consumption of the good accompanied by a correspondingly large tax bill, while those with a lesser demand for the local public good would reside in communities whose levels of consumption and tax bills were significantly less.

This scheme would tend to receive excellent marks on the efficiency criteria presented earlier. Since the tax-price paid by the consumer reflects accurately the cost of the public goods he consumes, this system of finance introduces no incentives for inefficient behavior. There is no way the consumer can avoid payment for the public goods he consumes; he must pay directly the cost of the resources he absorbs in consuming the local public good. Moreover, this implies that, in maximizing his welfare, the individual will adjust his consumption of the public good to the point where the benefits derived from an additional unit of consumption of the good equal marginal cost. We have, in this case, a clear benefit, earmarked tax, and the result is allocative efficiency.[12] In addition one would

[12] Note that, in contrast to Chapter Two, where unrestricted mobility led to certain inefficiencies, mobility here leads to an efficient solution, because a new entrant does not impose any costs of congestion on

guess that this form of local taxation would involve relatively low administrative and compliance costs.

One likely objection to this solution to the local finance problem concerns the incidence of municipal head taxes. If we had in the system an equitable distribution of income, the solution just described would probably be quite acceptable to most. Assume, for example, that there exists a perfectly equal division of income in the economy: all families have an identical real income. In this case there would probably be little objection to the use of head taxes to finance local public goods. Some individuals would pay more taxes than others, but they would be those who chose to live in communities offering a higher level of consumption of the public good. Problems arise where the distribution of income is not regarded as satisfactory and where, as a result, it seems desirable to adopt a tax system that compensates for this somewhat. If, for example, the members of society feel that an ability-to-pay standard is most suitable for taxes at all levels of government, we will probably find a heavier reliance on income, wealth, or property taxes rather than on a head tax. A cursory survey of revenue systems at decentralized levels of government suggests that this is largely the case. Subcentral governments have adopted a wide variety of instruments to generate receipts—including property, sales, and income taxes—in addition to an imaginative array of user charges such as tolls and license fees. A particular favorite of local governments in many countries is the property tax; in the United States it is the source of close to 90 percent of local tax revenues. Therefore, it seems worthwhile to explore, in terms of the local finance model, the implications of the taxes most often used by decentralized units of government.

The use of nonbenefit taxes
by local governments

Let us suppose, for example, that a single community in this system chose to finance its expenditures on public goods

---

existing residents. More precisely, an entrant, through his tax payment, restores the level of consumption of the local public good to its previous level so that he compensates, in effect, those in the locality for the costs of congestion he imposes.

through the imposition of a proportional income tax, while other communities continued to employ a head tax. Economists are well versed in the first sort of inefficiency that such a tax might introduce: a distortion in the choice between work and leisure.[13] A local tax of this type may also result in a second and more serious source of excess burden: it may distort the selection of a community of residence. The tax-price to a consumer of public goods would depend, in this case, not only on his level of consumption of the good, but also on the individual's income. High-income residents would pay a higher tax-price than would poorer residents. This implies that the adoption of the tax would immediately establish some pecuniary incentives for relocation: the wealthy would have an incentive to move to localities where they could obtain local public goods more cheaply. Conversely, poorer persons would tend to move into this community because they could consume public goods for a relatively low tax-price. As a result the local income tax could induce an inefficient pattern of location of individual economic units, as well as possibly introducing some distortion in the work-leisure choice. The point here is that individual decisions as to location and the consumption of local public goods would no longer accurately reflect the cost of providing these goods. In consequence, we would expect a pattern of location to emerge that does not correspond to an efficient allocation of resources. Moreover, the movement of the wealthy out of the community and the influx of the poor would necessitate a rising income-tax rate, which would further hasten the departure of the rich and subsequently provide little advantage for the poor. Consumer mobility would thus not only introduce allocative inefficiencies but would also largely frustrate the attempt to attain a more desirable incidence of local taxes.

Let us run this experiment again, but this time assume that the community under consideration replaces its head tax with an ad valorem sales tax on the purchase of all goods and services. As before, the introduction of the new tax would mean that some individuals, those with relatively high levels of expenditures, would pay a higher tax-price than others. Again, the former would have an incentive to migrate to other communities, while individuals with low levels of expenditures would tend to move into the locality. The local sales tax, like

---

[13] See, for example, Musgrave, *The Theory of Public Finance*, ch. 13.

the income tax, would thus tend to generate excess burden resulting from inefficient locational decisions. Since people with relatively high levels of expenditures are usually those with large incomes, we would expect that the use of a sales tax by our sample community would produce roughly the same results as a proportional income tax. There may be a significant difference, however, if purchases can be made outside the jurisdiction at a nominal cost. In this case, rather than relocate, some individuals may find it more desirable to go to the trouble of traveling outside the community to purchase goods and services. The excess burden, then, will take the form primarily of the increased time and money costs of making these purchases.[14] Note also that to the extent that this takes place, it again tends to prevent the realization of the intended incidence of the tax.

Local taxes in this model may not only introduce distortions in residential location patterns but may also result in inefficient patterns of production of private goods. Assume, for instance, that a community levies a tax on net business income generated within its jurisdiction. Following Arnold Harberger's treatment of the corporation income tax, I will assume that this tax is equivalent to a tax on the use of capital in this particular community.[15] To keep the analysis simple, assume further that in the system as a whole there are only two factors of production—labor and capital; that the units of each are perfectly homogeneous; that these factors are in perfectly elastic supply at the same price to all communities; and that production functions for private goods are the same in all communities and exhibit constant returns to scale. A tax on the use of capital would initially make the production of goods and services more expensive in this community than elsewhere; it would thus create an incentive for business enterprise to move

---

[14] The effects of even relatively small differentials in local sales taxes on the geographical purchasing patterns of consumers may in some circumstances be quite substantial. In one study of sales taxes in New York City, it was estimated that increases in the city's sales-tax rate of 1 percent on past occasions had led to approximately 6-percent declines in the level of taxable sales. See William Hamovitch, "Effects of Increases in Sales Tax Rates on Taxable Sales in New York City," in Research Report of the Graduate School of Public Administration, New York University, *Financing Government in New York City* (New York: 1966), pp. 619–33.

[15] "The Incidence of the Corporation Income Tax," *Journal of Political Economy*, vol. 70 (June, 1962), pp. 215–40.

elsewhere or, perhaps even more important, for new business investment to seek other locations. To a large extent this explains why public officials at decentralized levels of government are reluctant to rely heavily on these kinds of taxes.

There is, however, a somewhat more subtle effect that could operate in this model—namely, that business might find itself able to obtain labor more cheaply in this locality than elsewhere. Residents of this community no longer pay any local taxes; therefore, they consume local public goods free of payment. If we assume that commuting costs (both time and money costs) to jobs elsewhere are not negligible, it is possible that people will be willing to work for lower wages than elsewhere in exchange for free consumption of the local public good. Residents of the community will, in effect, pay for the public good by accepting a lower wage rate than they could receive in other communities. In this case, given an elastic supply of capital to firms in the community, the effective price of capital to these firms will rise by the amount of the tax per unit, while the wage rate may tend to decline. This implies that, as a result of the tax, the relative price of capital in terms of labor in this community will differ from that in other communities; capital here will be relatively expensive. As a result competitive forces will lead to the adoption of more labor-intensive techniques of production than elsewhere (that is, the capital-labor ratio for any given industry will tend to be lower than in other localities). But this implies that the marginal product of capital will be higher and the marginal product of labor lower in this community than elsewhere in the system.[16] The tax will therefore result in an intercommunity differential in the marginal products of the two factors. Such differentials, moreover, represent an obvious inefficiency in the system, for they imply that the national product could be increased simply by relocating some units of labor and capital. More precisely, real national output could in this case be increased by bringing more units of capital into the community that has a higher marginal product of capital than elsewhere, or, alternatively, by sending units of labor to jobs in

---

[16] With two factors of production and a production function exhibiting constant returns to scale, the marginal product of each factor depends only on the relative quantities of the factors, not on the scale of production. See James Henderson and Richard Quandt, *Microeconomic Theory* (New York: McGraw-Hill, 1958), pp. 62–63.

other localities, where their marginal products would be increased. Thus it would seem that, in a system of decentralized finance characterized by a high degree of mobility of economic units, taxes on production can result not only in an inefficient locational pattern of business firms, but also in the adoption of inefficient factor proportions in the processes of production.[17]

Let us consider finally the case of the most popular of all local taxes: the property tax. Specifically, assume that one of the communities in the system adopts an ad valorem tax on land and the structures on the land to replace its existing head tax. The traditional analysis of the economic effects of the property tax suggests that the tax will tend to depress property values, at least in the short run, since net income accruing to the owner of the property will fall because of his annual tax liability. However, this analysis does not readily apply to a system of decentralized finance, for an individual's property-tax payment is, in effect, the price he pays for his chosen level of consumption of the local public good. The point is that people will be willing to pay higher rents to live in a community that provides superior public services. As a result, landlords may be able to increase rents sufficiently (or perhaps even more than sufficiently) to restore their real or imputed net rental income. This implies that property values need not fall in response to the levying of a local property tax.[18]

In terms of the example here, the community's removal of the head tax will increase the demand for rental dwellings in the locality, since renters will now be able to consume the local public good for no charge. As a result, gross rents will rise; residents of the community will, in effect, pay for the local public good through these higher levels of rental payments.

[17] By altering the relative prices of factor inputs, a tax on the use of capital may also induce patterns of comparative advantage and thus a geographical pattern of production that does not correspond to the one implied by real opportunity costs. In this regard, some evidence suggests that factor proportions, at least among the states in the United States, are responsive to some extent to differences in relative factor prices. Matityahu Marcus, in a cross-sectional study of manufacturing industries across the states, found that there was a significant negative correlation between capital-labor ratios and price of capital relative to that of labor. See his "Capital-Labor Substitution Among States: Some Empirical Evidence," *Review of Economics and Statistics*, vol. 46 (Nov., 1964), pp. 434–48.

[18] For a recent empirical study that suggests local property values are not depressed by higher property taxes where the revenues are used to improve local public schools, see the appendix to this chapter.

Landlords will thus recoup at least part of their tax liability in the form of increased gross rental income. Such a property tax would, however, introduce at least two types of inefficiencies. First, since the price an individual pays for the local public good depends on the rental price of the dwelling he selects, there exists an extra pecuniary incentive to try to economize on expenditures for dwellings. To purchase an extra unit of housing services, an individual must pay more than the marginal cost of the unit: he must also make an additional contribution to the public treasury. As a result, residents of the community will tend to purchase less than efficient levels of housing.

Second, while it may be true that aggregate property values in the community will not decline significantly, the tax will tend to alter the relative values of different sites and structures. As in the case of the local income tax, the relatively wealthy, who typically occupy residences of higher value, will find that their tax-price at the new rent levels exceeds the head tax they paid previously and the tax-price they would have to pay for similar levels of consumption in nearby communities. Conversely, those living in relatively low-value dwellings will find, for a time, that their position is improved, since their tax-price is less than under the head tax. As a result there will be an increase in demand for lower-price dwellings accompanied by a fall in demand for housing of higher quality. This will tend to reduce the range of rent levels in the community: superior quality residences will now become cheaper relative to more humble dwellings.

Two features of this outcome are worthy of note. First, the property tax *may* have some advantage on efficiency grounds over local income or sales taxes. As noted earlier, the imposition of a proportional, or progressive, income tax, for instance, will tend to induce an exodus of the relatively wealthy to other communities where they can purchase local public goods for a lower tax-price. The property tax is likely (at least in the short run) to induce less in the way of movement of this kind because of the probable capitalization of the tax. The reduced demand for relatively expensive housing resulting from the imposition of a local property tax will lower the rental prices for high-grade housing in the community; net rents and, therefore, the market value of superior quality residences will decline or, in other words, the tax will be capitalized. The owners of such residences will therefore experience a capital loss on the value of their property. However, it is impossible for them to escape the tax by movement to another community: through the process of capitalization, the entire loss of future rental income is reflected in an immediate fall in the value of the property at the time the tax is levied.[19] In contrast, the owners of relatively cheap housing units will experience a windfall gain. With the change in demand, gross rents on their property will tend to rise by an amount in excess of their tax liability so that the stream of future net income and therefore the capitalized value of their property will rise.[20]

Second, the pattern of incidence of this tax may be a peculiar one in terms of the size distribution of income. On first glance, if the community feels that its relatively wealthy should pay a greater absolute sum in taxes than poorer individuals, the incidence of the tax may appear favorable. However, this need not be the case; it could easily be true that among the wealthiest members of the community are owners of relatively inexpensive dwellings, most rented to lower-income families. The rise in rents means that the occupants will tend to benefit little from the shift from the head tax to the property tax; the gains will come to the owners of low-rent property, who may already be among the high-income groups. It is true, however, that if all members of the community owned their own dwellings, the tax would generally require residents of relatively valuable housing units to pay more in taxes than those living in more modest units.

The analysis thus suggests that, in a Tiebout world of perfect mobility in response to economic incentives, the adoption of nonbenefit taxes at highly decentralized levels of government

---

[19] For a further explanation of the process of the capitalization of a tax, see Musgrave, *The Theory of Public Finance*, pp. 382–85. Available evidence does, incidentally, suggest that differentials in property taxes among neighboring municipalities (unaccompanied by an offsetting superior program of public services) are capitalized in the form of reduced property values or net rental income. See Larry Orr, "The Incidence of Differential Property Taxes on Urban Housing," *National Tax Journal*, vol. 21 (Sept., 1968), pp. 253–62; John Heinberg and Wallace Oates, "The Incidence of Differential Property Taxes on Urban Housing: A Comment and Some Further Evidence," *National Tax Journal*, vol. 23 (March, 1970), pp. 92–98; and the appendix to this chapter.

[20] To some extent this may be offset in the long run by the failure to replace more expensive dwelling units and by an expansion in the number of lower-quality units.

may come at a high cost in terms of excess burden. The ease of intercommunity movement means that a community's imposition of a tax whose pattern of incidence diverges significantly from the pattern of benefits of local public services will establish a set of pecuniary incentives for some persons and/or business units to move out of the community and others to move in. And the incentives to movement will reflect not the true resource costs of consumption of these publicly provided goods, but rather the particular set of purely pecuniary inducements present in the structure of the tax. Moreover, the realization of both economic efficiency and the distributional objectives of the tax is likely to be frustrated by this mobility. Attempts to tax the relatively wealthy more heavily than the poor will fail to some degree because of the departure of those on whom the tax places the largest liability.

The discussion of decentralized taxation in this chapter has been based on a highly artificial, simplified model involving the frictionless movement of economic units among jurisdictions in response to economic incentives. For this reason, I would not for a moment argue that all the various effects of the local taxes examined here are in fact of genuine importance in the real world. Even at the analytic level, some of these effects stand out sharply only because we have assumed that a single jurisdiction employs an income tax or a property tax while others continue to impose head taxes.

What is of interest, nonetheless, is that such a model does make clear the variety of incentives and the often subtle results that *can* occur when the customary forms of taxation are employed at decentralized levels of government. There is, moreover, little doubt that under some circumstances these effects have been important both in terms of introducing distortions in patterns of resource use and location and in frustrating the distributional intent of local revenue programs. In particular, the evidence suggests that the fiscal disparities between the central cities and suburban communities of many metropolitan areas have contributed to an exodus of the relatively wealthy and the middle class from the cities, with a resulting deterioration in the public economy of the cities. What the analysis would seem to suggest is that, where individual economic units are sensitive to local fiscal treatment in terms of locational decisions, it would appear wise for local governments not to depart too radically from at least rough approximations to benefit forms of taxation.

The magnitude of the undesired allocative and distributional distortions from local nonbenefit taxation will tend to vary directly with the degree of interjurisdictional mobility of individuals and other factors of production. To the extent that such mobility is absent, there exists, of course, less risk in departing from benefit taxes, for the use, for instance, of ability-to-pay forms of taxation. In the case where immobility is quite high, the problem of local taxation differs little in character from that at the central level of government. In this instance, we need concern ourselves primarily with the efficiency and equity implications of changes in behavior under the chosen structure of taxes within the locality, not with the movement of economic units to other jurisdictions.

The degree of mobility present among various jurisdictions depends on a number of economic, sociological, and technological variables; among the most important are the geographical size of the jurisdiction and the availability of rapid and inexpensive modes of transport. The smaller the jurisdiction and the better the system of transport, the fewer should be the obstacles to interjurisdictional movement. This suggests, first, that the smaller the units of government in terms of area governed, the more severe will be the constraints on revenue policies stemming from the mobility of economic units. The preceding analysis, for example, is certainly more relevant to a suburban municipality in Los Angeles County than to the entire State of California. The adoption of a moderately progressive income tax, for example, is clearly more feasible for California than for a municipality in the Los Angeles metropolitan area. This means that as we proceed from the central government to government units with progressively smaller jurisdictions, it becomes continually more important to place increased reliance on benefit forms of taxation.

Second, as technical advances in systems of transportation continue to increase the ease of movement among jurisdictions, one would expect nonbenefit taxes at decentralized levels of government to result in growing welfare losses and increasing distortion of intended patterns of incidence. Municipalities may have been able to pursue a relatively independent fiscal course several decades ago, but this is becoming continually less true; today an individual who works in the central city of a metropolitan area typically has a wide choice of suburban municipalities in which to reside, and there is growing evidence that the fiscal programs of the suburban communities are an important factor in his choice of locality of residence.[21]

Some further problems in local taxation

In the preceding section, we have considered the troublesome allocative and distributive problems that may arise when, in a system characterized by a high degree of mobility of individuals and capital, localities adopt forms of taxation under which benefits for individual economic units diverge significantly from the unit's local tax liability. It should be emphasized, however, that, even where individuals are wholly immobile among localities (at least with respect to fiscal differentials), a high degree of mobility of capital can itself lead to serious problems for decentralized taxation.

Charles McLure, in an excellent series of theoretical and empirical studies, has explored the problems of allocative efficiency and incidence associated with decentralized taxes in the framework of a general-equilibrium model.[22] McLure is concerned for the most part with a system in which the locational choices of households are not sensitive to regional tax differentials, but flows of capital are. In such a system regional taxes on the use of capital, or more generally on production (for example, a regional value-added tax), can introduce inefficiencies in resource allocation along with some curious distributional effects.

As McLure demonstrates, taxes on regional or local production may to some extent be shifted to residents of other jurisdictions through increases in the prices of local output, some units of which are sold outside the taxing jurisdiction. In this way residents of a particular locality may be able to get out-

---

[21] See, for example, the empirical study in the appendix to this chapter.
[22] See his "The Inter-Regional Incidence of General Regional Taxes," *Public Finance*, vol. 24, no. 3 (1969), pp. 457–83; "Taxation, Substitution, and Industrial Location," *Journal of Political Economy*, vol. 78 (Jan.–Feb., 1970), pp. 112–32; and "The Interstate Exporting of State and Local Taxes: Estimates for 1962," *National Tax Journal*, vol. 20 (March, 1967), pp. 49–77.

siders to absorb part of the cost of their own local services. This McLure calls "the exporting of taxes." Such a procedure is likely to be particularly effective where a locality produces a highly specialized commodity purchased primarily by non-residents. One common form of tax exportation is the imposition of sizeable levies on restaurant and hotel bills in tourist centers so that visitors pay a large sum into the local treasury. A tax specialist in Florida, for instance, observed recently that "we have done an excellent job of shifting a large portion of the tax burden to tourists—the tax system is designed to tax the service industries quite heavily." [23]

Similarly, when a variant of the value-added tax on productive activity was adopted in Michigan, some state officials thought that one result of the tax would be a rise in the price of automobiles, causing residents of other states to pay much of the tax. Taxes of this kind, however, can be a tricky business. The Michigan value-added tax, for example, could in the long run induce a greater dispersal of the automobile industry into other states so that the short-run advantages of tax exporting may, in cases such as this, carry with them a substantial long-run cost in terms of the loss of new investment.

Tax incidence in an open system can, therefore, be an extremely complicated problem. Taxes levied in one jurisdiction may ultimately be paid largely by residents of other areas, and as a result it may be very difficult to determine even roughly the actual pattern of incidence of many taxes at decentralized levels of government. The extent of the exportation of taxes appears to be very considerable. McLure has estimated that within the United States approximately 20 to 25 percent of state taxes are shifted to the residents of other states.[24] One interesting implication of this phenomenon is that the residents of a particular jurisdiction may not have to bear the full cost of their own public programs and may as a result have an incentive to push the output of local services beyond the efficient level. The point is that, where taxes are exported, the marginal cost to the residents of the jurisdiction

---

[23] C. H. Donovan, "Recent Developments in Property Taxation in Florida: A Case Study," in Harry L. Johnson, ed., *State and Local Tax Problems* (Knoxville, Tenn.: University of Tennessee Press, 1969), p. 59.
[24] "The Interstate Exporting of State and Local Taxes: Estimates for 1962."

is less than the full marginal cost of the program. However, to maximize the welfare of their constituency, officials should expand expenditures to the point where the benefits from a marginal dollar of spending equal only the portion of an additional dollar of taxes that is borne by residents of the jurisdiction. Spending may therefore tend to be pushed past the point where marginal benefits equal true marginal costs.[25]

Local or regional taxation of capital may, in addition to its implications for incidence, induce inefficiencies in resource use. As discussed earlier, a tax on the use of capital in one jurisdiction will tend to discourage the employment of capital there and to divert its use to other locations. The result is interjurisdictional differences in the marginal product of capital and, consequently, a loss of national output.

It can also have serious effects on the levels of income and employment within the taxing jurisdiction. The diversion of capital through excessive taxation, particularly the loss of potential new business investment, is typically a matter of great concern to local officials, and there is the contention that this has given rise to the problem of "tax competition." Local officials, in an attempt to attract new investment to stimulate local employment and income, compete with neighboring jurisdictions by holding down local tax rates. This is, however, an oversimplified view of the problem. The benefits as well as the costs of public programs are clearly of some importance in the locational decision. A more extensive program of public services (including such things as a superior system of roads) will serve to entice business enterprise to locate in the community. Nevertheless, it is true that there are some forms of local expenditures, notably those for public welfare programs, that increase tax liabilities without providing offsetting benefits for local business firms. These kinds of programs are therefore particularly dangerous from the standpoint of a single local jurisdiction. It is by no means clear just how important local fiscal programs are in the location decisions of firms,[26] but local public officials appear to think that fiscal incentives

[25] The exporting of taxes may not have undesirable allocative and distributive effects in all cases. Taxation of tourists, for example, may be justified on the grounds that the visitors make use of local public services and therefore should bear part of the cost.

[26] For a survey of the available evidence on this, see John Due, "Studies of State-Local Tax Influences on Location of Industry," *National Tax Journal*, vol. 14 (June, 1961), pp. 163–73.

for location are significant, and this is what matters, for it means that these officials will tailor fiscal programs to avoid locational disincentives for existing (and, probably more important, for potential) local business activity.

The result of tax competition may well be a tendency toward less than efficient levels of output of local public services. In an attempt to keep tax rates low to attract business investment, local officials may hold spending below those levels for which marginal benefits equal marginal costs, particularly for those programs that do not offer direct benefits to local business. More systematic empirical work is needed to determine just how pervasive this phenomenon is. However, casual empiricism (for example, newspaper advertisements and subsidies to new business) does suggest that tax competition among decentralized levels of government is widespread in the United States, and the effect of this competition may be to restrict public output below efficient levels.

As we have stressed, the source of these problems in decentralized taxation is the interjurisdictional mobility of economic units; this mobility provides an avenue of escape from local taxation with the resulting inefficiencies in resource use and frustration of distributional objectives. To avoid these difficulties, decentralized governments can try to seek out immobile bases for taxation. What is mobile and immobile depends on a number of factors, particularly the size of the jurisdiction. For relatively large provinces or states, for example, labor may be, for all practical purposes, immobile with respect to modest levels of taxation of personal income. In the case where the supply of labor is perfectly inelastic within a state or region, a tax on labor income, as McLure shows formally, will be wholly capitalized in the form of reduced disposable income to labor in the taxing jurisdiction.[27] In this case both the intended incidence of the tax and the avoidance of excess burden can be realized.

For small jurisdictions, however, there may be no immobile factors to tax save one: land. A tax on site values long ago captured the fascination of some economists, notably Henry George and his followers, largely because of this characteristic.[28] A tax on land values will, according to economic theory,

---

[27] "The Inter-Regional Incidence of General Regional Taxes," p. 469.
[28] See George's famous *Progress and Poverty* (New York: Robert Schalkenbach Foundation, 1942).

be a neutral tax; since the supply of land is fixed, a tax on the income from land (or on its value) will be fully capitalized in terms of a reduced market value of the land. There is no escape from the tax and hence no excess burden. Local taxation of land values has also been defended on equity grounds. Since local public services provide benefits for users of local property and thereby enhance the value of this property, a land tax may provide a rough form of taxation according to benefits. Moreover, since the ownership of substantial amounts of valuable land is normally associated with a high level of wealth, a land tax may get reasonably good marks according to ability-to-pay criteria for taxation.

For these reasons and the fact that the property tax applied to structures seems to have discouraged both new construction and the maintenance of existing dwelling units, there has been a recent revival of interest in the possibility of a larger role for land taxation in local finance.[29] It is extremely doubtful whether land itself constitutes a large enough tax base to finance the bulk of local services, but there does at least appear to be some merit in placing a relatively greater reliance on land taxation as a local revenue source. In the City of Pittsburgh, for example, the value of the site and the structure are distinguished in the assessment procedure, and the tax rate on the site value is twice the rate on the value of the structures.

In concluding this section on the problems of decentralized taxation, it should also be stressed that the administrative and compliance costs of taxation at decentralized levels of government are frequently greater than those of the central government. The property tax, for example, is a relatively expensive tax to administer, since it requires the assessment of all taxable property. Existing wide variations in assessment practices can, moreover, lead to substantial inequities and discontent among taxpayers. Tax collection and administration appears to be an activity with considerable economies of scale,

[29] For a number of interesting papers on the feasibility of land taxation, see Daniel Holland, ed., *The Assessment of Land Value* (Madison, Wisc.: University of Wisconsin Press, 1970). There is not much hard evidence on the extent to which local property taxes have retarded the construction and maintenance of housing. However, the high levels that effective tax rates have attained in some United States cities (on the order, in some instances, of 5 percent of the true market value) imply an excise tax on building of approximately 50 percent. It is hard to believe that such rates would not seriously reduce levels of construction and maintenance activity.

and for this reason a heavy reliance on taxation by decentralized levels of government may often carry with it a real cost.

The case for tax harmonization

In the preceding sections the inefficiencies and distorted patterns of incidence of various local taxes stood out in sharp relief, because we assumed at each stage of the argument that only one community adopted the tax while all other localities employed some other form of taxation (for example, a head tax). One can imagine the distortions if all the communities were to adopt widely varying forms of taxation. Each individual and business firm would in this case have an incentive to reside in that community whose particular system of taxes gave him the best tax break. Clearly, this could seriously interfere with the attempt to reach a solution in which individuals locate according to their preferences for levels of output of public services and where the factors of production are employed in their most efficient use and place. Rather, both location patterns of individuals and other factors of production and the levels and techniques of production might be dominated by the particular pecuniary advantages afforded under varying kinds of taxes.

To minimize these distortions one can make a strong case for a substantial degree of "tax harmonization"—that is, for a cooperative effort to secure a system of taxation that minimizes excess burden and yields a desirable pattern of incidence. One promising move in the direction of such harmonization is for governments at the same level to adopt at least roughly similar revenue systems. If, for example, all municipal governments (as is close to true in many countries) place primary reliance on the property tax, there would be much less incentive for an individual to choose a community of residence on the basis of its tax program. In the limiting case where all governments at one level (for example, municipal, state, provincial, etc.) employ the same taxes with identical rate structures, the taxes become equivalent to national taxes levied by the central government on all residents of the country.

Typically, however, even if all local governments use the same tax, they will not adopt the same set of rates, since they generally provide varying levels of consumption of public services and have differing tax bases. As we discussed in Chapter Three, varying tax rates resulting from significant differences in levels of income or wealth among communities can themselves give rise to distortions in patterns of location. Where nonbenefit forms of taxation are employed, there will typically exist a pecuniary incentive to locate in wealthier communities in order to hold down one's tax bill.[30]

It is therefore clear that the use of nonbenefit taxation by decentralized levels of government is bound to introduce some inefficiencies and inequities, but this is to be expected. As Musgrave puts it,

> The very purpose of fiscal federalism . . . is to permit different groups living in various states to express different preferences for public services; and this, inevitably, leads to differences in the levels of taxation and public services. The resulting differentiation in tax levels may interfere with the most efficient allocation of resources and location of industries for the region as a whole; but such is the cost of political subdivision, be it on an intranational or international level.[31]

Tax harmonization does not, therefore, imply perfect uniformity in the rates and the forms of taxation across jurisdictions. Rather, it refers to the development of systems of taxation that, *subject to the economic objectives of the individual jurisdictions* (that is, each community's chosen levels of its

[30] An interesting and predictable reaction of many wealthy communities to this incentive has been to try to prevent the construction of more modest dwellings through the enactment of various zoning regulations and building codes that, in effect, limit construction to residences of only high value. In this way the existing residents are in some instances able to prevent the entry of those who would, under the existing tax structure, make a lesser contribution to the public treasury. Another technique for establishing a tax haven under the property tax consists of forming a jurisdiction with only a few families and a substantial amount of industrial or commercial property. The huge tax base, accompanied by the need to supply only a small number of persons with such services as public education, may allow extremely low rates of taxation. One striking example of such a tax haven has been the municipality of Teterboro in New Jersey, which had a population of twenty-two in 1960. The value of commercial and industrial property per resident was at that time close to $1.5 million. As a result, the "true" (adjusted for assessment ratio) tax rate in Teterboro was only 0.81 percent as compared with an average true rate of 2.20 percent for Bergen County as a whole.

[31] *The Theory of Public Finance,* pp. 179–80.

local services), serve to promote efficient resource use and an equitable pattern of incidence. As we have seen, a local jurisdiction is seriously constrained in its capacity to carry out successfully a strongly redistributive fiscal program. Some redistribution, however, is feasible if all jurisdictions at a given level of government pursue roughly similar redistributive programs so that economic units will not find certain localities much more attractive than others for purely distributional reasons.

A first guideline for tax harmonization, therefore, is that, where the interjurisdictional mobility of certain economic units is of a high degree, taxation of these units, if it is employed, should be of a similar form across the jurisdictions. Moreover, the rates at which these units are taxed locally should not vary greatly among the jurisdictions *except* to the extent that differences in rates are compensated at least roughly by differences in benefits to these units from the services provided. In this way distortions in both resource use and incidence resulting from the tax system itself can be kept to a minimum consistent with the other fiscal objectives of the individual jurisdictions.

Second, as we discussed earlier, it is desirable, where possible and where consistent with distributional objectives, to rely heavily on taxation of immobile economic units—those whose location is relatively insensitive to fiscal differentials across jurisdictions. In the limiting case of complete immobility and a fixed supply, taxation falls wholly on the units on which the tax is levied; no shifting or distortions in resource use occur. Since economic units that may be quite responsive to fiscal differentials across some small jurisdictions (for example, individual households in municipalities within the same metropolitan area) may be highly immobile with respect to the same tax when it is levied over a larger jurisdiction (such as states or provinces), the taxation of such units, at least to a modest extent, may be far less costly in terms of excess burden and frustrated distributional objectives for the larger localities than for the smaller ones. We might expect, therefore, that the most effective forms of taxation will differ among the various levels of government.

This brings us to the issue of the "vertical harmonization" of the tax system: the choice of taxes at different levels of government. I have argued that for the horizontal harmonization of taxation, different jurisdictions at the *same* level of government will generally find it desirable to adopt similar systems of taxation. In contrast, much greater variation in the tax structures at different levels of government is likely. At one extreme, some specialists in taxation have advanced the so-called doctrine of the separability of sources. Each level of government, according to this position, should have its own sources of revenues, or tax bases, that are not available to other levels of government. The central government, for example, might finance its expenditures through an income tax; the states or provinces could rely on sales and excise taxes; and local governments could tax the value of property. In this way there would be no overlapping of taxation by different levels of government with regard to the same tax base; each level of government would have its own source of revenues and would not encroach on the revenue base of another tier of government.

There is little in the way of economic logic, it seems to me, to support a firm adherence to the separability of sources. One may argue on political grounds that such a separation affords a certain degree of protection for the exercise of power at the different levels of government. In particular, it might conceivably prevent a gradual expansion of the powers of the central government at the expense of more decentralized public units. As we have seen, the scope for taxation with minimal allocative and distributive distortions is typically greatest at the level of the central government, and one might argue that, without constraints on the access to sources of revenue, the central government would gradually draw away the fiscal resources of decentralized levels of government.

The force of this argument is hard to evaluate, but it is surely far from self-evident, as will be seen in Chapter Six. Moreover, the rigid maintenance of separate revenue sources may be quite costly. Recent experience in a number of countries suggests that the coordinated taxation of the same tax base by different levels of government may in many instances be a very effective and inexpensive procedure. In the United States, for example, counties or metropolitan areas in some cases may add an additional percentage point or so to an existing state sales tax. The tax is collected in the normal way by the state tax authorities who then turn back the appropriate share of the receipts to the local government. By placing such a levy piggyback on a tax base already in use by another level of government, considerable economies in the administration and collection of revenues can be realized.

In addition this procedure may permit highly decentralized levels of government to make use of certain taxes that would otherwise be too costly to employ. Local sales or income taxes are a case in point. The argument in this chapter suggests that the scope for small local governments to use these taxes is quite limited because of the high degree of mobility of the units subject to the tax. Such governments may, however, be able to impose these taxes *at very low rates* such that incentives for the adjustment of behavior of the taxed units is too small to have serious distorting effects. The costs, however, of administering such a tax independently may not make it, on net, worthwhile; if, in contrast, the bulk of the administrative costs can be avoided by coordinating collections with another level of government, the tax may become a useful local revenue source.

For these reasons the case for separability of sources is not, it seems to me, a very persuasive one. The most effective tax system under a federal form of government may well involve vertical, as well as horizontal, coordination of taxation such that different levels of government may find it useful in certain instances to tax the same revenue base. Moreover, in view of the advantages larger jurisdictions possess in terms of taxing capability, it may be desirable to go one step further. A greater share of the responsibility for taxation can be placed with more centralized levels of government that in turn pass on some of these revenues in the form of grants to more decentralized public units.

A further role for intergovernmental grants: revenue sharing

Earlier in this chapter we outlined a model of local finance in the Tiebout tradition that possessed certain highly desirable characteristics. Mobile consumers in this system seek out a community providing the most suitable level of output of an impure public good for which they pay a tax-price equal to the cost of extending the consumption of this good to them. In this sense each individual pays a price equal to the marginal cost of the good. While this solution is an attractive one on our efficiency criteria, its acceptability is seriously impaired by the absence of an optimal distribution of income. Society may feel that, given the existing distribution of income, it is unfair to charge all members of a particular jurisdiction the same tax-price for the consumption of public services. Consequently, decentralized governments may, and have, turned to nonbenefit forms of taxation partly to attain a more equitable distribution of the tax burden.

The problem with this solution to the distribution problem is that the adoption of nonbenefit taxes by decentralized levels of government may involve serious inefficiencies. The imposition by a locality of a progressive income tax is, as we have discussed, likely to result in a severe distortion of locational decisions. Moreover, the induced movements of economic units can largely frustrate the attempt to establish a more desirable pattern of incidence of local taxes. Property taxes, by virtue of their capitalization, appear to have some advantages over income or sales taxes for avoiding excess burden, but they also are far from immune to this line of criticism. In addition, heavy reliance on decentralized taxation may involve further costs and distortions in incidence resulting from tax competition, the exporting of taxes, and relatively high costs of administration and compliance.

The most attractive solution to this whole problem (at a formal level at least) is that suggested in Chapter One: let the central government resolve the distribution problem and allow decentralized levels of government to provide public services that they finance with benefit taxes. The use of ability-to-pay taxation by local government, instead of a national negative income tax, may well involve a very high cost both in terms of excess burden and the failure to realize distributional objectives.

An alternative solution is the separation of the responsibility for raising revenues from that for determining levels of output of public services. Alvin Hansen and Harvey Perloff have argued forcefully that decentralized levels of government, while determining the composition of their respective budgets, need not also levy their own taxes.[31] The functions of public spending and taxation are separable; the central government

[31] *State and Local Finance in the National Economy* (New York: W. W. Norton, 1944), ch. 7.

could raise the bulk of the revenues and, through a program of intergovernmental grants, provide decentralized governments with needed funds. This sort of fiscal structure has real appeal, for by shifting the task of levying taxes to governments encompassing larger jurisdictions, many of the problems discussed in this chapter can be avoided or at least reduced in magnitude. Several countries, including Australia and Canada, have moved in this direction in recent years. The recognition of the many advantages, both in terms of economic efficiency and equity, of a more centralized system of taxation has led these countries to substitute centrally levied taxes for those at the provincial or state level. In return, the provinces or states receive from the central government large grants to assist in the financing of public programs. The United States is also considering a program of this type involving revenue sharing by the federal government with the states and localities.

While this separation of the spending and tax functions does offer real promise for circumventing some of the major deficiencies in a system of decentralized finance, we should recognize that this type of fiscal structure may tend to impede effective collective decision-making. We have emphasized that where possible it is generally desirable to maintain a clear and explicit link between spending and taxation so that individuals are in a position to evaluate the costs and benefits of public programs. If local governments do not raise their own funds but acquire them in the form of grants from the central government, there is an incentive to undertake almost any public program for which funds can be obtained, since the cost of the program to the community in question is likely to be close to zero. The transfer of the responsibility for raising revenues to the central government may for this reason discourage effective resource use within the public sector as a whole.

This problem, however, can be largely resolved through a properly designed system of unconditional intergovernmental grants. If only a portion of local revenues is provided by the central government, subcentral governments wishing to expand the provision of public services will still have to finance the *marginal* units of the public services entirely from their own revenues. Such grants, as discussed in Chapter Three, have only income effects, so that decisions at the margin will have to take into account the full cost of additional units. The essential feature of these grants is that they do not vary in amount with the budgetary decision of the recipient; as a result, they have no effect on the marginal cost to the locality of providing public goods.[32] In this way a partial separation of the revenue and expenditure functions may be achieved without seriously distorting the incentives for an effective use of public resources.

However, some observers have argued that the centralization of taxation leads inevitably to the eventual centralization of expenditure functions as well. They contend that without independent revenue authority, decentralized levels of government become so dependent on the central government that they ultimately lose their other powers as well. We shall examine this issue in the concluding chapter, but the point here is that a real question exists as to whether the centralization of the revenue system under a federal form of government is desirable. Such a step possesses both weighty advantages and disadavantages that are likely to vary in importance among different countries. It may be, for example, that the obstacles to geographic mobility are sufficient in some countries to keep the inefficiencies and inequities stemming from local taxation in accordance with ability to pay at a tolerable level. In this case there may be little need to centralize the system of taxation. In other situations the distortion stemming from heavy local taxation may be serious enough to merit increased centralization of the revenue function. In addition, where significant disparities exist across jurisdictions in levels of per-capita income and wealth, increased centralization of taxation combined with a program of equalizing grants can promote horizontal equity and the realization of acceptable national standards of important local services. The choice is obviously one of great importance in a federal system of government, and curiously enough it is not one that has received much attention from theorists in public finance. Moreover, with the evidence accumulating from the experience of countries with widely varying degrees of centralization of taxation, it should

---

[32] This is in contrast to the case where spillover benefits are present in the provision of particular local public goods. Where this condition exists, matching grants are needed for the explicit purpose of reducing the marginal cost to the locality of providing the good.

become increasingly possible to reach some reasonably firm conclusions on this issue.

Debt finance in a federal system

The primary purpose of debt finance by the central government in a federal system differs fundamentally from its function in the fiscal operations of decentralized levels of government. For the central government, the basic role of debt finance is to help the public sector regulate the level of aggregate demand so as to stabilize the economy at a high level of employment with stable prices. To stimulate the level of total spending, the central government may find it desirable to allow its expenditures to exceed its tax revenues and to finance the deficit by issuing bonds. The central bank (the Federal Reserve Banks in the United States) can then, to the extent deemed appropriate, purchase some of these bonds and thereby inject new money into the economy. In this way the operations of the treasury and central bank determine the size and composition of the national debt. At the central government level, debt finance is thus primarily a means for the control of the level of aggregate demand and, therefore, for the resolution of the stabilization problem.[33]

At the local level, however, debt finance plays an entirely different role. In Chapter One and its appendix, I argued that the task of countercyclical policy should generally rest with the central government. The function of local government from this perspective is to provide outputs of public services in accordance with the preferences of local residents. And it is in the realization of this objective that local debt finance can be extremely useful.

The conventional view is that local governments should issue bonds for one basic purpose: to finance capital projects. Capital projects are by definition long-term investment programs with benefits spread over the years to come. New water reservoirs or an expanded highway system, for example, can be

[33] For useful analyses of the countercyclical function of debt policy, see Musgrave, *The Theory of Public Finance*, ch. 24; and James Tobin, "An Essay on Principles of Debt Management," in Commission on Money and Credit, *Fiscal and Debt Management Policies* (Englewood Cliffs, N.J.: Prentice-Hall, 1963), pp. 143–218.

expected to provide services extending several decades into the future. This means that not only present residents of a locality, but also future residents will consume the services provided by the project. In this case the benefit principle of taxation suggests that future residents should share the costs of the program. For this purpose bond finance seems quite appropriate, for it offers a means through which payments for capital projects can be spread over the life of the structure so as to coincide more closely with the stream of future benefits. A local government can borrow the funds to finance the construction of the project and can then repay principal plus interest in a series of payments in future years.

There is, as was pointed out in Chapter One, a fundamental asymmetry between debt finance by the central government and debt finance by local governments. Since the bonds issued by the central government are held primarily by residents of the country, these holdings constitute an internal debt; the issuance of such bonds does not in itself imply a shifting of the burden of the debt to later generations. Future residents of the country will admittedly pay back the principal and interest, but they will also receive the payments. In contrast, the debt issues of local government are normally held primarily by residents of other localities. Therefore, local debt is largely an external debt and as such will require at a future date a transfer of income from residents of the locality to nonresidents. This implies that the use of debt finance by a locality, in contrast to the national debt, places a real burden on future residents, for they will have to repay the loan but generally will not be the recipients or beneficiaries of the payments.

However, this makes debt finance ideally suited for the funding of capital projects. Creating an external debt to cover the cost of capital programs places some of the real financial burden on the future residents who will realize many of the benefits flowing from the program. By virtue of its external character, bond finance at decentralized levels of government would thus appear to provide a means to an equitable allocation of the costs of capital projects among those who will share the benefits of the programs.[34]

---

[34] This view of the function of local debt finance is advanced, for example, by Musgrave, *The Theory of Public Finance*, p. 575. Musgrave also points out in ch. 23 of his book, that, subject to certain assumptions, the use of debt finance by the central government may allow some

It is useful, however, to examine somewhat more closely this conventional view of the effects of local public debt. In particular, let us return to a model of local finance characterized by mobile household units. Assume that we have a system of the Tiebout type in which individuals move without cost among localities in response to fiscal differentials. In equilibrium, this implies that any fiscal advantages available in a particular community will become capitalized in the form of higher local property values; the demand for residences in such a community will bid up the value of a local property to the point where it exceeds the value of similar properties elsewhere by the present discounted value of the future stream of additional fiscal benefits accruing to a resident of that particular community. At this point the fiscal advantages of the community will be precisely offset by the higher price of its residences so that there will be no remaining inducement for further locational adjustments.

In this framework consider two communities that are in every way identical. Assume that each decides to undertake a capital project and that the benefits and costs associated with these projects are the same in the two localities. The sole difference is that community A decides to finance the project out of the revenues available during the current year, while community B chooses to employ debt finance so as to spread out the payments for the project over future years. At the end of the current year, A and B both have their projects complete and anticipate equal benefits from these projects in future years. However, in A the cost of the project is fully paid, while the residents of B have a future tax liability equal to this sum. If we compare the position of a typical resident of A with that of a typical resident of B, we find that the former has one obvious advantage in terms of his local fiscal future: he has the same expected future stream of fiscal benefits as his counterpart in B, but he has no corresponding future tax liability. In our frictionless world we would expect the capitalization of this fiscal differential so that the value of a typical residence in A would soon exceed that in B by the present discounted value of the additional future tax liability of the household in B.

spreading over time of the burden of public expenditures. The counter-cyclical function of public debt finance has, however, become of primary importance for central governments.

In this world, debt finance does not allow the present residents of B to shift the cost of the project to future residents, because the future tax liability becomes capitalized in the form of lower property values in B. In fact, if individuals had free access to capital markets at the same rate of interest as the local government, it would be a matter of complete indifference to the individual household whether the local government employed tax or debt finance for the capital project. Suppose a resident of A preferred to defer his tax liability for the project. He could simply borrow the funds—that is, sell his own bonds —to pay his taxes in the current year and then repay this sum over future years thereby achieving a position equivalent to a resident of B, who will make his tax payments for the project in later years. Conversely, a resident of B who wishes to meet his liability for the project in the current year could simply buy a bond, the future proceeds from which would cover his future tax payments. In our model of perfect mobility and costless access to capital markets at a single rate of interest, it makes no difference to the individual whether his local government chooses debt or tax finance; he can achieve whatever combination of present and deferred payments he prefers through adjustments in his own asset portfolio in the existing market for bonds. Moreover, it is clear that the process of capitalization implies that bond finance does not permit the shifting of costs to future residents relative to tax finance, since the deferred tax payments are reflected in reduced local property values.[35]

It is to be emphasized that the value of the future benefits from the project, as well as the associated future tax liability, are capitalized in terms of local property values. A marginal project, for example, whose future benefits to an individual household precisely equal its tax liability, will have no net effect on the value of local property; in this case, the capitalization of the tax liability, which depresses local property values, is precisely offset by the capitalization of the future stream of benefits. The individual simply pays in taxes a sum equal to the fiscal benefits received. Note that should an individual move away from this community, he realizes no gain or loss; the new resident of the community will be compensated

[35] This argument is developed by George G. Daly, "The Burden of the Debt and Future Generations in Local Finance," *Southern Economic Journal*, vol. 36 (July, 1969), pp. 44–51.

for any differentials between the remaining tax liability and the residual stream of benefits from the project by an off-setting adjustment to the price he pays for the local property. In this model there is payment in accordance with fiscal benefits received.[36] But the interesting point is that it occurs regardless of whether the locality uses bond finance or current taxation to meet the costs of the project.

What, then, is left of the conventional case for local debt finance and the argument that bond issues facilitate an equitable temporal pattern of payments among present and future residents over the life of the project? The preceding analysis suggests that benefit pricing over time and hence an equitable intertemporal pattern of payments will take place under either tax or debt finance. To answer this question, we must examine the assumptions that gave rise to this equivalence of taxation and bond finance, which were: (1) sufficient mobility of households in response to fiscal differentials such that these differentials do in fact become capitalized in terms of local property values; and (2) costless access to capital markets at the same rate of interest for all economic units.

First, if fiscal differentials among jurisdictions are not capitalized, then pay-as-you-go tax finance will place the full burden of financing the project on present residents while many of the benefits will accrue to future residents. If capitalization does not occur, the conventional argument for local debt finance, therefore, remains valid. Some recent evidence suggests that for municipalities within the same metropolitan area, differentials among jurisdictions, both in terms of tax rates and out-puts of local services, are largely capitalized.[37] For small local jurisdictions this assumption may thus be reasonably realistic, and both debt and tax finance may result in intertemporal

---

[36] Should a community use debt finance for a project that produces a surplus of benefits over costs, local property values in this model would clearly rise. Conversely, the undertaking of inefficient projects, those for which costs exceed benefits, would depress the value of local property. To keep the argument as simple and clear as possible, I have deliberately avoided the issue of the distribution of the benefits from the project by assuming implicitly that they accrue to each household in proportion to that household's local tax share. Where this is not the case, it is possible that a particular capital project in the context of the local revenue system could enhance the value of some local properties while depressing the value of others.

[37] See the appendix to this chapter, and Heinberg and Oates, "The Incidence of Differential Property Taxes on Urban Housing."

equity. However, I would judge that for larger jurisdictions, such as states or provinces, such mobility is much less, and as a result the capitalization of fiscal differentials takes place to a much smaller extent. For relatively large jurisdictions, therefore, the traditional role for debt finance is probably quite legitimate.

Second, it is clear that the assumption of free access to capital markets at a single market rate of interest is a serious oversimplification. Government units typically can borrow funds at rates of interest significantly below those available to individual households.[38] Individuals may, for example, have to pay relatively high interest costs to borrow against prospective future earnings. In addition, some people simply have a strong aversion to personal indebtedness. This implies that to the extent local residents wish to spread out the payments for projects over future years, there are real gains to be realized from undertaking the necessary borrowing collectively through local government bond issues. Savings in interest and also in transaction costs may, therefore, make local borrowing to finance capital projects a desirable procedure even in the presence of a high degree of interjurisdictional mobility of households.

Moreover, there is generally some merit in minimizing the fluctuations in local tax rates over time to avoid what Musgrave calls "tax friction," the costs resulting from uncertainty as to the future levels of tax rates.[39] Since large, nonrecurrent expenditures on capital projects can be the source of considerable instability in levels of spending, reliance on tax finance could involve substantial fluctuations over time in tax rates. Through the use of debt finance for capital projects, a locality can avoid this source of variations in tax rates by, in effect, spreading out the payments for these projects.

This brings us, at a very pragmatic level, to what is perhaps the most compelling reason for a substantial reliance on bond

[38] This is particularly true in the United States, where the interest income from state and local bond issues is exempted from taxation under the federal income tax. As a result, states and localities can normally obtain funds at rates of interest well below those on issues of other borrowers. This is not to say that such an implicit subsidy to state and local government borrowing is desirable—it is not. See David Ott and Allan Meltzer, *Federal Tax Treatment of State and Local Securities* (Washington, D.C.: Brookings Institution, 1963), chs. 1–3.
[39] *The Theory of Public Finance*, p. 567.

finance for local capital programs: for many worthwhile projects, bond issues are frequently the only practical way to acquire the necessary funds. Capital programs, such as the construction of roads or universities, typically involve very high costs that must be met over a relatively short time span. For this reason it is often very difficult to finance these programs out of current revenues. This problem, incidentally, is by no means peculiar to the public sector. Private corporations are continually making decisions on long-term investment projects, and these corporations, given the prospect of an attractive return from a potential investment program, are seldom reluctant to approach the capital market with their own bonds. Even at the level of the family, we find that long-term investments, such as the purchase of a house, normally involve the issuance of a mortgage. Debt finance in such instances is sound finance.

Where prospective capital programs are clearly in the public interest (that is, where they promise a stream of future benefits whose value exceeds the cost of the project), they should not be pushed aside because of the inadequacy of current tax revenues. Rather than deprive both the present and future residents of a locality of valuable public services, the government should feel justified in turning to bond finance. Where local governments either refuse or are prohibited by law from engaging in debt finance, many desirable but expensive investment projects will probably not be undertaken simply because of limitations imposed by levels of current tax revenues.

The experience with debt finance by state and local levels of government in the United States seems to conform at least roughly to the principles developed in this section. The reliance on state and local debt finance has increased rapidly in the last few decades. The outstanding debt of state and local governments in the United States has grown more than eightfold—from $15.9 billion to $133.5 billion—over the years 1946–1969, a rate of increase well in excess of even the rapid expansion in state and local expenditures.

The great bulk of this oustanding debt (over 90 percent in 1969) consists of long-term bonds issued to finance capital programs—largely highways and school construction. It is interesting, moreover, that state and local governments have chosen increasingly in recent years to issue "serial" bonds; these are bonds that require each year a payment not only of interest charges, but also a part of the principal. A thirty-year issue of serial bonds, for example, might require, in addition to interest costs, the payment each year of one-thirtieth of the principal. The actual life of most of these bonds is typically matched (very roughly) with the expected useful life of the asset (or, in the case of revenue-producing projects, the period over which it is expected that the revenues realized from the asset will be sufficient to repay principal and interest) ; bond issues to cover the construction of water and sewer projects, for instance, are often of the thirty-year variety.

There is, however, immense variation in the practices among the different states and localities.[40] Some, for example, have adopted formal "capital budgets." This procedure involves the separation of the budget into two parts: a capital budget, which lists new investment projects to be undertaken, and a current budget, which contains operating and maintenance expenditures plus allocations of funds to service and retire outstanding debt. The financing procedure, then, typically consists of bond issues to finance the capital budget and tax levies to fund current spending.

In other states, however, there is little in the way of systematic planning and reliance on bond issues to finance capital programs. While it is true that state and local governments employ bond issues almost exclusively to finance capital programs, not all state and local projects are financed by bond issues. In fiscal year 1969, for example, total capital outlays by all state and local governments in the United States were $28.2 billion. Long-term bond issues by these governments, however, were only $15.5 billion. It is therefore clear that many state and local governments are to a substantial extent drawing on current revenues to fund investment projects.

A strong reluctance to use debt finance for capital programs or legal obstacles to such funding seem to increase the likelihood that potentially beneficial projects will be passed up because of the drain they would place on current revenues. One series of empirical tests indicated that the ability and willingness of state and local governments to engage in debt finance, as measured by a number of different variables, dis-

---

[40] For a detailed description of the capital budgeting procedures of the various states in the United States, see A. M. Millhouse and S. K. Howard, *State Capital Budgeting* (Chicago: Council of State Governments, 1963).

played a strong positive correlation with levels of public capital formation.[41] Those states that for one reason or another have not placed much reliance on debt finance have exhibited relatively low levels of public investment. Both for attaining an equitable intertemporal pattern of payments for the services from public investment programs and for realizing an efficient level of public capital formation, it appears that debt finance, along with taxation, should be an integral part of local fiscal operations.

[41] See my "The Theory and Practice of Bond Finance," in Economic Policy Council and Office of Economic Policy, Department of the Treasury, State of New Jersey, *Second Annual Report* (June, 1969), pp. 21–29. Thomas Pogue has also found recently that constitutional restrictions on the use of local debt finance appear to have had some effect in holding down levels of local expenditure. See his "The Effect of Debt Limits: Some New Evidence," *National Tax Journal,* vol. 23 (March, 1970), pp. 36–49.

Appendix

The effects of property taxes and local public spending on property values: an empirical study of tax capitalization and the Tiebout hypothesis[1]

This appendix presents some empirical findings on a problem for which we presently possess only the scantest of evidence: the effects of local public budgets on property values in the community. There do exist several studies of the incidence of property taxes, the mainstay of local revenue systems in the United States, but in nearly all cases these studies are based on assumptions concerning the degree to which the tax on various components of property is capitalized. However, we have little hard empirical evidence indicating whether property taxes are in fact capitalized and, if so, to what extent.[2] This deficiency might not seem very serious if we had a single, compelling theory of the shifting and incidence of property taxes, a theory that suggested a definite solution to the problem. The truth is, however, that the theory of the shifting of property taxes points to a wide range of possibilities. Under some circum-

[1] Reprinted by permission of the *Journal of Political Economy*, vol. 77, no. 6 (Nov.–Dec.), © 1969, pp. 957–71, and The University of Chicago Press. I am indebted to the Ford Foundation for support of that work, and I am also grateful to William Baumol, David Bradford, Lester Chandler, Thomas Frederick, James Heckman, John Heinberg, E. Philip Howrey, Harry Kelejian, James Litvack, and the members of the graduate seminar at Princeton University for many extremely helpful comments on earlier drafts of the paper.
[2] The paucity of empirical work on this problem is readily apparent from Dick Netzer's survey of the evidence in his comprehensive study of the property tax (*Economics of the Property Tax* [Washington, D.C.: Brookings Institution, 1966], ch. 3).

stances the whole of the tax may be reflected in a reduced rental income (and hence lower property values) for landlords, while in other situations the tax may result primarily in increased rents to tenants, with little impact on the market value of property.

Some years ago, Charles Tiebout[3] developed a formal model involving consumer location in accord with preferences for local public goods and services. He suggested that at least at a theoretical level we can envision a system in which we get something resembling a market solution to the production and consumption of local public goods. Very simply, Tiebout's world is one in which the consumer "shops" among different communities offering varying packages of local public services and selects as a residence the community that offers the tax-expenditure program best suited to his tastes. The obstacles to such consumer mobility (including job commitments and family ties) are obviously great; as a result several economists have expressed serious reservations as to the likely explanatory power of the Tiebout model. On the other hand, with the growing urbanization of society, there is some reason to believe that the Tiebout hypothesis may be relevant to the real world. Individuals working in a central city frequently have a wide choice of suburban communities in which to reside, and the quality of the local public schools, for instance, may be of real importance in the choice of a community of residence. If this is true, its outputs of public services (as well as taxes) should influence a community's attractiveness to potential residents and should thereby affect local property values.

The following section develops briefly the conceptual framework for examining the effects of property taxes and local expenditure programs on property values. This will provide the background for the subsequent empirical study of fifty-three residential communities in northeastern New Jersey. The results of the study, which suggest the direction of the effects of tax and expenditure programs on local property values, together with rough estimates of orders of magnitude, have some interesting implications for local government finance.

[3] "A Pure Theory of Local Expenditures," *Journal of Political Economy*, vol. 64 (Oct., 1956), pp. 416–24.

Local public budgets and the Tiebout model

There is an extensive literature on the theory of the shifting of property taxes that examines the probable effects of property taxes on the value of land and structures.[4] The traditional, or "classical," theory suggests (subject to numerous qualifications) that the part of the tax falling on the land would, since the income from land is a pure economic rent, be absorbed by the land owner (that is, this part of the tax would be capitalized in the form of reduced property values). In contrast, the portion of the tax applicable to structures would in the long run be "shifted" forward to purchasers, as the tax would depress the net return on investment in the construction industry and would thereby result in a diminished stock of structures in future periods.

This literature, however, deals largely with the case of a single tax rate applicable to all land and structures. If, in contrast, we consider a system (as is the case in the United States and several other countries) in which localities have varying tax rates and offer differing levels of output of public services, a quite different approach and set of conclusions suggest themselves. In terms of the Tiebout model, we can conceive of a utility-maximizing consumer who weighs the benefits stemming from the program of local public services against the cost of his tax liability and chooses as a residence that locality which provides him with the greatest surplus of benefits over costs. From this standpoint the individual's tax liability (that is, the value of his house and lot multiplied by the property tax rate) becomes the price of entry into the community, the price of consuming the local output of public services. It is the present value of the future stream of benefits from the public services *relative* to the present value of future tax payments that is in this case important.

This general-equilibrium approach to the problem implies that, if a community increases its property tax rate in order to expand its output of public services, *net* rental income (actual

[4] For an excellent critical survey of the theories of the shifting and incidence of the property tax, see Herbert Simon, "The Incidence of a Tax on Urban Real Property," *Quarterly Journal of Economics*, vol. 57 (May, 1943), pp. 398–420. Reprinted in American Economic Association, *Readings in the Economics of Taxation* (Homewood, Ill.: Richard D. Irwin, 1959), pp. 416–35.

or imputed) to property owners need not decline and may well increase.[5] Moreover, this suggests a way to determine whether the Tiebout hypothesis of consumer location in accordance with preferences for local budgetary programs has any relevance to actual behavior. If consumers, in their choice of locality of residence, do consider the available program of public services, we would expect to find that, other things being equal (including tax rates), gross rents (actual or imputed) and therefore property values would be higher in a community the more attractive its package of public goods. Individual families, desiring to consume higher levels of public output, would presumably tend to bid up property values in communities with high-quality programs of public services. As C. F. Bickerdike noted, "Some things, such as lighting and cleaning of streets, are advantages visible to the eye; they may be taken into account when a man is choosing a house, though they are apt to be forgotten when the rate-collector calls."[6] In contrast, if local expenditure programs have no impact at all on locational decisions, we would not expect local property values to depend on spending variables, for in this case the demand and supply for local property would presumably be independent of these programs. The next section of this appendix is an attempt to see if we can discern empirically the effects or absence of effects of local property taxes and public expenditures on

[5] A superb treatment of the incidence of property taxes is to be found in Appendix G of Alfred Marshall's *Principles of Economics*, 8th ed. (New York: Macmillan, 1948). Marshall is careful to distinguish between the case of a national property tax and a system of local taxes on property. Contrasting "onerous rates" (those that yield no compensating benefits) with "remunerative rates" (those that confer benefits on those who pay them), Marshall argues that for local rates

> onerous taxes on site values tend to be deducted from the rental which the owner, or lessee receives: and they are accordingly deducted, in so far as they can be foreseen, from the ground rent which a builder, or anyone else, is willing to pay for a building lease. Such local rates as are remunerative, are in the long run paid by the occupier, but are no real burden to him (*Principles of Economics*, p. 797).

Marshall notes further that "such rates [remunerative], ably and honestly administered, may confer a net benefit on those who pay them; and an increase in them may attract population and industry instead of repelling it" (*Ibid.*, p. 794).

[6] "Taxation of Site Values," *Economic Journal*, vol. 12 (Dec., 1902), pp. 472–84. Reprinted in American Economic Association, *Readings in the Economics of Taxation* (Homewood, Ill.: Richard D. Irwin, 1959), pp. 377–88.

local property values and, if so, whether we can get some rough approximations concerning the relative strength of the two effects.

An empirical study

The study presented here is a cross-sectional analysis of a sample of communities that aims to determine, other things being equal, the relationship between property values and local property taxes and expenditures. The problem (as usual in these kinds of experiments) is that within a sample of communities other things are not equal. It therefore becomes necessary to specify the other determinants of local property values and then to attempt to hold these constant while observing the partial relationship among the variables of concern. In addition to the level of property tax rates and the output of public services, one would expect the value of residences in a particular community to depend on a number of other variables. First, within a metropolitan area, the accessibility of the community to the central city should be of importance. Since the central city is the primary source of employment in the area, individuals should, other things being equal, prefer living close to the city to minimize the cost in both time and money of traveling to their place of employment (and to make the leisure activities of the city more accessible). Therefore, we would expect property values to vary inversely with distance from the central city.

Second, the character of the residences themselves is an obvious determinant of value. Large houses in an excellent state of repair and in a pleasant location will tend to sell at higher prices than smaller, run-down residences in unattractive areas. For this study I will thus assume that the value of dwellings in a particular community depends on the physical characteristics of the residences and area, on the proximity of the community to the central city, on the property tax rate, and on the level of output of public services in the locality. The sample under study consists of a group of fifty-three municipalities in northeastern New Jersey, all of which are located within the New York metropolitan region.[7] To maintain some semblance of

[7] For a description of the sample of communities and of the sources of data, see the notes at the end of this appendix.

homogeneity, the sample is limited to "residential" communities. A residential community is defined as one with an employment-residence ratio of less than 100 (that is, a municipality in which a larger number of residents go outside the community to their place of employment than come into the community to work from other places of residence).

The next task is to locate operational measures of the variables. As an index of proximity to the central city, I have used simply the linear distance of the municipality from midtown Manhattan. The physical characteristics of the property, including the attractiveness of the neighborhood as a place of residence, are more difficult to quantify. Some data are available on the quality of the housing stock in each community.[8] As a measure of size, the study employs the median number of rooms per dwelling. To measure the age (and presumably to some extent the state of repair) of the housing stock, I have used as an independent variable the percentage of the houses in the community built since 1950. However, this still leaves unconsidered the various intangible characteristics of a house: its physical charm or beauty and the attractiveness of the particular neighborhood or community as a place to live. As a proxy variable for these intangibles, the study uses family income. Wealthier families will presumably select higher-quality residences—better houses in more desirable neighborhoods. The median family income of the community therefore represents a measure of the intangible features of the houses in the community.

In the choice of fiscal variables, one cannot use the nominal property tax rate, because the wide variation in assessment ratios across communities implies that the actual rate at which communities tax property is not likely to bear a systematic relationship to the nominal rate. Instead, I have used the "effective" tax rate (that is, the nominal rate times the assessment ratio), which should provide a better measure of the true rate at which property is taxed in the locality.[9] The major

[8] United States Bureau of the Census, *1960 Census of Housing,* vol. 7, Part 6 (Washington, D.C.: U.S. Government Printing Office, 1963).
[9] Official assessment ratios for each community are determined by the State of New Jersey for use in the school aid equalization program. These ratios are arrived at by comparing the actual prices at which individual homes in the various communities are bought and sold with the value at which these homes are assessed for tax purposes. In 1960 assessment ratios ranged all the way from 11 percent to 104 percent.

problem in the selection of variables is determining a reasonable index of output for local public services. Those who have worked in this area are familiar with the difficulties in obtaining operational measures of output in the public sector. Frequently the only feasible proxy for public output is some measure of inputs. Per-capita public expenditure immediately suggests itself; further reflection, however, suggests that this is likely to be a rather unsatisfactory measure of the level or quality of output. Public spending per capita in two communities may vary, for example, as a result of differing relative sizes of the school population; a community with a relatively large number of children will typically have to spend more per capita to provide a school system of the same quality as a community with an older age distribution of the population. And these variations in spending may have nothing to do with the quality of public output provided.[10]

By far the largest single item in local public budgets (and no doubt the most important to families with children) is primary and secondary education. Again no direct measure of output is available, but comprehensive data on inputs, more precisely on costs, are published annually. I have, as a result, used expenditure per pupil as a proxy variable for the level of output of educational services. While this is by no means a perfect variable for my purposes (in part because it neglects the noneducational public services provided locally), there is some reason to expect that, for a group of residential communities in the same section of a metropolitan area, the quality of local school systems should vary directly with expenditure per pupil.[11] If this is the case and if (as the Tiebout model

In the regressions, I have used a simple average of effective tax rates for each community over the period 1956–60, which serves to smooth out any aberrations resulting from an unrepresentative sample of homes sold in a particular year. See Morris Beck, *Property Taxation and Urban Land Use in Northeastern New Jersey*, Urban Land Institute Research Monograph 7 (Washington, D.C.: Urban Land Institute, 1963).

[10] In the actual regression runs, the coefficient of the per-capita public-expenditure variable was not significantly different from zero.

[11] Herbert Kiesling, in a recent study of a sample of school districts in New York State, had only modest success with a per-pupil expenditure variable in explaining the level of achievement as measured by the test scores of pupils in the sample districts. (See his "Measuring a Local Government Service: A Study of School Districts in New York State," *Review of Economics and Statistics*, vol. 49 [Aug., 1967], pp. 356–67.) It may still be the case, however, that *perceived* benefits in terms of smaller classes, better libraries, etc., are closely related to expenditure per pupil,

suggests) individuals consider the quality of local public services in making locational decisions, we would expect to find that, other things equal (including tax rates) across communities, an increased expenditure per pupil should result in higher property values.

Using the multiple-regression technique, my procedure was to regress the median value of owner-occupied dwellings (including house and lot) in the various communities on the median number of rooms per house, the percentage of houses constructed since 1950, median family income, the distance in miles from Manhattan, the annual expenditure per pupil in the public schools, the effective property tax rate, and the percentage of families in the community with an income of less than $3,000 per year.[12] The inclusion of the last variable, the percentage of low-income families, is necessitated by the character of the data. Poorer families are more likely to reside in rental dwellings in suburban communities than are wealthier families. Consequently, in a community with a relatively large number of low-income families, median family income will tend to understate significantly the actual median income of homeowners. And it is this latter figure that is needed for the study, since

---

and that this is what counts in terms of the evaluation of different schools by parents. For purposes of determining whether individuals consider the benefits from public services in selecting a community of residence, expenditure per pupil may for this reason be a satisfactory variable. In computing expenditure per pupil, I, like Kiesling, used a weighted average of enrollments to take account of the increased cost of pupils at higher grade levels. Following Kiesling and incorporating information from New Jersey sources, I employed the following weights to determine a "weighted pupil enrollment" for each school district: kindergarten pupils $= .5$, elementary school pupils (grades 1–8) $= 1$, secondary school pupils (grades 9–12) $= 1.25$, special pupils (mentally retarded, etc.) $= 2$. Expenditure per pupil for each school district was then calculated by dividing the weighted enrollment into the annual current costs of the district. For data sources, see Note B at the end of this appendix.

[12] The dependent variable in the analysis is the median value of single-unit, owner-occupied dwellings (including the value of both house and lot) in the community that is provided by the United States Bureau of the Census, *1960 Census of Housing*. The value of residences is based on appraisals by owners and may, as a result, be subject to considerable error. However, the typical or average value for residences in a municipality seems to be reasonably accurate. Leslie Kish and John Lansing, for example, found that the difference between the mean of appraisers' and owners' estimates for over 500 residences was only $350. See their "Response Errors in Estimating the Value of Homes," *Journal of the American Statistical Association*, vol. 49 (Sept., 1954), pp. 520–38.

we are trying to explain the median value of owner-occupied dwellings. We would therefore expect the median value of owner-occupied houses to be higher relative to median family income in the community as a whole for those municipalities where a relatively large number of low-income families reside.

Before presenting the regressions, it is important to stress that the variation in the dependent variable, the value of owner-occupied dwellings, is likely to be quite substantial in the presence of capitalization of the tax. If, for example, we consider two identical houses in two identical communities, where both dwellings have an expected life of forty years and rent for $2,000 annually, the difference in the market value of the houses, if one were subject to a 4-percent property tax and the other to a 2-percent tax, would be in excess of $5,000 if the tax were fully capitalized.[13] As a result, we are not likely to be faced with the difficult task of isolating minute differences in property values, differences that could easily be obscured by minor imperfections in the explanatory variables.

Employing ordinary least squares (OLSQ), equation 1 indicates that, with other things constant, property values bear a significant negative relationship to the property tax rate and a significant positive association with expenditure per pupil.[14]

---

[13] For property of a finite life, in this case forty years, we have:

$$\text{(N1)} \qquad V = \sum_{i=1}^{40} \frac{Y_n}{(1+r)^i} = \sum_{i=1}^{40} \frac{(Y - tV)}{(1+r)^i},$$

where V = market value of the property, Y = gross annual rental income, Y_n = net (after tax) rental income, r = rate of discount. Solving for V, we get:

$$\text{(N2)} \qquad V = \frac{Y \left[\sum\limits_{i=1}^{40} \frac{1}{(1+r)^i} \right]}{1 + t \left[\sum\limits_{i=1}^{40} \frac{1}{(1+r)^i} \right]}.$$

Using a rate of discount of 5 percent, the difference cited in the text is calculated from the expression:

$$V = \frac{\$2,000m}{(1 + .02m)} - \frac{\$2,000m}{(1 + .04m)} = \$25,550 - \$20,350 = \$5,200,$$

where:

$$m = \sum_{i=1}^{40} \frac{1}{(1 + .05)^i} = 17.1591.$$

[14] The tax, expenditure, and distance variables are employed in log form, which somewhat enhances their explanatory power. This would appear

170

(1) $V = -21 - 3.6 \log T + 3.2 \log E - 1.4 \log M + 1.7R$
$\quad\quad (2.4)\quad (4.1)\quad\quad\quad (2.1)\quad\quad\quad\quad (4.8)\quad\quad\quad\quad (4.1)$

$$+ .05N + 1.5Y + .3P$$
$$(3.9)\quad (8.9)\quad (3.6)$$

(Note: The numbers in parentheses are the absolute values of the t-statistic for the coefficients. All the coefficients are statistically significant at a 5-percent level of significance.)

$$R^2 = .93,$$

where V = median home value in thousands of dollars (1960); $\log T$ = natural log of the effective percentage tax rate (the rate used is a simple average of effective rates over the years 1956–60); $\log E$ = natural log of annual current expenditures per pupil in dollars (1960–61); $\log M$ = natural log of the linear distance in miles of the community from midtown Manhattan; R = median number of rooms per owner-occupied house (1960); N = percentage of houses built since 1950 (1960); Y = median family income in thousands of dollars (1959); P = percentage of families in the community with an annual income of less than \$3,000 (1959). These results thus appear to suggest some capitalization of the tax and appear consistent with the Tiebout hypothesis.

Some further thought, however, suggests good reason to be suspicious of the results in equation 1. One could make a good case for the argument that the negative association between tax rates and home values stems from a dependence of tax rates on property values, rather than the reverse. Given the

---

to make sense. As suggested by equation N2 in the preceding footnote, we would not expect property values to vary linearly with the absolute level of the tax rate; rather, the higher the tax rate, the smaller should be the impact of a given absolute change in the rate. Similarly, we might expect that additional expenditures per pupil would tend to yield successively diminishing increments of benefits. Finally, a log form for the distance variable seems reasonable, since being an additional mile from the central city would presumably be more important to someone who was quite close to the city than to an individual who was already twenty miles away. I also experimented with two other variables from the *1960 Census of Housing* (United States Bureau of the Census, 1963), variables that one might expect to influence the value of owner-occupied houses in a community: the "homeowner vacancy rate" and the percentage of owner-occupied units deemed "sound" by the census takers. Neither variable, however, was statistically significant or had any appreciable effects on the results.

level of public spending, the higher the property values in a community, the lower are the tax rates needed to generate the revenues to finance the program. A more complete model would have to include another equation in which the tax rate is treated as a dependent variable, presumably as a function of the level of local public spending, the size of the tax base, and the extent of public issues of debt, if any. Moreover, the level of spending per pupil in the local public school system probably also depends to some extent on the wealth and income in the community.

What all this means is that equation 1 may well contain some simultaneous-equation bias, since the supposed independent variables, the tax rate and expenditure per pupil, probably depend to some extent on the dependent variable, home values. If this is true, the coefficients of log T and log E in equation 1 will be correlated with the error term, and the results in equation 1 may be spurious. To provide a more reliable test of the capitalization and Tiebout hypotheses, I reestimated equation 1 using two-stage least squares (TSLS).[15] The TSLS version appears as equation 2.

$$(2) \quad V = -29 - 3.6 \log T + 4.9 \log E - 1.3 \log M + 1.6R$$
$$\quad\quad\quad (2.3) \quad (3.1) \quad\quad (2.1) \quad\quad (4.0) \quad\quad (3.6)$$
$$\quad\quad\quad\quad\quad\quad\quad\quad + .06N + 1.5Y + .3P$$
$$\quad\quad\quad\quad\quad\quad\quad\quad\quad (3.9) \quad (7.7) \quad (3.1)$$

$$R^2 = .93.$$

[15] To "purge" the tax and expenditure variables of their correlation with the error term, it is necessary to derive "predicted" tax and spending variables by regressing log T and log E on the other independent variables in equation 1 and on some additional predetermined variables. These new predicted variables are then used to reestimate equation 1. On this procedure, see, for example, John Johnston, *Econometric Methods* (New York: McGraw-Hill, 1963), ch. 9. The additional predetermined variables employed in generating the new tax and expenditure variables were: the median number of years of school completed by males of age twenty-five or more, population density, percentage of dwellings owner-occupied, the percentage of change in population from 1950 to 1960, the percentage of the population enrolled in public elementary and secondary schools, a dummy variable with a value of one for those communities in Hudson County and a value of zero for municipalities in other counties, and the value of commercial and industrial property per resident. In the complete model, these variables would appear as exogenous variables in other equations that determine the levels of tax rates and public expenditures.

The results in equation 2 differ little from those in equation 1 except that the coefficient on the public-expenditure variable is somewhat larger. It is interesting to try to get some idea of the orders of magnitude implied by the coefficients of the tax and expenditure variables. Equation 2 indicates that, with public output held constant, an increase in local property tax rates from 2 percent to 3 percent will reduce the market value of a house by about $1,500.[16] Considering a typical house with a market value of $20,000 and an expected life of forty years, and using a rate of discount of 5 percent, full capitalization of the increase in the tax would imply a reduction in value to about $17,740.[17] Equation 2 thus suggests that a substantial portion of the tax increase, approximately two-thirds (that is, $1,500/$2,260) in this case, is being capitalized in the form of depressed property values.[18]

[16] The mean value of the effective property tax rate for the sample of communities is 2.4 percent.

[17] The capitalized value of the house is calculated with the use of equation N2 in footnote 13. The first step is to employ equation N2 to determine the value of the annual rent, Y:

(N3) $$\$20,000 = \frac{Ym}{1 + .02m} \qquad \text{yields} \qquad Y = \$1,566,$$

where

$$m = \sum_{i=1}^{40} \frac{1}{(1 + .05)^i} = 17.1591.$$

Then, using this equation again with the computed value of Y and a tax rate of 3 percent, we find the value to be:

$$V = \frac{\$1,566m}{1 + .03m} = \$17,739.$$

The mean value of an owner-occupied house in the sample is $19,200.

[18] Ronald Ridker and John Henning have recently studied the determination of residential property values in the St. Louis metropolitan area. (See their "The Determinants of Residential Property Values with Special Reference to Air Pollution," *Review of Economics and Statistics*, vol. 49 [May, 1967], pp. 246–57.) Using 1960 census data, they find important some of the same variables I have used in this study. Although they did not employ any property-tax or public-spending variables, the authors did include a dummy variable to distinguish between census tracts in Illinois and Missouri. Property taxes are significantly higher in Illinois than in Missouri, and Ridker and Henning found that, other things being equal, property in the St. Louis metropolitan area is of higher value if it is located in Missouri rather than in Illinois. Therefore their results also suggest some capitalization of local property taxes.

In addition, by assuming typical values of the variables, it is possible to get some feeling for the relative strength of the tax and expenditure variables. For this purpose, consider the following experiment. Assume that the community is composed of identical homes, each worth $20,000 and each housing one public-school pupil. Assume next that the community decides to raise its effective property tax rate from 2 percent to 3 percent to provide a balanced expansion in spending on all locally provided services. Since roughly half of the local public budget goes into education, this implies that expenditure per pupil in the school system will rise by $100 (that is, $20,000 [.01/2]). Again using typical values of the variables, assume that this allows spending per pupil to rise from $350 per annum to $450. Placing these values into equation 2, one finds that the impact of the tax increase is to reduce the value of each house by $1,500. On the other hand, the increase in expenditure per pupil from $350 to $450 pushes house values up by roughly $1,200. Equation 2 thus suggests that the half of the budget increase going into the school system almost in itself offsets the depressive effects of the higher taxes on home values. This makes no allowance for the presumed positive impact on property values of the improved quality of other locally provided services. If we had considered a rise in tax rates for the sole purpose of improving the quality of the school system, equation 2 would (for average values of the variables) suggest that the effect on property values of the benefits from the improved services would more than offset the depressive influence of higher property taxes. The evidence therefore suggests that the benefits forthcoming from the primary service provided by local government, the public school system, do in fact exert a positive influence on local property values; better schools, other things being equal, appear to enhance the value of local residential property. One clearly should not take seriously the precise outcome of the example just considered; rather, the results should be regarded as indicating no more than orders of magnitude. In this light, equation 2 suggests that the impact of increased benefits on property values from an expansion in spending on the local school system approximately offsets the depressive effects of the higher taxes required to finance the expanded program. If property values do provide a reasonably accurate reflection of the benefits from local public services, these results would seem to suggest that these communities have, on the average, expanded public spending to the point where (very roughly) the benefits from an additional unit of output equal marginal cost.

While the benefits from better schools may cancel out the effects on residential property values of higher taxes, equation 2 does imply that increases in property tax rates *unaccompanied* by an expanded program of public services will depress local property values. This is important for comparing the effects of property taxes across communities; it means, for example, that if one community (because of houses of lower value or as a result of a relatively large population of children) levies higher tax rates than a neighboring municipality in order to provide the *same* quality of public services, property values in the former community will be depressed relative to those in the adjacent community where tax rates are lower. Consumers thus appear to some extent to "shop" for public services. If one community can provide a given program of public services more "cheaply" (that is, with lower tax *rates*) than another, at least some individuals appear willing to pay more to live there.

I should comment briefly on some problems inherent in the approach adopted in this study and on deficiencies in the available data. Most studies of the effects of taxes (for example, the shifting of the corporation income tax) have relied on time-series data to isolate the effects over time on relevant variables of changes in tax rates. In contrast, I have adopted cross-sectional techniques. This latter approach would appear best suited to the problem under investigation: we are asking what effect a change in tax rates and/or expenditures has on the equilibrium value of residential property. The problem is thus one of comparative statics for which cross-sectional estimation is the appropriate technique. Implicit in the use of cross-sectional regression analysis is the assumption that the observations do in fact represent points of equilibrium. This, of course, is seldom if ever strictly true and, especially where an adjustment period of some length is likely, it is possible that the results may be distorted to some extent.[19] It could be, for

[19] On this problem see Edwin Kuh, "The Validity of Cross-Sectionally Estimated Behavior Equations in Time Series Applications," *Econometrica*, vol. 27 (April, 1959), pp. 197–214; and Yehuda Grunfeld, "The

example, that the negative association we have observed between property taxes and home values is primarily a short-run phenomenon, which would disappear over a longer period of time. Unfortunately, time-series data to investigate the nature of the adjustment process are not available. Ultimately, however, time-series studies of the adjustment process would provide a valuable supplement to cross-sectional studies of the effects of local taxes.

I should also like to recognize explicitly the imprecision of several of the operational measures of the variables. This, along with the problems inherent in the use of simultaneous-equation estimation techniques, suggests that some caution is in order concerning the degree of reliability that we can attribute to the results.

To summarize, this appendix reports the findings of a cross-sectional study of the effects of local property taxes and local expenditure programs on property values. Using the two-stage least-squares estimation technique in an attempt to circumvent the likely presence of some simultaneous-equation bias, the regression equation indicates that local property values bear a significant negative relationship to the effective tax rate and a significant positive correlation with expenditure per pupil in the public schools. The size of the coefficients suggests that, for an increase in property taxes unaccompanied by an increase in the output of local public services, the bulk of the rise in taxes will be capitalized in the form of reduced property values. On the other hand, if a community increases its tax rates and employs the receipts to improve its school system, the coefficients indicate that the increased benefits from the expenditure side of the budget will roughly offset (or perhaps even more than offset) the depressive effect of the higher tax rates on local property values.

These results appear consistent with a model of the Tiebout variety in which rational consumers weigh (to some extent at least) the benefits from local public services against the cost of their tax liability in choosing a community of residence; people do appear willing to pay more to live in a community that provides a high-quality program of public services (or

---

Interpretation of Cross-Section Estimates in a Dynamic Model," *Econometrica*, vol. 29 (July, 1961), pp. 397–404.

in a community that provides the same program of public services with lower tax rates).

Note A: The sample of communities

The group of communities used in the empirical study consists of all residential New Jersey municipalities of population size 10,000 to 50,000 (according to the 1960 Census of Population) in the New York metropolitan region with the exception of those in Monmouth County. This county was omitted from the outset because it includes a large number of beach-resort communities with seasonal residences.[20] By residential community is meant a municipality with an employment-residence ratio of less than 100 according to *The Municipal Yearbook*.[21] This procedure produced a group of fifty-three municipalities, which were included in the study and are listed below.

Bergen County	*Essex County*	*Morris County*
Bergenfield	Maplewood	Madison
Cliffside Park	Millburn	Parsippany-Troy Hills
Dumont	Montclair	
East Paterson	Nutley	*Passaic County*
Fair Lawn	Orange	Hawthorne
Fort Lee	South Orange	Totowa
Garfield	Verona	Wayne
Glen Rock	West Orange	
Hasbrouck Heights		*Somerset County*
Lodi	*Hudson County*	Bound Brook
Lyndhurst	Secaucus	North Plainfield
Maywood	Weehawken	Somerville
New Milford	West New York	
North Arlington		
Palisades Park	*Middlesex County*	*Union County*
Ridgefield Park	Edison	Cranford
Ridgewood	Highland Park	New Providence

[20] For a definition of the New York metropolitan region, see Edgar Hoover and Raymond Vernon, *Anatomy of a Metropolis* (New York: Doubleday, 1962), p. 8.
[21] Orin Nolting and David Arnold, eds., *The Municipal Yearbook, 1963*, vol. 30 (Chicago: International City Managers' Association, 1963), Table 3.

River Edge	Metuchen	Roselle
Rutherford	Middlesex	Roselle Park
Teaneck	South Plainfield	Summit
Tenafly	South River	Westfield
Waldwick		

Note B: The sources of data

The sources of data for the variables used in the estimations are as follows:

VARIABLE	SOURCE
1. Median value of owner-occupied dwellings	Census of Housing, 1960
2. Median number of rooms per owner-occupied dwelling	Census of Housing, 1960
3. Population	Census of Population, 1960
4. Median number of years of school completed by males of age twenty-five and over	Census of Population, 1960
5. Effective property tax rates	Beck (1963)
6. Value of commercial and industrial property per resident	Beck (1963)
7. Population density	Beck (1963)
8. Median family income	Beck (1963)
9. Percentage of dwellings built since 1950	*Municipal Yearbook, 1963*
10. Percentage of dwellings owner-occupied	*Municipal Yearbook, 1963*
11. Percentage of population with family incomes under $3,000	*Municipal Yearbook, 1963*
12. Percentage change in population from 1950 to 1960	*Municipal Yearbook, 1963*
13. Linear distance in miles from midtown Manhattan (that is, Fifth Avenue and 34th Street)	Measured in *Rand McNally Road Atlas*, 43rd ed. (1967)
14. Municipal expenditure data	*Twenty-Third Annual Report of the Division of Local Government*, State of New Jersey, 1960

15. School district enrollment and
    expenditure data

*Tenth Annual Report of the
Commission of Education,
Financial Statistics of
School Districts*, School
Year 1960–61, State of
New Jersey

Chapter five
An empirical study of federal finance

There is a limit to the extent of country which can advantageously be governed, or even whose government can be conveniently superintended, from a single centre

John Stuart Mill, REPRESENTATIVE GOVERNMENT

The preceding chapters have presented a primarily theoretical discussion of the way governments ought to behave in order to maximize economic welfare. In this sense the analysis has been primarily normative: we have concerned ourselves with divisions of functions among levels of government and with sets of policies designed to achieve an efficient allocation of resources and an equitable distribution of income. At this point, we will shift the focus of the analysis to an investigation of the ways in which governments are actually organized and the manner in which they function. The issue here is whether or not it is possible to use the body of theory we have developed to help understand the international similarities and differences in intergovernmental fiscal relations.

A number of political scientists have reached essentially negative conclusions on this matter; the division of functions among different levels of government, they argue, is the result of a bargaining process, the outcome of which is generally unpredictable:

What functions are vested in the general government, and what left to the regions, what activities are expressed and what implied, what activities are protected, and what activities denied only emerge from an elaborate system of political "horse-trading" in which the variety of interests seeking expression must be compromised. . . . There is neither science nor theory in this process. It is not a mathematical division where high exactitude is possible. There is only the skill of translating precedent to local circumstance, and the draftsmanship to express the compromised purposes of the key bargainers in language to satisfy them.[1]

They would contend, therefore, that it is impossible to determine any general principles by which to understand the division of functions within a federal system of government. McGregor Dawson's description of the formation of the Canadian federal system seems to sum up this position:

The original allocation of power was not made . . . on any *a priori* basis; it represented the greatest common measure of agreement that could be formulated among conflicting interests at the time, and the primary test it had to meet was the approval it could command from the federating colonies.[2]

My own findings suggest that there is more than a little truth in such conclusions. As one examines the development of different countries and notes, for example, the sorts of considerations that led to the establishment of a particular federal government, it becomes clear that the unique historical experiences and circumstances of each country have led to a differentiation in governments that is difficult if not impossible to explain in terms of a simple set of general principles.[3] It

[1] Rufus Davis, "The 'Federal Principle' Reconsidered," in Aaron Wildavsky, ed., *American Federalism in Perspective* (Boston: Little, Brown, 1967), p. 10.
[2] *Ibid.*
[3] In some countries, such as Australia, sheer geographical size was clearly important in the decision to adopt a more decentralized form of government. In contrast, a small country like Switzerland also found a federal system attractive; where size might have suggested a unitary form of government, the linguistic, religious, and cultural differences among the regions in Switzerland resulted in a political and economic system with considerable local autonomy.

may yet be the case, however, that beneath the bargaining process to which the political scientists refer there do exist some fundamental considerations that exert an important and, to some extent, predictable effect on the structure of the public sector. The preceding analysis would seem to suggest that this could well be the case. For this reason it does seem worthwhile to explore the fiscal structure and activities of existing governments to see if they conform significantly to the normative theory developed in the preceding chapters.

In the first two sections of this chapter, I examine some admittedly fragmentary evidence on the stabilization and redistributive policies of a few federal countries. The findings do seem to indicate (as theory would lead us to expect) a prominant role for the central government in performing these functions. The main body of the chapter consists of an econometric study of the degree of fiscal centralization in fifty-eight countries, including both federal and nonfederal governments, in which I make an attempt to generate and test some hypotheses based on the earlier theoretical discussion. Since this is an area where there exists very little quantitative empirical work, this study is of a tentative and exploratory character. The findings themselves are not always consistent with our expectations; nevertheless, some empirical relationships of interest do emerge, which suggest, to some extent, both the potential and the limitations of an economic explanation of the structure and operation of the public sector.

Public policy for high employment and stable prices

The contention in the first chapter was that the resolution of the stabilization problem must generally be the job of the central government. The constraints on effective counter-cyclical policy by subcentral governments in the form of an absence of control over the money supply, the relatively small fiscal multipliers resulting from the openness of regional or local economies, and the largely external character of the debt issues of such governments, mean that the scope for efficacious programs to generate full employment with stable prices is quite limited. In contrast, the central government has at its disposal powerful fiscal and monetary instruments for this task. The responsibility for stabilizing output and prices at high levels of employment must, therefore, fall primarily on the central government.

But have governments in fact behaved as this argument would suggest? If so, we would expect to find that in federal countries the central government has been the primary agent for countercyclical policy; subcentral governments presumably take levels of employment and prices as pretty much beyond their control and devote the bulk of their efforts to providing outputs of basic public services for their constituencies. The evidence is, I think, reasonably consistent with this view of public countercyclical activities. Since the Great Depression of the 1930's, when both the need for public programs to reduce fluctuations in the level of economic activity and the potential of fiscal and monetary policies to achieve this goal became apparent, central governments have taken the lead in meeting this task of the public sector.

In the United States, for example, the experience seems to have been along these lines. State and local governments emerged from the 1930's with a record of having contributed directly to the severity of the contraction in the economy: as the level of economic activity declined and their tax revenues fell off, these governments responded by attempting to restore budgetary balance through reductions in spending and increases in taxation. The remarkable fact is that, in spite of the tremendous contraction in the economy, state and local governments in the aggregate moved from a budgetary deficit in 1929 to a surplus by 1934 on the National Income and Product Accounts.[4] This led in the 1940's to the formulation by Alvin Hansen and Harvey Perloff of the "fiscal perversity" hypothesis by which they suggested that the fiscal activities of state and local governments could be expected to accentuate rather than dampen fluctuations in the level of economic activity.[5]

Since the principles of compensatory finance were not well understood in the 1930's, what is far more relevant here is the fiscal behavior of state and local government in the post World War II period. Robert Rafuse sought, some twenty years after

[4] An excellent study of United States fiscal policy in the 1930's, both at the federal and state-local levels, is available in E. Cary Brown, "Fiscal Policy in the 'Thirties': A Reappraisal," *American Economic Review*, vol. 46 (Dec., 1956), pp. 857–79.
[5] *State and Local Finance in the National Economy* (New York: W. W. Norton, 1944), ch. 4.

the work of Hansen and Perloff, to reevaluate the fiscal-perversity hypothesis in terms of the record of state and local governments in the United States since the end of World War II.[6] Rafuse found that during the period from 1945 to 1961 the record of state-local spending and revenues was essentially one of unbroken and rapid increases. The intense demands placed on state and local governments for important public services during these years led to continued rises in expenditures and receipts with practically no relation to the state of the economy.[7] State and local budgetary activities in the United States in recent years thus appear to have been basically neither pro- nor countercyclical; rather, they have been generally neutral with regard to the aggregate level of economic activity.[8] This evidence should not, I think, lead to a complete rejection of the perversity hypothesis. In particular, the United States has not seen a really serious depression over this period; should one occur there remains good reason to expect that state and local governments would eventually cut back on spending in response to an extended contraction in their tax bases.

The evidence does suggest that state and local governments in the United States have not engaged extensively in explicit countercyclical policies.[9] In a few instances, some efforts have been made in this direction, but they seem not to have amounted to much. The State of New York, for example, established a

[6] "Cyclical Behavior of State-Local Finances," in Richard Musgrave, ed., *Essays in Fiscal Federalism* (Washington, D.C.: Brookings Institution, 1965), pp. 63–121.
[7] State and local government debt issues also expanded very rapidly over this period; outstanding state and local debt increased from about $16 billion in 1946 to $81 billion in 1962. These debt issues were not, however, the result of expansionary countercyclical policies. Rather, state and local governments have used issues of bonds to finance long-term investment projects, of which many are self-financing over the long run (for example, toll-financed highways). As noted in Chapter Four, debt issues for long-term capital projects provide a means to spread out payments equitably among both present and future beneficiaries of the projects.
[8] To the extent that increases in spending matched by identical increments in revenues are expansionary (through the balanced-budget multiplier), one could argue that the overall effect of the growth in state and local spending and revenues has been somewhat inflationary.
[9] The kinds of programs typically adopted by state or local governments to increase employment involve fiscal incentives to encourage new business investment in the jurisdiction. Such programs, while perhaps contributing to the long-run development of an area, are not very suitable for countercyclical purposes.

Tax Stabilization Reserve Fund in 1946. The idea was that, during boom years, surplus tax revenues would be accumulated in the fund so that, in recession years when revenues were insufficient, the fund could be tapped to maintain levels of spending. The Fund has never, however, proved important in the state's fiscal activities. In particular, the financial demands on state and local governments have been so intense over this period that there has been little opportunity to set aside funds in reserve.

The federal government, in contrast, assumed explicit responsibility for economic stability in the Employment Act of 1946:

> The Congress hereby declares that it is the continuing policy and responsibility of the Federal government to use all practicable means . . . to promote conditions under which there will be afforded useful employment for those able, willing, and seeking to work, and to promote maximum employment, production, and purchasing power.[10]

This is not to say that the record of the federal government in the United States is one of consistently sensitive and effective stabilizing fiscal and monetary policies. The record is, rather, a highly mixed one, including such contrasting episodes as the apparently overly restrictive policy stance of the late 1950's, which permitted excessive levels of unemployment and the tax cut of 1964 which (from the viewpoint of some observers at least) was highly successful in pushing the economy toward a full-employment level of output.[11] I do not propose here to enter the current debate on the relative effectiveness of fiscal and monetary policy or of rules versus discretionary policy. My point is rather that, regardless of the position one takes on these issues, it is generally thought at a policy level that

[10] Quoted by Lester Chandler, "Economic Stability," in Edgar Edwards, ed., *The Nation's Economic Objectives* (Chicago: University of Chicago Press, 1966), pp. 38–39.

[11] For a useful study of United States fiscal policy in recessions during the period from 1948 to 1962, see Wilfred Lewis, Jr., *Federal Fiscal Policy in the Postwar Recessions* (Washington, D.C.: Brookings Institution, 1962). Arthur Okun has provided a quantitative examination of the 1964 tax cut in his "Measuring the Impact of the 1964 Tax Reduction," in Walter Heller, ed., *Perspectives on Economic Growth* (New York: Random House, 1968), pp. 27–49.

the federal government, including the central monetary authority, bears the primary responsibility for excessive unemployment or rapid price inflation, and federal fiscal and monetary policies are, as a result, formulated with economic stabilization as a major objective.

The experience in several other federal countries has paralleled at least roughly that in the United States. In both Canada and Australia, for example, the central government has formally recognized its responsibility for maintaining high and stable levels of economic activity. In 1940 the Royal Commission on Dominion-Provincial Relations in Canada reported:

> The Dominion is the only government which can meet, in an equitable and efficient manner, the large fluctuating expenditure due to unemployment. Its unlimited powers of taxation give it access to all the incomes which are produced. . . . With its control over the monetary system the Dominion is able to finance the temporary deficits that may arise . . . without suffering such a drastic weakening of credit as occurs when the budgets of local governments get seriously out of balance. The monetary and taxation powers of the Dominion would enable it to follow a planned budgetary policy of deficits during depressions, and surpluses and debt repayment during prosperity—a policy which is generally impracticable for provinces and municipalities. . . . It is not suggested that it is within the powers of government to do away with depressions, particularly in a country like Canada which is so largely dependent upon foreign markets, but governments can do a great deal to minimize the huge losses in national income. . . . Implementation of the Commission's recommendations would throw all the extreme fluctuations of Canadian public finance on the Dominion. This is essential if fiscal, monetary, and economic policies are to be coordinated with a view to reducing Canadian overhead costs and to minimizing and helping control the swings of the business cycle. . . . The Dominion would have to budget for the business cycle rather than for any specific fiscal period. This would lead to integration of fiscal policy with monetary and economic policies in a manner which could be made highly beneficial to the general welfare.[12]

[12] Ian Drummond, *The Canadian Economy: Organization and Development* (Homewood, Ill.: Richard D. Irwin, 1966), p. 97.

This was followed in 1945 by the issuance of a White Paper on Employment and Income by the Dominion government which stated:

> The Government will be prepared, in periods when unemployment threatens, to incur the deficits and increases in the national debt resulting from its employment and income policy, whether that policy in the circumstances is best applied through increased expenditures or reduced taxation. In periods of buoyant employment and income, budget plans will call for surpluses. The Government's policy will be to keep the national debt within manageable proportions, and maintain a proper balance in its budget over a period longer than a single year.[13]

Likewise in Australia, the central government in a White Paper in 1945 asserted that "full employment is a fundamental aim of the Commonwealth Government."[14] This was further reflected in the Reserve Bank Act of 1959, which directs the central bank to adopt policies that "will best contribute to: (a) the stability of the currency of Australia; (b) the maintenance of full employment in Australia; and (c) the economic prosperity and welfare of the people of Australia."[15]

While the central governments of federal countries have explicitly acknowledged their fundamental role in resolving the stabilization problem, it is not the case that appropriate policies have in all instances been forthcoming. In Canada, for example, following a strong Keynesian orientation in the 1940's, there appeared some reluctance on the part of the Dominion authorities to adopt aggressive expansionary policies to stimulate a relatively depressed economy in the late 1950's. In part the problem seems to have been one of an improper mix of fiscal and monetary policy: operating under a system of floating exchange rates during these years, an expansionary monetary policy, which would have depreciated the Canadian dollar, was critical to increasing aggregate demand. Canadian officials, however, chose a relatively tight monetary policy combined with budgetary deficits, a policy that in retrospect

---

[13] *Ibid.*, pp. 97–98.
[14] A. J. Hagger, *Price Stability, Growth, and Balance: Australia's Economic Objectives* (Melbourne, Australia: F. W. Cheshire, 1968), p. 1.
[15] *Ibid.*

seems ill-suited to the situation.[16] In more recent years, with the return to fixed exchange rates, the Dominion government has behaved more in line with Keynesian prescriptions: income taxes, for example, have been cut with the explicit aim of stimulating aggregate expenditure. The policies of the provincial governments have, in contrast, shown little regard for countercyclical considerations.

These conclusions find support in a recent study of Canadian fiscal policy. Examining the period from 1952 to 1965, T. R. Robinson and T. J. Courchene found that the great bulk of countercyclical changes in the total public budget emanated from the level of the central government.[17] In particular, their calculations indicate that during this period the federal share in countercyclical changes in the surplus of the entire public budget, including both automatic and discretionary budgetary adjustments, was 85 to 90 percent. Provincial governments showed slight countercyclical budgetary changes—however, these were automatic changes in tax receipts, not changes in expenditures—while shifts in municipal budgets were roughly neutral with respect to cyclical movements in the aggregate level of economic activity.

D. A. L. Auld has found that, during the postwar period in Australia, both the built-in and discretionary budgetary policies of the Commonwealth government have in general been stabilizing.[18] In addition, through its influence in terms of loans and grants to the state governments, central authorities have been able to minimize somewhat any accentuations of cyclical forces by the fiscal activities of subcentral levels of government. Representatives of the Commonwealth government, for example, have considerable influence in the Loan Council, which determines the level of loans to the states to finance public-works programs; in this way, the spending of

[16] See Drummond, *The Canadian Economy*, chs. 4 and 5. For a formal analysis of problems in the use of fiscal and monetary policy under both fixed and floating exchange rates, with some observations on the Canadian experience, see Ronald I. McKinnon and Wallace E. Oates, *The Implications of International Economic Integration for Monetary, Fiscal, and Exchange-Rate Policies*, Princeton Studies in International Finance, no. 16 (Princeton, N.J.: Princeton University Press, 1966).

[17] "Fiscal Federalism and Economic Stability: An Examination of Multi-Level Public Finances in Canada, 1962–1965," *Canadian Journal of Economics*, vol. 2 (May, 1969), pp. 165–89.

[18] "A Measure of Australian Fiscal Policy Performance, 1948–49 to 1963–64," *Economic Record*, vol. 43 (Sept., 1967), pp. 333–53.

state governments can to some degree be stimulated in periods when aggregate spending lags and restrained during times of excessive aggregate demand.[19]

This brief overview of stabilization policy in federal countries suggests that central governments have usually recognized explicitly that they must play the primary role in achieving the goal of high employment with stable prices. While the record shows lapses in the pursuit of this objective, central governments have with increasing frequency adopted fiscal and monetary policies with the stated objective of regulating aggregate demand so as to attain high levels of employment with reasonably stable prices. Subcentral governments, in contrast, do appear, as expected, to have been much less active in the pursuit of countercyclical budgetary policies.

Public redistributive activity

A second function of the public sector is the establishment of the socially desired distribution of income. As earlier, let us assume that this entails achieving a somewhat more equal distribution of income than that which emerges from the unfettered operation of the market system. The argument advanced in previous chapters suggests that, as in the case of stabilization policy, constraints on decentralized activity to redistribute income are very real; the mobility of economic units prevents any particular locality from embarking on an aggressive redistributive program because of the likelihood that those from whom income is being transferred will relocate in areas where they can obtain more favorable fiscal treatment.

If this view of public redistributive activity has any relevance to actual public policy, we would expect to find that the budgets of central governments in federal countries have a more pronounced redistributive impact than those of decentralized governments. This is not an easy matter to determine at an empirical level, for it requires that we find at each level of government and for every income class the level of tax payments and the benefits from public expenditure programs; both are difficult to calculate. In the absence of a set of market prices and data on the quantities purchased at different income

[19] Burgess Cameron, *Federal Economic Policy* (Melbourne, Australia: F. W. Cheshire, 1968), chs. 1 and 2.

levels, we can only make plausible guesses as to the benefits members of different income classes derive from public programs. Determining the distribution of tax payments is equally problematical: the process of shifting greatly complicates the determination of just who bears the burden of a particular tax. Nevertheless, by adopting certain reasonable assumptions concerning the distribution of benefits and the incidence of various taxes, we can develop some rough ideas as to the redistributive nature of public budgets.

W. Irwin Gillespie has made such a study for the United States using 1960 data.[20] First, Gillespie found (as had others before him) that the pattern of incidence of state and local taxes in the United States is distinctly regressive: poorer families typically "pay" a larger percentage of their income in the form of state and local taxes than do wealthier families.[21] Of greater interest, however, was Gillespie's finding that state and local expenditure programs have a strongly "pro-poor" orientation; by this Gillespie means that, when the expenditure side of the budget is allocated among income classes, the benefits as a percentage of income are considerably higher for lower-income families. On net, Gillespie found some redistribution in favor of the lowest-income groups, but for families with incomes above $4,000, Gillespie concluded that state and local budgets are roughly neutral in terms of their redistributive impact: expenditures received (whether in the form of transfer payments or imputed benefits from public services) are approximately equal to taxes paid for the typical family with an income over $4,000. This finding would appear to be consistent with the discussion in the preceding chapter, where it was argued that, at decentralized levels of finance, the pattern of benefits from public services should not diverge radically from that of taxes paid so as not to create fiscal incentives for relocation.[22] At the federal level in the United States,

[20] "Effect of Public Expenditures on the Distribution of Income," in Richard Musgrave, ed., *Essays in Fiscal Federalism* (Washington, D.C.: Brookings Institution, 1965), pp. 122–86.
[21] George Bishop, for example, reached this result in his "The Tax Burden by Income Class, 1958," *National Tax Journal*, vol. 14 (March, 1961), pp. 41–58.
[22] While benefits may not differ greatly from tax payments on the average, there are, no doubt, sizeable divergences for some individuals. A married couple with no children, for example, may still have to pay property taxes to support the local public schools; for such people there is a fiscal incentive to locate in areas with a relatively small proportion

Gillespie found that lower-income families are net beneficiaries from fiscal operations, while, in contrast, high-income families appear to pay considerably more in taxes than they receive in benefits from public programs; for the highest-income group (families with incomes over $10,000 in 1960), Gillespie found, for example, that, on net, public expenditures and taxes by the federal government resulted in a reduction of over 13 percent of money income.[23]

While complete studies of fiscal incidence of the sort made by Gillespie are not to my knowledge available for other countries, there are in some instances studies of the incidence of taxation by income classes. If we assume that patterns of benefits from public expenditures are pro-poor in the sense defined above, we would expect to find that more decentralized levels of government adopt more regressive systems of taxation so that taxes paid would more closely approximate the benefits received from spending programs. This does appear to be the case in Canada. Table 5-1 indicates that in Canada in 1957 local systems of taxation were more regressive than the taxes of the federal government. Indeed, federal taxes were distinctly progressive; provincial taxes were roughly proportional over lower-income groups and slightly progressive at higher levels of income; and municipal taxes were regressive at low levels of income and approximately proportional above a family income level of $3,000.

A further bit of evidence on this matter is provided by Frederic Pryor in his comparative study of the structure of the public sectors of a number of countries.[24] In the study, Pryor examines the extent of the centralization of several different public functions by comparing the share of central government in total public expenditures for each of these functions. What is of interest here is that among the eleven countries for which he had data, Pryor found that spending on welfare programs, which consists largely of transfer payments, was, in every case except the USSR, more highly centralized than the fiscal activities in the public sector as a whole —that is, the central government's share of welfare expendi-

---

of children and/or a relatively low expenditure per pupil in the public schools.
[23] Gillespie, "Effect of Public Expenditures on the Distribution of Income," p. 162.
[24] *Public Expenditures in Communist and Capitalist Nations* (Homewood, Ill.: Richard D. Irwin, 1968).

TABLE 5-1
Taxes as a percentage of income,
by level of government, Canada, 1957

INCOME LEVEL	UNDER $1,000	$1,000–2,000	$2,000–3,000	$3,000–4,000	$4,000–5,000	$5,000–6,000	$7,000 & OVER	ALL CLASSES
FEDERAL	11.6	13.0	13.8	14.1	16.0	17.5	24.3	18.3
PROVINCIAL	2.9	2.9	3.0	3.0	3.2	3.3	4.4	3.6
MUNICIPAL	7.3	5.0	4.2	3.7	3.8	3.7	3.7	3.9
ALL GOVERNMENTS	21.9	20.9	21.0	20.9	23.0	24.5	32.4	25.8
PERCENTAGE OF TAXPAYER UNITS IN EACH INCOME CLASS	10.8	14.0	15.6	17.1	13.8	16.3	12.5	100

SOURCE I. J. Goffman, *The Burden of Canadian Taxation* (Toronto: Canadian Tax Foundation, 1962 [Canadian Tax Papers, no. 29, July, 1962]), pp. 10, 15. Reprinted by permission.

tures was greater than its share of total public spending. In most cases the degree of centralization was quite striking; in eight of these eleven countries, for example, the central government's share of welfare expenditures was 85 percent or more.[25]

It is interesting in this regard that history shows a trend toward the increasing centralization of explicitly redistributive programs, a trend that has greatly accelerated in recent decades. The care of the poor in the history of England, the United States, and a number of other countries, was originally envisioned as a local responsibility; each community was to take care of its own. With growing industrialization and, particularly, technological advances in transportation and communications, the geographical mobility of the populations increased; communities were no longer insulated against the effects of local policies to the degree they had been previously. To some extent this no doubt discouraged the establishment of generous public support for the poor because of the fear of inducing an influx of undesirables while at the same time creating incentives in the form of high local tax rates for an exodus of the well-to-do.[26] Partly for these reasons, welfare programs of substantial magnitude appear in most instances to have awaited an active role by the central government.

One finds in the present century and particularly since the 1930's that central governments in many countries have assumed primary responsibility for and have extended the scope of redistributive programs.[27] And there remain strong pres-

[25] Pryor, *Public Expenditures in Communist and Capitalist Nations*, p. 177.

[26] In the minority report of the Royal Commission on Local Taxation, vol. 34 (Scotland: 1902), W. Penny, General Superintendent of the Poor, observed:

> Another point which has long caused anxiety is the unequal pressure of the Poor Rate assessment. The miserably poor parish of Walls in Shetland has to pay nearly 12/– in the £ as a Poor Rate while many much wealthier parishes escape with less than half of the number of pence, with the inevitable result that the able-bodied men are driven from it to work in less heavily taxed districts only returning when health and strength alike fail.

From Lawrence Boyle, *Equalization and the Future of Local Government Finance* (Edinburgh and London: Oliver and Boyd, 1966), p. 29.

[27] An excellent description of the development of social programs in three federal countries is available in A. H. Birch, *Federalism, Finance, and Social Legislation in Canada, Australia and the United States* (Oxford,

sures for even further centralization of this function. In the United States, for example, the current fiscal crisis of the large cities has been greatly exacerbated by the huge cost of local welfare programs, in most cases funded only in part by the federal and/or state governments.[28] To some extent these welfare loads are the result of a migration of the rural poor to the cities, in part motivated by the availability there of relatively generous welfare payments. The recognition of the contribution of this phenomenon to the United States urban crisis has led to the assumption by several state governments of a greater part (or, in some cases, all) of the subcentral welfare burden and, more recently, to consideration of a further expansion of the role of the federal government—perhaps in the form of a national guaranteed minimum level of income. Public redistributive (like stabilization) programs thus do appear to have become increasingly a responsibility of central governments.

An econometric study of the degree of fiscal centralization

In contrast to the preceding sections, which involved an examination of particular public functions, the purpose here is to explore with quantitative techniques differences in the overall extent of fiscal centralization in the public budgets of a substantial number of federal and nonfederal countries. The obstacles to this undertaking, both conceptually and in terms of obtaining reliable data, are very real ones; as a result, the findings of this particular study must be taken as highly tenta-

England: Clarendon Press, 1955). Kjeld Philip points out that this shift from local to federal responsibility for welfare programs also took place in Denmark and Sweden. See his *Intergovernmental Fiscal Relations* (Copenhagen: University of Copenhagen, 1954), pp. 56–58, 62. The course of the centralization of the welfare function has varied somewhat among countries. In some, the United States for example, the job of administering the programs has been left largely to local officials, with the federal government providing guidelines and the funding, in whole or in large part, for the programs. In other countries the central government has taken over the administrative function as well.

[28] Of a population of about eight million persons in New York City in 1969, over one million were on welfare. As a result, welfare expenditures constituted over 30 percent of the city's budget.

tive. Nevertheless, there are at least a few empirical relationships that stand forth with some clarity and may prove useful in suggesting further approaches to quantitative studies of the public sector.

The first task is to define an operational measure of the degree of fiscal centralization. As mentioned briefly in Chapter One, there are, even aside from the problem of available data, a number of serious conceptual ambiguities inherent in such a measure. Where there exist several different levels of government, for example, there is the need to develop some type of weighting scheme. Is a country, for instance, that places many fiscal functions in the sphere of relatively large regional governments more or less centralized than one that divides decision-making responsibility almost equally between a central government and small local governments?

A second major problem is the association of budgetary information with the appropriate decision-making units. Fiscal data are typically available on a revenue and an expenditure basis, and there exists a fundamental question as to which classification provides the most useful measure of fiscal centralization. Should funds be attributed to the level of government that collects the revenues or the one that spends them? As Richard Musgrave has pointed out, "Local governments which act as central expenditure agents do not reflect expenditure decentralization in a meaningful sense, just as centrally collected but shared taxes do not constitute true revenue centralization." [29]

This raises the whole issue of whether or not we can hope to develop reliable measures of the degree of centralization on the basis of budgetary data. Herbert Kaufman, for example, suggests a long list of plausible measures of the extent of centralization in decision-making, most of which do not involve, at least directly, fiscal magnitudes.[30] What we presumably want is a measure of the amount of independent decision-making power in the provision of public services at different levels of government. A perfect measure of this (could such be devised) would no doubt have a number of dimensions, only some of which would involve fiscal variables. Nevertheless,

[29] *Fiscal Systems* (New Haven, Conn.: Yale University Press, 1969), p. 342.
[30] *Politics and Policies in State and Local Governments* (Englewood Cliffs, N.J.: Prentice-Hall, 1963), pp. 12–13.

the extent of a public authority's activities in taxation and in the expenditure of public funds is surely a component of fundamental importance in determining its influence on the allocation of resources. For this reason, the use of a measure of centralization based on fiscal information may represent a reasonably satisfactory, although admittedly somewhat imperfect, procedure.

Moreover, fiscal information is frequently about all that we have available. Public budgetary regulations normally require a systematic recording of disbursements and receipts so that such data are available for many countries. This makes fiscal data one of the more accessible sources of information for the construction of indices of centralization. If all this is accepted, we must confront the problem of making the most sensible use of the available budgetary data, which brings us back to the question of whether to measure the relative fiscal importance of a level of government through the revenues it raises, or, alternatively, by the expenditures it makes.

In terms of available data, the issue here is how to treat intergovernmental grants. To the extent that the grantor directs in some detail the purposes for which the funds are to be used, the presumption is that the grants should be attributed to the level of government that collects the revenues. On the other hand, where the grants are unconditional (or where the restrictions accompanying the grants do not really constrain the recipient), logic suggests that the funds be included in the share of the government making the expenditure.

Available cross-sectional data for most countries do not facilitate a very satisfactory resolution of some of these problems. For the most part these data are subdivided only between all subcentral governments as a group and the central government, so that a more precise measure involving a weighting of each of the several tiers of government is impossible. For this reason, I use here what Frederic Pryor has called a "centralization ratio," a measure of the share of the central government in the total public sector.[31]

Moreover, existing data do not readily permit, for a large number of countries, a distinction between unconditional grants and those for which the grantor specifies in detail just how the funds are to be used. As a result, one must choose, in de-

[31] Pryor, *Public Expenditures in Communist and Capitalist Nations*, p. 70.

fining the fiscal share of the central government, to attribute all intergovernmental grants either to decentralized levels of government or to the central government itself. The procedure I have adopted in this study is to try both approaches.

In fact, I have used four different definitions of the degree of fiscal centralization. The first is the percentage of total public revenues collected by the central government. Relying on the United Nations and some additional sources, the Economics Department of the International Bank for Reconstruction and Development (IBRD) has provided these percentages for the early or mid-1960's for fifty-eight countries. In addition, this same source provides, for a slightly smaller sample of forty-four nations, the share of the central government in current public expenditures; this measure attributes grant funds to the share of decentralized levels of government and thus constitutes a measure of the degree of fiscal centralization on the expenditure basis.[32]

There is, however, a serious deficiency in the manner in which both these measures are computed. According to existing United Nations accounting conventions, contributions and expenditures for social security programs are included in the totals for the public sector but are excluded from the share of the central government. Since in most instances the central government plays an active role in these programs, this convention would appear to misrepresent the true allocation of fiscal functions among levels of government. This is not, moreover, a small matter; in some instances, contributions for social security account for over 30 percent of government current revenues, and, as a result, this in itself can make a striking difference in the centralization ratios across countries. Since available data do not permit satisfactory correction of the centralization ratios themselves, I have included, as an independent variable in all the regression equations using these two centralization ratios, the percentage of general government current revenue in the form of social security contributions. This procedure presumably separates out the effect of this definitional aberration on the centralization ratios and

---

[32] These percentages, along with a wealth of other economic data, appear in the IBRD, *World Tables* (Dec., 1968). The centralization ratios used in this study appear in *World Table* no. 6, cols. 13 and 14. The data I have used are for 1964 or 1965 and in a few instances for 1960.

permits us to assess more accurately the statistical influence of the other independent variables.

As an alternative I have also used two fiscal centralization measures that exclude transfer payments altogether. From the *United Nations Yearbook of National Accounts Statistics* (1968), I was able to determine, for a group of thirty-eight countries, the percentage share of the central government in "current consumption expenditure." This is essentially the central government's share of public expenditures on wages and salaries of public employees and on current purchases of goods and services from private enterprises. Finally, from this same United Nations source, I calculated for twenty-nine countries the share of the central government in "civil consumption expenditure" (that is, current consumption expenditure for nondefense purposes). All four centralization ratios (in addition to the other data used in this study) appear in the data appendix at the end of the book.

The objective of the following empirical work is to see to what extent certain variables suggested by the theoretical analysis in preceding chapters can explain statistically the variation among countries in the degree of fiscal centralization. One conclusion that emerged is that, regardless of which of the four centralization ratios is employed, the results both qualitatively and in terms of order of magnitude are highly similar. To simplify the presentation of the results, the text of this chapter will include only the equations for one of the centralization measures: the percentage share of the central government in total current revenues. This is the measure for which I was able to obtain the largest sample of countries—fifty-eight. Where the results differ substantially according to the measure of fiscal centralization employed, I will so indicate. The complete set of regression equations, including the results for all four centralization ratios, appear in the appendix to this chapter.

Prior to an analysis of the division of public finances among levels of government, it will prove useful to classify the sources of intereconomy differences in the degree of fiscal centralization. There are three such sources. First and most obvious, a function assigned to the central government in one country may be the responsibility of decentralized levels of government in another nation. A system in which education is provided publicly by the central government will obviously tend to be more centralized—to have a higher centralization ratio—than one in which education is financed by subcentral governments. Second, even if there exists an identical allocation of functions among levels of government across two countries, their centralization ratios will generally differ if they do not have the same relative expenditure patterns on these functions. A country, for example, with an unusually large portion of its resources devoted to national defense will have, other things equal, a relatively high degree of fiscal centralization. Third and last, centralization ratios may differ because certain services provided publicly in one economy are provided in the private sector in another. Two economies whose public sectors are otherwise identical will have differing degrees of fiscal centralization if in one, local governments provide certain recreational facilities, while in the other, all such facilities are provided privately.

It is worth noting here that both the extent to which the provision of services is placed in the public sector and the levels of expenditures on these services appear to depend to some degree on the level of affluence of the society. Wagner's Law asserts that, as the level of per-capita income in a society increases, public expenditure will increase even more than proportionately. Although this proposition lacks a sound theoretical basis and is subject empirically to a number of qualifications, there is some evidence in its support.[33] While Wagner's Law has no direct implications for the extent to which we would expect the public sector to be centralized, it does suggest that centralization ratios between high- and low-income countries may well vary because of significantly differing patterns of expenditures on services provided publicly in these countries.

The next task is to try to derive from the theoretical discussion a set of determinants of the optimal degree of fiscal centralization. The earlier treatment of economies of scale and costs of decision-making suggests that one important factor influencing the extent of centralization should be the size of

[33] For an interesting treatment of this issue, see Alison Martin and W. Arthur Lewis, "Patterns of Public Revenue and Expenditure," *The Manchester School of Economic and Social Studies*, vol. 24 (Sept., 1956), pp. 203–44. A more recent summary of the evidence on Wagner's Law is available in Pryor, *Public Expenditures in Communist and Capitalist Nations*, pp. 50–53, 451–54.

the nation in terms of population and perhaps also geographical area.

In a relatively small country, for example, there are likely to be real cost-savings in centralizing a substantial portion of the activity in the public sector. As a nation becomes larger, however, it becomes efficient for decentralized jurisdictions, because of their own significant size, to provide their own outputs of a wide range of public services. Moreover, as a country grows in size, central administration becomes more difficult and is likely to result in a less effective use of resources within the public sector. For these reasons we would expect the degree of fiscal centralization to vary inversely with the size of a country.

The second class of variables suggested by the analysis in Chapter Two and its appendix relates to the diversity in demands for goods and services provided publicly. A major attraction of a system of decentralized finance is its potential for adjusting the composition of public outputs to the demands of each jurisdiction. If the demand for public goods is very similar in all areas, there may be little to be gained from extensive decentralization. In the appendix to Chapter Two, I derived (following Yoram Barzel) as corollaries of the Decentralization Theorem the propositions that the gains from decentralized finance vary directly with the variance in individual demands for public goods and with the extent to which individuals with similar demands are grouped together so as to consume collectively the same units of output. The point here is simply that the incentives in terms of potential welfare gains for the decentralized provision of a public good will tend to be greater the more the population is arranged geographically in groups where individual demands are similar within each group but where these demands vary significantly among groups. Where we have evidence that the demand for public services is likely to be quite different across jurisdictions, the theory would therefore lead us to expect a higher degree of decentralization in the public finances.

To examine this proposition empirically, we need some means to identify those cases where diversity in demands for public services is likely to be pronounced and those where it will be more uniform. In this regard economic theory suggests that the demand of an individual for a particular good, public or private, will depend on his tastes and level of income. Where individual preferences and/or levels of income vary widely, we would anticipate an increased diversity in the demand for public services. Unfortunately, comparable and reliable data on the degree of inequality in the distribution of income are not available for a large group of countries; for this reason, attempts to relate it to the degree of fiscal centralization are not presently viable.[34]

There are, however, some measurable variables one might expect to be associated with a substantial variation in preferences for at least some public services. For example, one of the major areas of public expenditure in most countries is education. The character of education demanded, both in terms of content and technique, tends to vary greatly among groups with differing religious and cultural values. We would, therefore, expect the incentives for the decentralized provision of education to be much more compelling in countries composed of jurisdictions with different religious, lingual, and cultural institutions.[35] This would suggest that variables indicating the extent of geographical differences in religious, racial, linguistic, and other cultural characteristics could serve as proxy variables for measuring diversity in demands among jurisdictions for public services. In this regard Arthur Banks and Robert Textor have classified some 115 countries according to a vast number of characteristics, including such things as the degree of religious, linguistic, and racial homogeneity of the

[34] E. Ahiram (using data assembled by Simon Kuznets) and Irving Kravis have computed Gini coefficients (measures of the degree of inequality in the distribution of income based on the Lorenz Curve) for groups of fourteen and eleven countries, respectively, based on income data from the late 1940's and the 1950's. The difficulties in obtaining comparable intercountry estimates are revealed by the striking differences in their results. Not only does the size of the coefficient for a given country frequently differ widely in the two studies, but the ranking of countries is in some cases quite different. According to Ahiram's sample of fourteen countries, for example, Great Britain had the lowest Gini coefficient—that is, the most equal distribution of income; Kravis, in contrast, finds that Great Britain ranked fifth on this scale in his list of eleven nations. See Ahiram, "Income Distribution in Jamaica, 1958," *Social and Economic Studies*, vol. 13 (Sept., 1964), pp. 333–69; and Kravis, *The Structure of Income* (Philadelphia: University of Pennsylvania Press, 1962), p. 238.

[35] We could, for example, treat education in Catholic and Protestant schools as separate goods. From this perspective the demand for the former good would be relatively high and for the latter practically nil in Catholic-dominated localities, and the reverse pattern of demand would exist in primarily Protestant communities.

population.[36] Using these variables along with measures of size and income levels, we proceed next to a regression study of intercountry variations in the degree of fiscal centralization. All the equations that follow, both in the text and appendix, were estimated by ordinary least squares.

Equation 1 indicates that, in line with our expectations, the degree of fiscal centralization bears a significant inverse relationship to the population of the country: the more people, the more decentralized the public finances. The population variable (while statistically significant at a .01 level of confidence) can explain, however, only a modest fraction of the variance in the degree of fiscal centralization.[37] There are in this respect a few striking exceptions to this relationship. Switzerland, for example, a relatively small country both in terms of population and land area, possesses the lowest centralization ratio in the sample (32.7).

$$(1) \qquad C = \underset{(11.5)}{108} - \underset{(3.0)}{3.1 \ln P} - \underset{(5.2)}{0.7Z}$$

$$N = 58 \qquad R^2 = .41 \qquad \bar{C} = 73.1$$

where

C = central government percentage of total government current revenues
$\bar{C}$ = mean value of C
$\ln P$ = natural log of population, in thousands
Z = contributions to social security as a percent of total public current revenue
N = sample size
R^2 = coefficient of determination.

---

[36] *A Cross-Polity Survey* (Cambridge, Mass.: M.I.T. Press, 1963). All but four of the fifty-eight countries in the sample used in this study are included in the Banks-Textor survey. For these four I was in most cases able to determine the appropriate classification on the basis of supplementary information. Where for certain variables it was unclear in which category the country belonged, I omitted the country from those regressions that included the variable in question. In a few instances Banks and Textor also chose not to classify certain countries because of ambiguities. For these reasons the reader will note that for some of the regression equations in the text the number of observations is slightly less than fifty-eight.

[37] A simple regression of C on Z yields an R^2 of .31; the addition of $\ln P$ to the equation raises the R^2 from .31 to .41. The explanatory power of

(Note: The numbers in parentheses are the absolute values of the t-statistic for the coefficient.)

Equation 2 adds to 1 a variable indicating the geographical size of the nation (A = thousands of square kilometers). While A has a negative sign, which is consistent with the expectation that larger geographical size is associated with increased fiscal decentralization, it adds little to the explanatory power of the first equation, and using a one-tail test is only barely significantly different from zero at a .05 level of confidence. In working with other measures of fiscal centralization and additional independent variables, the population variable was consistently a more powerful explanatory variable than was geographical size; aside from the second equation, the latter was never statistically significant, and for this reason I have used the population variable as the measure of national size in the later multiple-regression equations.

$$(2) \qquad C = \underset{(10.4)}{102} - \underset{(2.0)}{2.2 \ln P} - \underset{(1.8)}{.001A} - \underset{(5.5)}{0.7Z}$$

$$N = 58 \qquad R^2 = .44$$

Equation 3 introduces, in addition to the log of population size, a measure of per-capita income (Y = gross domestic product per capita in United States dollars). The income variable, which is easily significant statistically, suggests that wealthier countries tend to be more decentralized in their public finances than poorer countries.[38] It is interesting in this regard that a number of students of federalism, such as Kenneth C. Wheare, have argued that the decentralization of public activity is a costly enterprise and that as a result a coun-

---

the population variable is, incidentally, considerably enhanced in the log form.

[38] The population and income variables have considerably larger coefficients and greater explanatory power in the regression equations that exclude transfer payments from the dependent variable. See the appendix to this chapter, equations 3A–3D. This seems to result in part from the presence of the control variable, Z (social security contributions), in the equations using the central government's share in the total budget; Z and Y are themselves significantly correlated, and the insertion of Z reduces somewhat both the explanatory capability and the size of the coefficient of Y. Pryor also found a statistically significant relationship among these variables using data from the mid-1950's. See his *Public Expenditures in Communist and Capitalist Nations*, p. 74.

$$(3) \qquad C = 111 - 3.0 \ln P - .006Y - 0.5Z$$
$$(12.6) \quad (3.2) \qquad (3.1) \quad (4.0)$$
$$N = 58 \qquad R^2 = .50$$

try must be relatively affluent to adopt a highly decentralized form of government. In Wheare's words, "federalism is expensive, and it is always a question whether the independence it gives is worth the price that must be paid for it." [39] In the literature on economic development, one finds a variation on this argument which asserts that greater centralization is necessary in underdeveloped countries because of the scarcity of qualified government personnel.[40] For these reasons it may not be surprising to find that wealthier countries typically exhibit a relatively high degree of fiscal decentralization.

The next step, after allowing for the effects of population size and the level of income, is to examine the statistical influence of a set of variables intended to serve as proxies for the degree of diversity in demands for public services. As suggested earlier, it would seem reasonable to expect considerable differences in individual demands for types and levels of public education and probably of other potential regional or local services, such as recreational facilities, where there exist wide differences in individual cultural characteristics. To explore this matter, equations 4–7 incorporate a series of dummy variables indicating whether, according to Banks and Textor, a country is homogeneous (1) or heterogeneous (0) in terms of the linguistic, racial, and religious characteristics of its population. In equation 4, for example, the variable L is given a value of one if the country is classified as linguistically homogeneous and a value of zero if heterogeneous. Equations 5 and 6 include a similar test in terms of R (a measure of racial homogeneity) and T (homogeneity of religion). Finally, in equation 7 the variable H takes on a value of unity if the country is homogeneous in terms of language, race, and religion (that is, if the country has a value of one for all these variables in the earlier equations) or a value of zero if the country is

---

[39] *Federal Government,* 4th ed. (Oxford, England: Oxford University Press, 1963), p. 51.
[40] In this regard, Martin and Lewis, "Patterns of Public Revenue and Expenditure," p. 231, found that "the weakness of local government in relation to central government is one of the most striking phenomena of under-developed countries."

classified as having a heterogeneous population by any of these measures. The results are disappointing. In no instance is the additional variable significantly different from zero, and in all cases but one, L, the variables have negative rather than the expected positive signs.[41]

(4) $C = 110 - 3.0 \ln P - .006Y + 0.3L - 0.5Z$
          (12.3) (3.2)   (3.0)   (0.1)   (3.9)

          $N = 58$ $R^2 = .50$

(5) $C = 112 - 3.0 \ln P - .006Y - 3.1R - 0.6Z$
          (12.6) (3.1)   (2.8)   (0.9)   (3.9)

          $N = 55$ $R^2 = .53$

(6) $C = 112 - 3.1 \ln P - .006Y - 1.2T - 0.5Z$
          (12.2) (3.2)   (3.0)   (0.4)   (3.6)

          $N = 56$ $R^2 = .49$

(7) $C = 114 - 3.4 \ln P - .006Y - 4.0H - 0.5Z$
          (12.1) (3.3)   (2.7)   (1.0)   (3.2)

          $N = 55$ $R^2 = .51$

These results are not consistent with our expectations, but I should note at least one major deficiency of these data. The dummy variables employed in equations 4–7 refer to the existing diversity in cultural characteristics among the population as a whole. For the gains from decentralized finance to be

---

[41] The Banks-Textor structure of classification is in some instances a bit finer than indicated here. Under the category of linguistic homogeneity, for example, Banks and Textor employ a three-way classification: homogeneous (majority of 85 percent or more speaking a single language; no significant single minority); weakly heterogeneous (majority of 85 percent or more; significant minority of 15 percent or less); and strongly heterogeneous (no single group of 85 percent or more). I collapsed this classification into two categories by first calling only those countries in their first grouping linguistically homogeneous and second by extending this definition to include the first two Banks-Textor groupings. The results reported in equation 4 in the text refer to those obtained by giving the dummy variable, L, a value of one for their group of homogeneous countries and a value of zero for those nations classified as either weakly or strongly heterogeneous. The variable was, however, likewise insignificant when I employed the other grouping.

maximized, however, such diversity must be reflected in geographical groupings of the population; it is by catering to groups, each of which is composed of individuals with similar tastes, that regional or local provision of public services is of the greatest value. A high degree of diversity across the whole population, as measured by L, R, T, and H, does not, however, necessarily mean that the economic incentives for decentralization are relatively large.[42]

The one classification Banks and Textor provide that does relate to geographical groups is what they call sectionalism, a measure of the extent to which people in geographical subareas of a country identify "self-consciously and distinctively with that area." [43] While this is admittedly a highly imperfect proxy variable for geographical diversity in tastes for public services, I have included in equation 8 a dummy variable, S, that has a value of one for those countries exhibiting a high degree of sectionalism and a value of zero for the others. We find that in this case the dummy variable is both statistically significant and has the expected sign: countries with strong sectional forces appear to have centralization ratios that are on the average twelve or thirteen percentage points less than countries without a pronounced sectionalism. To the extent that this

$$(8) \qquad C = \quad 99 - 1.4 \ln P - .006Y - 12.5S - 0.6Z$$
$$\qquad (10.6) \ (1.3) \qquad (3.1) \qquad (3.4) \qquad (4.2)$$
$$N = 50 \qquad R^2 = .58$$

variable does reflect the presence or absence of regional groups with varying preferences for public services, the results in equation 8 are consistent with the economic view of decentralized finance developed in earlier chapters. Even if this is the case, however, equation 8 still explains only about half the variance in C; it seems clear that there are plenty of other considerations—many, no doubt relating to the unique historical

[42] These results might also be explained by certain political forces. In some societies, a high degree of cultural heterogeneity may generate divisive tendencies that public authorities find it advisable to suppress through an increased centralization of decision-making authority. In such cases, a substantial centralization of the public sector may be viewed as necessary to provide social and political cohesion, although at the expense of the economic gains from greater decentralization.
[43] A Cross-Polity Survey, printout 113.

experience of each country—that have influenced the division of fiscal activity among levels of government.[44]

In Chapter One, it was suggested that, although the formal constitutional structure of a nation is not in itself of primary interest for an economic study of federal finance, it may nevertheless be the case that the legalistic framework of a society imposes a set of constraints on decision-making procedures that may have an important impact on the extent of decentralization in fiscal decisions. This does in fact seem to be the case; for example, countries that have adopted the federal form of government do appear to have a relatively low degree of fiscal centralization. Daniel J. Elazar, in the new edition of the *International Encyclopedia of the Social Sciences*, lists sixteen formally federal nations in the world at the present time.[45] Of these, thirteen countries are included in the sample of fifty-eight nations used here. The mean centralization ratio for this group of thirteen federal countries is 58.7 as compared to a mean of 77.3 for the forty-five nonfederal countries, a difference that is easily significant at a .01 level, using a simple test for the difference between means.[46] Moreover, if we add to the equation a dummy variable, with a value of one for federal countries and a value of zero for nonfederal countries, we find that it is highly significant and possesses the expected sign; equation 9 suggests that after allowing for the effects of population size and income, federal countries on the average have

$$(9) \qquad C = \underset{(12.0)}{96} \ - \underset{(1.3)}{1.2 \ln P} \ - \underset{(2.3)}{.004Y} \ - \underset{(4.7)}{15.9F} \ - \underset{(5.5)}{0.6Z}$$

$$N = 58 \qquad R^2 = .65$$

[44] The dummy variable for sectionalism, while still possessing the anticipated negative sign, has a substantially smaller coefficient and a reduced explanatory power in those equations including only exhaustive public expenditures in the measure of fiscal centralization. See the appendix to this chapter, equations 8A–8D.

[45] "Federalism," *International Encyclopedia of the Social Sciences*, vol. 5 (New York: Macmillan, 1968), pp. 353–67. The sixteen federal countries are Argentina, Australia, Austria, Brazil, Cameroon, Canada, West Germany, India, Libya, Malaysia, Mexico, Nigeria, the Soviet Union, Switzerland, the United States, and Yugoslavia. Of these, all but Libya, the Soviet Union, and Yugoslavia are in the sample used in this study.

[46] The test used for the difference between means is described in John E. Freund, *Modern Elementary Statistics*, 3rd ed. (Englewood Cliffs, N.J.: Prentice-Hall, 1967), pp. 254–57.

fiscal centralization ratios that are roughly sixteen percentage points less than those of nonfederal countries.

Decentralization and the size of the public sector

In view of the ready availability of the data used in the preceding section, it seems worth investigating empirically another aspect of federal finance: the impact of decentralization on the size of the public sector as a whole. If it is true that decentralization is expensive because of the loss of potential economies of scale (particularly in terms of an increased number of public employees resulting from a multiplicity of public units), we would expect to find the degree of decentralization directly related to the relative size of the public sector. There are, however, some reasons to believe that this may not be the case. Centralization may, for example, lead to a higher level of public spending because of the likely weakening of the link between expenditures and tax payments. The point is that, under a system of local finance where local residents pay taxes to finance the provision of the public services they receive, there is a real incentive to hold down local spending so as to prevent high levels of local taxation. In contrast, if under a more centralized system of finance the central government provides the bulk of public services, local residents are likely to try, through the various political channels available to them, to get as high a level of public services for their locality as possible. Since these services are financed mainly by the central government, the marginal cost to the residents of the locality may be close to zero, so that there may exist incentives to seek greater than efficient levels of output of these services.

We find in equation 10 that, for the sample of fifty-eight countries, the size of the public sector relative to the size of the economy as a whole, G, as measured by tax revenues as a percent of national income, does in fact bear a significant inverse correlation to the centralization ratio: countries with more decentralized systems of public finance do appear to have relatively large public budgets.[47] There is, however, a good reason

[47] The data for the variable G come from IBRD, *World Table* no. 3, col. 12.

to be suspicious of the finding in equation 10, because other

(10)
$$G = 49 - .33C$$
$$(6.7) \quad (3.4)$$
$$N = 57 \quad R^2 = .17 \quad \overline{G} = 24.6$$

where

G = tax revenues as a percentage of national income
$\overline{G}$ = mean value of G.

things have not been held equal. In particular, we know that wealthier countries tend both to have more decentralized forms of government and (in line with Wagner's Law) to have higher levels of public spending relative to the size of national income. This latter relationship is in fact quite a strong one; equation 11 indicates that our measure of per-capita income can account

(11)
$$G = 16 + .011Y$$
$$(9.7) \quad (7.6)$$
$$N = 57 \quad R^2 = .52$$

statistically for more than one-half the variance in G. Moreover, when we employ a multiple-regression test, including both C and Y as independent variables in equation 12, we find that

(12)
$$G = 21 + .011Y - .06C$$
$$(2.9) \quad (6.2) \quad (0.7)$$
$$N = 57 \quad R^2 = .52$$

the degree of fiscal centralization no longer has a significant relationship with the size of the public sector; the earlier significance of the centralization ratio would thus appear to have been the result of its reflection of the influence of the income variable on G. The tentative conclusion that emerges from this study is that, after allowing for the effects of the level of income on the size of the public sector, the degree of fiscal centralization does not appear to have a systematic effect on the relative size of public spending.[48] In equation 13 we find, more-over, that the dummy variable indicating a federal or non-federal government is likewise not significant in explaining the variation in G. The extent of decentralization in itself would, therefore, appear to have little effect on the overall level of public expenditure.

$$(13) \qquad G = \underset{(9.8)}{16} + \underset{(7.8)}{.012Y} - \underset{(1.3)}{3.7F}$$

$$N = 57 \qquad R^2 = .53$$

My aim in this chapter has been to see to what degree the theoretical view of federalism developed in earlier chapters can be used to understand the actual fiscal activities of govern-ments in federal and, to some extent, in nonfederal countries. My feeling is that the theory does provide some insights into the structure and functioning of the public sector. The first two sections suggest that, at least in recent decades, central governments in the federal countries examined have come to play the dominant role in public policy directed toward stabiliz-ing the economy and inducing a more desirable distribution of income. Theory indicates that there are sound reasons for these developments and that the continued and growing primacy of central governments in performing these functions is to be expected.

[48] It might be objected that a better measure of the dependent variable here would be so-called exhaustive public spending as a percent of GNP, rather than a measure using tax revenues. The former would presum-ably provide a more accurate indication of the fraction of the nation's resources directed into the public sector by omitting transfer payments that make up part of public revenues. To check this I replaced G with a variable measuring the percentage of total resources used by govern-ment. More precisely, the IBRD, in *World Table* no. 4, col. 4, provides, for fifty-seven of my fifty-eight countries, total government consumption expenditure—which omits transfer payments—as a percentage of total resources (gross domestic product plus net imports). Replacing G in equation 12 with this new dependent variable, we find that the cen-tralization ratio is again statistically insignificant, which suggests that the degree of fiscal centralization does not in itself influence the pro-portion of total resources going into the public sector. In addition, the explanatory power of the income variable is greatly reduced, and it would thus appear that the strong partial correlation between Y and G in equation 12 reflects in large part higher levels of transfer payments in wealthier countries.

The empirical work based on the earlier theoretical structure was, in contrast, considerably less successful in explaining the variation in the degree of fiscal centralization across a large number of countries. A few relationships of some interest do, however, stand out. The results suggest, as expected, that countries with larger populations typically exhibit greater decentralization; there are, however, a few striking exceptions, such as Switzerland, to this relationship. We found, in addition, a strong inverse association between levels of per-capita income and the degree of fiscal centralization: wealthier countries appear to have more decentralized systems of finance. There is, again, some theoretical justification for this phenomenon in terms of the costly character of decentralization and the need in the less developed countries to conserve on scarce administrative talent.

Attempts to explain the degree of fiscal centralization through the use of proxy measures for the diversity in demands for public goods were on the whole unsuccessful. However, this may in part reflect the failure of these variables to capture the extent to which such diversity is reflected in geographical groupings of the population. One attempt to do this by using a variable measuring the strength of sectional forces within each country did generate some interesting results; nations with a high degree of sectionalism appear to have more decentralized fiscal systems. In addition, it proved to be the case that countries with explicitly federal forms of government are more decentralized in fiscal terms than countries with other forms of government.

Finally, we found that, after allowing for the effects of other factors, neither the degree of fiscal centralization nor the presence or absence of a federal form of government appears in itself to influence the relative size of the public sector as a whole.

The overall impression that emerges from the empirical results is, it seems to me, that hypotheses based on conventional forms of economic analysis can explain to some extent the structure and functioning of federal fiscal systems. It is clear, however, that the amount of unexplained variance remains considerable; the unique experience of each country has no doubt left its own imprint on the structure of its government. One can hope, however, that theoretical and empirical study will enable us to do somewhat better than De Tocqueville's conclusion that it is "as impossible to determine beforehand, with any degree of accuracy, the share of authority which each of two governments [is] to enjoy, as to forsee all the incidents in the existence of a nation." [49]

[49] Quoted by A. H. Birch in *Federalism, Finance, and Social Legislation,* p. 3.

Appendix

Complete set of regression equations

In the text of this chapter, the results were presented for only one of the measures of the degree of fiscal centralization: the central government share in total public revenues. This appendix contains the corresponding equations for all four centralization ratios; as the reader will note, the results are typically quite similar for all four alternatives I have used in this study. The number of each equation refers back to the text, while the accompanying capital letter is associated with one of the particular measures of fiscal centralization. A glossary defining the symbols precedes the presentation of the regression equations. In addition, a comprehensive data appendix, which presents all the data and identifies their sources, is available at the end of the book.

Glossary

C = Central government share in general government current revenues (percentage)

CE = Central government share in general government current expenditure (percentage)

CC = Central government share in general government consumption expenditure (percentage)

CV = Central government share in general government nondefense (civil) consumption expenditure (percentage)

Z = Contributions to social security programs as a percent of general government current revenue

$\ln P$ = Natural log of population (thousands)

A = Geographical size (thousands of square kilometers)

Y = Gross domestic product per capita in U.S. dollars

L = Dummy variable: 1 = lingual homogeneity, 0 = lingual heterogeneity

R = Dummy variable: 1 = racial homogeneity, 0 = racial heterogeneity

T = Dummy variable: 1 = religious homogeneity, 0 = religious heterogeneity

H = Dummy variable: 1 = cultural homogeneity, 0 = cultural heterogeneity

S = Dummy variable: 1 = strong sectionalism, 0 = weak or no sectionalism

F = Dummy variable: 1 = federal government, 0 = nonfederal government

G = Tax revenues as a percent of national income

N = Number of observations

R^2 = Coefficient of multiple determination

Regression equations

(Note: As in the text, the number in parentheses under the regression coefficient is the absolute value of the t-statistic. In the equations involving C and CE, Z is included as an independent variable to correct for the exclusion of social security contributions from the share of the central government; this adjustment is not necessary for CC and CV, since they exclude all transfer payments.)

(1A)
$$C = 108 - 3.1 \ln P - 0.7Z$$
$$(11.5) \quad (3.0) \qquad (5.2)$$
$$N = 58 \qquad R^2 = .41$$

(1B)
$$CE = 106 - 3.4 \ln P - 1.0Z$$
$$(7.8) \quad (2.3) \qquad (4.4)$$
$$N = 44 \qquad R^2 = .39$$

(1C)
$$CC = 127 - 6.6 \ln P$$
$$(6.8) \quad (3.2)$$
$$N = 38 \qquad R^2 = .22$$

(1D)
$$CV = 142 - 9.7 \ln P$$
$$(5.2) \quad (3.2)$$
$$N = 29 \qquad R^2 = .28$$

(2A)
$$C = 102 - 2.2 \ln P - .001A - 0.7Z$$
$$(10.4) \quad (2.0) \qquad (1.8) \qquad (5.5)$$
$$N = 58 \qquad R^2 = .44$$

(2B)
$$CE = 101 - 2.7 \ln P - .001A - 1.0Z$$
$$(7.1) \quad (1.7) \qquad (1.2) \qquad (4.5)$$
$$N = 44 \qquad R^2 = .41$$

(2C)
$$CC = 121 - 5.7 \ln P - .002A$$
$$(6.3) \quad (2.6) \qquad (1.2)$$
$$N = 38 \qquad R^2 = .25$$

(2D)
$$CV = 131 - 8.2 \ln P - .002A$$
$$(4.7) \quad (2.6) \qquad (1.4)$$
$$N = 29 \qquad R^2 = .33$$

(3A)
$$C = 111 - 3.0 \ln P - .006Y - 0.5Z$$
$$(12.6) \quad (3.2) \qquad (3.1) \qquad (4.0)$$
$$N = 58 \qquad R^2 = .50$$

(3B)
$$CE = 113 - 3.7 \ln P - .009Y - 0.7Z$$
$$(9.0) \quad (2.7) \qquad (3.1) \qquad (2.9)$$
$$N = 44 \qquad R^2 = .51$$

(3C)
$$CC = 120 - 4.4 \ln P - .013Y$$
$$(7.8) \quad (2.5) \qquad (4.3)$$
$$N = 38 \qquad R^2 = .49$$

(3D)
$$CV = 138 - 7.0 \ln P - .019Y$$
$$(6.9) \quad (3.1) \qquad (4.9)$$
$$N = 29 \qquad R^2 = .63$$

(4A)
$$C = 110 - 3.0 \ln P - .006Y + 0.3L - 0.5Z$$
$$(12.3) \quad (3.2) \qquad (3.0) \qquad (0.1) \quad (3.9)$$
$$N = 58 \qquad R^2 = .50$$

(4B)
$$CE = 113 - 3.7 \ln P - .009Y + 0.4L - 0.7Z$$
$$(8.9) \quad (2.7) \qquad (2.9) \qquad (0.1) \quad (2.8)$$
$$N = 44 \qquad R^2 = .51$$

$$(4C) \quad CC = 120 - 4.4 \ln P - .014Y + 0.9L$$
$$ (7.7) \quad (2.5) \qquad (4.1) \qquad (0.2)$$
$$N = 38 \quad R^2 = .49$$

$$(4D) \quad CV = 138 - 6.8 \ln P - .019Y - 2.6L$$
$$ (6.7) \quad (2.9) \qquad (4.5) \qquad (0.4)$$
$$N = 29 \quad R^2 = .63$$

$$(5A) \quad C = 112 - 3.0 \ln P - .006Y - 3.1R - 0.6Z$$
$$ (12.6) \quad (3.1) \qquad (2.8) \qquad (0.9) \qquad (3.9)$$
$$N = 55 \quad R^2 = .53$$

$$(5B) \quad CE = 115 - 3.6 \ln P - .009Y - 4.0R - 0.7Z$$
$$ (9.0) \quad (2.6) \qquad (3.0) \qquad (0.7) \qquad (2.9)$$
$$N = 44 \quad R^2 = .52$$

$$(5C) \quad CC = 122 - 4.1 \ln P - .013Y - 6.6R$$
$$ (7.9) \quad (2.4) \qquad (3.9) \qquad (1.2)$$
$$N = 38 \quad R^2 = .51$$

$$(5D) \quad CV = 148 - 7.0 \ln P - .018Y - 12.8R$$
$$ (7.2) \quad (3.2) \qquad (4.9) \qquad (1.6)$$
$$N = 29 \quad R^2 = .66$$

$$(6A) \quad C = 112 - 3.1 \ln P - .006Y - 1.2T - 0.5Z$$
$$ (12.2) \quad (3.2) \qquad (3.0) \qquad (0.4) \qquad (3.6)$$
$$N = 56 \quad R^2 = .49$$

$$(6B) \quad CE = 112 - 3.7 \ln P - .009Y - 0.6T - 0.7Z$$
$$ (8.6) \quad (2.7) \qquad (3.0) \qquad (0.1) \qquad (2.7)$$
$$N = 42 \quad R^2 = .51$$

$$(6C) \quad CC = 118 - 4.3 \ln P - .013Y + 3.3T$$
$$ (7.2) \quad (2.4) \qquad (4.0) \qquad (0.7)$$
$$N = 36 \quad R^2 = .50$$

$$(6D) \quad CV = 129 - 6.1 \ln P - .020Y + 4.4T$$
$$ (5.6) \quad (2.4) \qquad (4.7) \qquad (0.6)$$
$$N = 27 \quad R^2 = .65$$

(7A) $\quad C = \begin{array}{llllll} 114 & -3.4\ln P & -.006Y & -4.0H & -0.5Z \\ (12.1) & (3.3) & (2.7) & (1.0) & (3.2) \end{array}$

$$N = 55 \qquad R^2 = .51$$

(7B) $\quad CE = \begin{array}{llllll} 114 & -3.7\ln P & -.009Y & -2.1H & -0.6Z \\ (8.4) & (2.6) & (3.1) & (0.4) & (2.5) \end{array}$

$$N = 43 \qquad R^2 = .52$$

(7C) $\quad CC = \begin{array}{llll} 118 & -4.1\ln P & -.014Y & +1.5H \\ (7.3) & (2.2) & (4.2) & (0.3) \end{array}$

$$N = 37 \qquad R^2 = .50$$

(7D) $\quad CV = \begin{array}{llll} 135 & -6.4\ln P & -.020Y & -0.3H \\ (6.3) & (2.7) & (5.1) & (0.0) \end{array}$

$$N = 28 \qquad R^2 = .65$$

(8A) $\quad C = \begin{array}{lllll} 99 & -1.4\ln P & -.006Y & -12.5S & -0.6Z \\ (10.6) & (1.3) & (3.1) & (3.4) & (4.2) \end{array}$

$$N = 50 \qquad R^2 = .58$$

(8B) $\quad CE = \begin{array}{lllll} 94 & -1.4\ln P & -.008Y & -17.5S & -0.7Z \\ (6.5) & (0.9) & (2.8) & (2.9) & (3.1) \end{array}$

$$N = 40 \qquad R^2 = .55$$

(8C) $\quad CC = \begin{array}{llll} 110 & -3.4\ln P & -.012Y & -8.3S \\ (6.1) & (1.7) & (3.6) & (1.2) \end{array}$

$$N = 34 \qquad R^2 = .44$$

(8D) $\quad CV = \begin{array}{llll} 129 & -6.3\ln P & -.017Y & -4.1S \\ (5.5) & (2.5) & (4.0) & (0.5) \end{array}$

$$N = 26 \qquad R^2 = .56$$

(9A) $\quad C = \begin{array}{lllll} 96 & -1.2\ln P & -.004Y & -15.9F & -0.6Z \\ (12.0) & (1.3) & (2.3) & (4.7) & (5.5) \end{array}$

$$N = 58 \qquad R^2 = .65$$

(9B) $\quad CE = \begin{array}{lllll} 102 & -2.2\ln P & -.007Y & -14.3F & -0.7Z \\ (8.3) & (1.6) & (2.6) & (2.7) & (3.5) \end{array}$

$$N = 44 \qquad R^2 = .59$$

(9C)
$$CC = 112 - 3.4 \ln P - .011Y - 14.1F$$
$$(7.4) \quad (1.9) \qquad (3.5) \qquad (2.2)$$
$$N = 38 \qquad R^2 = .55$$

(9D)
$$CV = 127 - 5.6 \ln P - .017Y - 14.1F$$
$$(6.3) \quad (2.5) \qquad (4.4) \qquad (1.8)$$
$$N = 29 \qquad R^2 = .67$$

(10A)
$$G = 49 - 0.33C$$
$$(6.7) \quad (3.4)$$
$$N = 57 \qquad R^2 = .17$$

(10B)
$$G = 48 - 0.32CE$$
$$(8.9) \quad (4.0)$$
$$N = 43 \qquad R^2 = .28$$

(10C)
$$G = 46 - 0.27CC$$
$$(7.1) \quad (3.0)$$
$$N = 38 \qquad R^2 = .20$$

(10D)
$$G = 40 - 0.19CV$$
$$(8.7) \quad (2.5)$$
$$N = 29 \qquad R^2 = .19$$

(12A)
$$G = 21 + .011Y - .06C$$
$$(2.9) \quad (6.2) \qquad (0.7)$$
$$N = 57 \qquad R^2 = .52$$

(12B)
$$G = 26 + .009Y - 0.1CE$$
$$(4.3) \quad (4.7) \qquad (1.5)$$
$$N = 43 \qquad R^2 = .54$$

(12C)
$$G = 17 + .011Y - .00CC$$
$$(2.1) \quad (4.5) \qquad (0.0)$$
$$N = 38 \qquad R^2 = .49$$

(12D)
$$G = 19 + .009Y + .01CV$$
$$(2.5) \quad (3.2) \qquad (0.1)$$
$$N = 29 \qquad R^2 = .41$$

Chapter six
The dynamics of federalism

*I am of the opinion that, in the democratic ages which
are opening upon us . . . centralization will be the
natural government*

> Alexis de Tocqueville, DEMOCRACY IN AMERICA

The epoch of federalism is over

> Harold Laski, THE NEW REPUBLIC (May 3, 1939)

The analysis to this point has concerned the division of fiscal
functions among levels of government under a given set of
conditions. I have argued, for example, that the optimal degree
of fiscal centralization, other things equal at some point in
time, will tend to vary inversely with the extent of interjurisdictional differences in levels of demand for potential local
public services. There remains, however, the issue of trends in
multilevel finance over time. As conditions change we would
expect the degree of fiscal centralization corresponding to the
most effective organization of the public sector to vary.

The problem here is whether or not there is much of a systematic nature to be said about the evolution of intergovernmental fiscal relations over time. Some students of the subject
have concluded, for example, that the public sector can be
expected to exhibit temporal tendencies toward increasing
centralization. As regards the federal form of government in
particular, Edward McWhinney cites what he calls " 'Bryce's
Law'—the proposition that federalism is simply a transitory

step on the way to governmental unity." [1] This position implies that federalism is basically an unstable form of government, that it represents part of a process of adjustment leading to the establishment of a unitary system. Or, in terms of our economic definition of federalism, this view suggests that, over time, public sectors will move in the direction of greater centralization in the provision of public services. To get at this issue, it will prove useful first to return to the theoretical structure we have developed earlier and see if from that framework we can derive any hints as to the likely course of multilevel finance over time. After expanding this treatment to include some additional arguments suggested by others, we shall turn to an examination of the historical trends in federal finance.

Dynamic tendencies in fiscal federalism

In the course of development through time, particularly in the process of industrialization and modernization, the economic and social structure of a country typically changes in ways that appear to have important implications for the organization and functioning of the public sector. Three aspects of this process are of special significance here: improved transportation facilities, more effective systems of communication, and a rising level of per-capita income. All three of these developments promote both a more widespread knowledge of conditions throughout the country and an increasing ability to respond to these conditions. As a result we would expect to find

[1] *Comparative Federalism*, 2nd ed. (Toronto: University of Toronto Press, 1965), p. 105. Although McWhinney associates Lord Bryce with the proposition that federal systems tend to become more highly centralized over time, this does appear, from what I have been able to determine, to misrepresent somewhat his true position on this issue. Bryce did note a tendency toward centralization in the United States during the nineteenth century in his monumental *The American Commonwealth* (New York: Macmillan, 1896) (see ch. 35). In his more general treatments of this issue, however, he suggests that there are both "centripetal" and "centrifugal" forces present within a federal system and that it is generally impossible to tell which set of forces will prove the stronger during future periods. See Bryce's *Studies in History and Jurisprudence*, "The Action of Centripetal and Centrifugal Forces on Political Constitutions" (New York: Macmillan, 1901).

over time a rising level of intranational mobility, a phenomenon likely to result in many pressures on the structure of the government sector of the economy.

The most basic determinant of the proper level of government to provide a particular public service is the geographical pattern of the effects of the output. It is quite likely for a number of services that increasing mobility will extend the spatial boundaries of the costs and benefits associated with the local consumption of a given service. This is especially true, as George Break has stressed recently, for public programs that influence the formation of human capital.[2] As mobility within a nation increases, the educational system in one area, for example, comes to have a greater impact on the welfare of those in other communities, since many of those educated within the locality will eventually live elsewhere. In an empirical study of the external effects of public education in the United States, Burton Weisbrod found:

> Whereas public primary and secondary education have been considered traditionally as matters to be dealt with locally according to the preferences of each community, we have found that the effects of these local decisions permeate the entire society. Population mobility and fiscal interdependence make education decisions in one part of the nation important to other, even distant, parts.[3]

For this reason, one would expect over time a growing role for the central government in the provision of public services that affect the development of human capital. This could take the form of either direct provision of the service by the central government or, perhaps more likely, the use of fiscal instruments, such as conditional grants, to stimulate local levels of activity on such programs.

We also noted earlier the sorts of constraints the mobility of economic units imposes on the fiscal activities of decentralized governments. In particular, higher degrees of mobility are likely to make it increasingly necessary to centralize re-

[2] "Changing Roles of Different Levels of Government," in Julius Margolis, ed., *The Analysis of Public Output*, National Bureau of Economic Research Conference (New York: Columbia University Press, 1970), pp. 163–209.
[3] *External Benefits of Public Education* (Princeton, N.J.: Princeton University, Industrial Relations Section, 1964), p. 117.

223

distributive fiscal programs. It seems to be the case, moreover, that the desire for redistributive programs rises with the level of per-capita income; wealthier countries typically do, at any rate, devote a much larger fraction of their public expenditures to transfer payments than do poorer nations.[4] This may reflect to some extent the capability of a relatively affluent society to eliminate the extremes of poverty, a capacity the less developed countries usually do not possess. Poverty in the midst of affluence is, moreover, likely to constitute a blight on the conscience of society and therefore to induce a greater willingness to engage in redistributive activities. For these reasons development over time is likely to bring with it both a rising level of redistributive payments and an increasing degree of centralization of such programs.

Closely related to these first two centralizing forces (and strongly emphasized by a number of authors) are growing pressures for improved levels of services in poorer areas.[5] Increasing knowledge and wealth call attention to glaring instances of substandard public services. As mentioned above, such deficiencies may in many cases impose real external costs on the residents of other jurisdictions. Consequently, there are likely to be pressures on central governments to assist, perhaps through programs of equalizing grants, poorer areas in providing satisfactory levels of key public services.[6]

The general point here is that the growing knowledge, mobility, and wealth that accompany economic development tend to reduce the scope for independent budgetary policies by decentralized levels of government. Local public officials find over

---

[4] Using IBRD data and a sample of fifty-five countries, a regression of the percent of general government current expenditures devoted to "transfers to households and nonprofit institutions" on per-capita gross domestic output yielded a significant and positive relationship between the two variables. The precise relationship was:

$$TR = 15 + .01\,Y$$
$$(7.3)\ (5.2)$$
$$R^2 = .34$$

with $N = 55$.

[5] See, for example, R. J. May, *Federalism and Fiscal Adjustment* (London: Clarendon Press, 1969).

[6] As discussed in Chapter Three, pressures of this kind in Australia, Canada, and, more recently, in the United States have in fact led to equalizing grants to decentralized levels of government.

time that they become less insulated from the policies adopted in other localities; to an increasingly greater degree they must take into account the impact their decisions will have on the inflow and outflow of economic units and business investment and on the well-being of their residents relative to those elsewhere. This suggests, first, that the inefficiencies, or excess burden, associated with varying local tax structures are likely to become accentuated over time. Second, public officials are likely to become increasingly sensitive to tax competition among jurisdictions, which, it has been suggested, will tend to result in less than efficient levels of output of local public services. All this points to a growing role for the central government in raising public revenues; since the inefficiencies associated with decentralized taxation may become magnified over time, it will become increasingly attractive for the central government to undertake a larger part of the function of taxation and to supply decentralized levels of government with funds through programs of intergovernmental grants.

Finally, it is also possible that technical progress over time will permit more effective centralized provision of some public services so that previously nonexistent economies of scale will come into being. Improved techniques in the construction and operation of dams, for example, made it desirable to shift the primary responsibility for flood control away from systems of locally provided levies to government agencies responsive to the interests of all parties affected by a particular system of rivers. To some extent improvements in transportation and communications systems may make it more feasible to exercise effective supervision and direction over operations covering larger areas and more persons.

What all this implies is that there may exist a formidable set of forces operating through time that promote an increasing degree of centralization within the public sector. What will be the likely form of this process of centralization? Alan Peacock and Jack Wiseman, on the basis of their study of the public finances in Great Britain, have suggested that the process will in all probability not be a smooth, continuous one.[7] Both the relative size and the structure of government, they contend, are

[7] *The Growth of Public Expenditures in the United Kingdom* (Princeton, N.J.: National Bureau of Economic Research, 1961).

likely to undergo little change through periods "when societies are not being subjected to unusually violent pressures or disturbances." [8] However, when major social crises arise, such as wars or serious depressions, there is likely to be a "displacement effect." By this Peacock and Wiseman mean that people will be willing to accept a much larger role for government than in normal times. Following such a period, the size of the public budget may fall somewhat but is unlikely to return to its previous level. The point is that, during such crises, governments will tend to take on additional responsibilities, some of which they are likely to retain following the period of turmoil. While a displacement effect does not itself imply increased fiscal centralization, Peacock and Wiseman suggest that "we should expect to find some relation (though not a precise or straightforward one) between the two." [9] Social disturbances, such as wars, typically magnify the relative importance of the central government and weaken the strength of local autonomy. We should not be surprised, therefore, to find that displacement effects typically result in a higher degree of centralization within the public sector. Kenneth C. Wheare seems to some extent to share this view. Writing at the conclusion of World War II, he argued:

> War and economic depression unavoidably produce an increase in the powers of general governments. If federations are to survive these crises successfully they must submit to a large measure of unitary control while the crises last. The price of victory in war and the price of economic recovery is at least temporary unification. Consequently war, or power politics, and economic crisis, or depression politics, are the enemies of federal government. Peace and prosperity are in truth prerequisites for the successful working of federal government. It may be said, therefore, that if wars and economic crises are to recur frequently the prospect is that federal government will not survive for long.[10]

Kjeld Philip, who also sees the development of the public sector as involving an increasing degree of centralization, sug-

[8] *Ibid.*, p. 26.
[9] *Ibid.*, p. 30.
[10] *Federal Government*, 4th ed. (London: Oxford University Press), p. 239.

gests a typical pattern for this process.[11] Philip distinguishes between three phases of public activity: administration, legislation, and finance; and contends that, as regards a particular public function, the centralization of each phase may well come at a different time. In particular, centralization of finance is likely to precede a major role for the central government in the other two phases. The most painful aspect of providing any public service is raising the funds to support it; as a result, decentralized levels of government will be least resistant to assistance from the central government in the area of funding. Sooner or later, however, controls are likely to accompany central funds: "State grants can be used as a battering-ram, which will enable the state [central government] after a time to capture the management and administration also." [12] Following its movement into the phase of financing a function, Philip thus suggests that the central government is likely to begin imposing controls on the use of these funds perhaps in the form of legislative guidelines. Even after the central government has assumed the responsibility for funding and for major policy decisions regarding the provision of the service, the actual administration of the function within each jurisdiction may remain, perhaps permanently, decentralized. Philip's view of the process of centralization is therefore one in which the central government accepts the responsibility for funding part of a local public service and then uses this role to gain increasing control over decisions concerning the provision of the service and, perhaps, ultimately acquires the actual job of administration of the service.

The view developed thus far is one of the likelihood of increasing centralization in the public sector over time. This is not, however, to be interpreted too inflexibly. None of the authors whose views have been discussed above would subscribe to a rigid interpretation of the position I have attributed to him; none, for instance, would regard a process of centralization as inevitable in the case of every country. Nevertheless, they do see a trend toward the growing centralization of government as the typical case. While not inevitable, there are, they would contend, good reasons for expecting an expansion

[11] *Intergovernmental Fiscal Relations* (Copenhagen: University of Copenhagen, 1954).
[12] *Ibid.*, p. 99.

227

over time in the relative importance of the central government within the public sector.

The earlier theoretical discussion does suggest, however, that, arrayed against these centralizing forces are at least two factors that should work in the opposite direction. First, I have argued that the potential welfare gains, and hence the incentives, for decentralized finance are enhanced by the congregation of individuals with similar tastes for public services. Such groupings of consumers should be encouraged by the growing mobility within a developing society. The Tiebout model discussed in Chapter Two (wherein we assumed consumers locate according to their preferences for levels of output of public services and thus strengthen the case for local finance) would appear far more applicable to an industrialized, affluent society characterized by a mobility of economic units of the kind that constitutes the adjustment mechanism in the model. The idea here is that over time the increasing mobility of individuals should facilitate the formation of jurisdictions composed of individuals with similar tastes for public services. To the extent that this is true, we would expect over time a continued or growing desire to provide certain public services at more decentralized levels of government.

There may, however, be an additional consideration which at least partially offsets this tendency: a growing homogeneity of individual tastes and perhaps income levels. One effect of improved systems of communication and transportation is to make the same sorts of information more widely available. As a result of this (particularly of the association with the same mass media), there may exist a tendency toward greater similarities in tastes for public services. To the extent that this is reinforced by an increasing equality in the distribution of income (a typical characteristic of economic and social development), one might expect individual demands for public services to become more homogeneous over time. This would tend to reduce the potential gains from decentralized finance and would therefore offset at least some of the welfare gains arising out of geographical groupings of those with similar demands.

A second possible force operating in favor of greater decentralization over time stems directly from increasing income. As discussed earlier, extensive decentralization of government can be expensive, especially in terms of manpower. For a country at an early stage of economic and social development with relatively low levels of income and education, extensive decentralization may simply be too costly to be worthwhile—particularly in terms of spreading thin a relatively small supply of administrative talent. As income and the general levels of skills rise over time, a more decentralized organization of the public sector may become appropriate. To some extent this may explain why the cross-sectional study in the preceding chapter found a strong inverse relationship between the level of per-capita income and the degree of fiscal centralization.

There is, moreover, some reason to be uneasy over the process of centralization outlined by Philip. In particular, it is far from clear that a larger role for the central government in raising revenues will typically lead to a later shift of expenditure functions to the central level. In fact, just the opposite may well be true; grants may permit decentralized levels of government to perform more satisfactorily, thereby slowing (or perhaps even stopping) a shift of functions to the central government. This is especially true where the grants are of an unconditional form so that the central government has little control over their use. However, even where the grants are conditional, they may frequently (as discussed in Chapter Three) constrain the recipient very little, since the local government may be able to redirect the use of its own funds in such a way as to nullify the attempts of the grantor to influence the locality's pattern of expenditures.

There do exist, therefore, some forces that over the course of time are likely to run counter to those inducing greater centralization in the public sector. For this reason it is extremely difficult to reach any firm conclusions concerning dynamic tendencies in fiscal federalism. The weight of the arguments, particularly the crucial phenomenon of growing interdependency over time, creates, I think, a presumption in favor of centralizing tendencies. This is, however, far from certain, and it would not be surprising to find that over some periods the trend has been toward greater fiscal centralization, while at other times the public sector was in the process of becoming more decentralized. To try to illuminate this matter further, we turn next to an examination of the actual historical trends in the extent of the centralization of public finances.

Historical tendencies in
fiscal centralization

An examination of what information we have on the history of fiscal centralization suggests that it is extremely difficult to generalize on this matter. The experience among countries and at varying times within the same country has in many instances been quite different. One's results, moreover, depend to some extent on the particular definition of fiscal centralization adopted—that is, whether the centralization ratio is defined as the central government's share of revenues or, alternatively, of public expenditures.

At the risk of oversimplification, however, there do seem to be some reasonably broad trends in the experience of a substantial number of countries during the present century.[13] Over the first half of the twentieth century, the overall trend in most countries appears to have been toward increased centralization of both public expenditures and revenues. It is interesting that this tendency is present in federal and nonfederal countries alike. In the United States, for example, we find that the federal government's share of direct public expenditures rose from 34 percent in 1902 to 60 percent in 1950; and the federal share of general revenues increased from 40 percent in 1902 to 68 percent in 1950.[14] The Australian experience has been similar to that in the United States. B. U. Ratchford, for example, found that the fiscal centralization ratio for Australia rose rapidly from 35 percent in 1928 and 1929 to 68 percent in 1949 and 1950, measured on a revenue basis, and from 28 percent to 52 percent in these same years when measured on an expenditure basis.[15] Pryor's work indicates that, in a third federal country, Canada, the degree of fiscal centralization was also increasing significantly over the first half of this century.[16]

[13] Among those countries for which he was able to obtain data, Frederic Pryor found "no pattern" in the movements of fiscal centralization ratios in the nineteenth century. See his *Public Expenditures in Communist and Capitalist Nations* (Homewood, Ill.: Richard D. Irwin, 1968), p. 73.
[14] The data for these calculations came from *Historical Statistics of the United States, Colonial Times to 1957*, series Y385, Y413, Y447, and Y493 (Washington, D.C.: United States Bureau of the Census, 1961).
[15] *Public Expenditures in Australia* (Durham, N.C.: Duke University Press, 1959), p. 225.
[16] *Public Expenditures in Communist and Capitalist Nations*, p. 72.

Some nonfederal countries exhibited the same tendency. Peacock and Wiseman have found a growing degree of fiscal centralization in the United Kingdom during the first half of the present century. More precisely, they have estimated that from 1910 to 1951 the share of the central government in public expenditures increased from 52 percent to 77 percent.[17] Rising fiscal centralization was also the experience of France and Germany over most of this period.[18]

Among the primary sources of this growth in the relative role of the central government seems to have been a rapid growth in transfer payments (which for reasons discussed earlier are typically relatively highly centralized) and, in some cases, a significant increase in the fraction of national resources directed into national defense. In the case of the United Kingdom, for example, J. Veverka has found:

> The majority of transfers are central government expenditure, whether it be national debt payments or social insurance transfers. Although the transfer payments are with the exception of the national debt connected with the central government, any large scale redistribution through governmental transfers must necessarily be through the central government as local authorities collect revenue in a limited territory. Thus the increasing importance of local expenditure in the nineteenth century brought about a growing share of direct spending of revenue by governmental agencies, which reached over 80 per cent around the turn of the century. The reversal of the trend since then is reflected in a faster increase in transfer payments.[19]

Pryor's impressions based on his study of centralization tendencies in several countries suggest that the experience of the United Kingdom is not atypical; in particular, Pryor notes that "the increasing relative importance of social security expenditures" has been an important force underlying the increasing degree of fiscal centralization.[20]

---

[17] *The Growth of Public Expenditures in the United Kingdom*, p. 107.
[18] Pryor, *Public Expenditures in Communist and Capitalist Nations*, p. 72.
[19] "The Growth of Government Expenditures in the United Kingdom Since 1790," *Scottish Journal of Political Economy*, vol. 10 (Feb., 1963), p. 120.
[20] *Public Expenditures in Communist and Capitalist Nations*, p. 77.

All this is probably not very surprising to most; we have come to accept a trend toward an increasing centralization of the public sector as a normal, if not inevitable, state of affairs. From this perspective, it does come as somewhat more of a surprise to find that in the years since 1950 this trend has in most countries reversed itself. An examination of the data source described in Chapter Five (that is, the *World Tables* of the IBRD) reveals that since 1950 fiscal centralization ratios in the great majority of countries have declined, in some instances quite significantly. Table 6-1, for example, displays for both 1950 and 1965 the central government's share in public current expenditures for all those countries for which the IBRD was able to assemble this information.[21]

TABLE 6-1
Central government share in general government current expenditure

COUNTRY	1950	1965
Australia	79.9	69.9
Austria	56.8	45.8
Canada	54.7	43.7
Finland	67.1	53.5
West Germany	29.5	26.6
Greece	79.0	58.9
Italy	57.9	43.8
New Zealand	86.7	82.2
Norway	66.2	69.6
South Africa	55.9	60.5
Sweden	52.6	43.3
Switzerland	31.4	22.3
United Kingdom	71.9	57.5
United States	52.7	57.1
Zambia	96.9	92.1

The table indicates that, with the exception of Norway, South Africa, and the United States, the centralization of public expenditures within these fifteen countries has declined. The IBRD figures for the United States appear, moreover, to be

[21] See *World Table*, no. 6, col. 14.

rather misleading. Using a variety of definitions of the centralization ratio (including measures based in some cases on the central government's share of expenditures and in other instances on its share of revenues), George Break has found that, regardless of the definition he employed, the degree of fiscal centralization in the United States declined between 1948 and 1966.[22]

Why has the trend in multilevel finance reversed itself since 1950 and proceeded in the direction of greater decentralization? The earlier discussion may suggest part of the answer; while disorder and turmoil have certainly not been absent over this period, it has not been a time of major wars or serious, widespread economic depressions. The two world wars and the Great Depression that marred the first half of the century provided, as Peacock and Wiseman and as Wheare have argued, a profound stimulus to increased economic activity on the part of the central government. Comparable stimuli have probably been lacking over the years from 1950 to 1965.

There is, moreover, another reason to expect that expenditures by decentralized levels of government might grow more rapidly than those of the central government during times of more moderate change. This stems from the pressures on the cost side of the budget. William Baumol has argued (and there is some evidence to support this contention) that much of the rapid increase in spending by state and local governments in the United States is the result of increases in the *relative* costs per unit of output.[23] Many of the services provided by these governments are labor intensive in character and are frequently of a kind for which significant advances in productivity are difficult to come by. As a result rising wages and salaries throughout the economy translate themselves into higher unit costs for such public services; in manufacturing, in contrast, much of the rise in the cost of labor is offset by increases in productivity. This implies that the costs of providing these public services will tend to rise more rapidly than those in the rest of the economy. We have found, for example, that, over

[22] "Changing Roles of Different Levels of Government," p. 164.
[23] "Macroeconomics of Unbalanced Growth: The Anatomy of Urban Crisis," *American Economic Review*, vol. 57 (June, 1967), pp. 415–26. For an empirical study that finds some support for Baumol's position, see David F. Bradford, Richard A. Malt, and Wallace E. Oates, "The Rising Cost of Local Public Services: Some Evidence and Reflections," *National Tax Journal*, vol. 22 (June, 1969), pp. 185–202.

the period from 1947 to 1967 in the United States, the current cost per pupil-day in public elementary and secondary schools rose at an annual, compound rate of almost 7 percent, compared to an annual rise of only 1.4 percent of the wholesale price index over this same period.[24]

Furthermore, one might expect these sorts of cost pressures to be more intense on decentralized levels of government than on the central government, because a much larger fraction of the budget of the latter typically takes the form of transfer payments, for which these pressures are less important. Such increases in costs would for this reason tend to result, other things being equal, in a more rapid expansion in spending by local governments than by the central government. In the case of the United States, it does appear that one can explain a major portion of the postwar increase in expenditures by state and local government in terms of increased unit costs.

An additional striking feature of fiscal development in the twentieth century (one that has continued and, in several instances, accelerated since 1950) is a growing reliance on the use of intergovernmental grants. This phenomenon is again apparent in the experience both of federal countries and those that have not adopted (at least not formally) federal systems of government. The experience in the United States, for example, clearly fits this pattern. At the turn of the century, federal grants to state and local governments were negligible; in 1902 they amounted to only $7 million, which accounted for less than 1 percent of state and local revenues. By 1927 they had increased to $123 million but still amounted to only about 2 percent of state-local funds. By 1950, however, federal grants to decentralized levels of government had risen to $2.3 billion (11 percent of state-local receipts), and they have continued to expand rapidly, reaching a level of $24.4 billion (about 20 percent of state-local receipts) by 1970. And all indications are that this is a trend that is likely to continue in the United States for the foreseeable future.[25]

A similar trend, although one with a much greater emphasis on unconditional grants, has taken place in Australia. In 1939,

[24] Bradford, Malt, and Oates, "The Rising Cost of Local Public Services," p. 190.
[25] The data for the United States come from *Historical Statistics of the United States*, series Y517 and Y519, and from *The Economic Report of the President* (Feb., 1971), Table C-66.

for example, the tax revenues of the states from their own sources were over three times the 15.6 million pounds they received from the Commonwealth in the form of both conditional and unconditional payments; by 1955, however, Commonwealth payments to the states had risen to 202 million pounds, which was over twice as much as state tax revenues.[26] Table 6-2 indicates the experience of a nonfederal country, the

TABLE 6-2
Expenditures and grants in the United Kingdom
(millions of pounds)

	LOCAL GOVERNMENT EXPENDITURES	CENTRAL GOVERNMENT GRANTS	GRANTS AS A PERCENT OF LOCAL GOVERNMENT SPENDING
1900	65.4	19.9	30
1929	298.7	120.6	40
1950	656.0	337.0	51
1955	1,006.0	545.0	54

SOURCE Alan Peacock and Jack Wiseman, *The Growth of Public Expenditures in the United Kingdom* (Princeton, N.J.: National Bureau of Economic Research, 1961), p. 197. Reprinted by permission.

United Kingdom. Here again, intergovernmental grants have come to account for an increasingly large proportion of the receipts and expenditures of decentralized levels of government. The findings on Canada are a bit different in that federal payments to the provinces were of great importance from the outset. In 1868, the year following the Confederation, the provinces received 54 percent of their revenues in the form of payments from the federal government. Although these payments grew significantly in absolute size, they came to constitute a smaller fraction of provincial revenues in the early twentieth century, reaching a low of 9 percent in 1930. By 1950, however, federal payments to the provinces were up to $241 million (24 percent of provincial revenues) and by 1962 had reached $1,148 million (40 percent of the receipts of the provinces).[27]

[26] Ratchford, *Public Expenditures in Australia*, p. 222.
[27] For excellent historical information on Canadian finance, see A. Milton Moose and J. Harvey Perry, *The Financing of Canadian Federation*,

Philip and some others might regard the growing importance of intergovernmental grants as further evidence of growing fiscal centralization and, more particularly, as pointing to an eventual shift of additional expenditure functions from decentralized governments to the central level of government. As I have suggested earlier, I think that this is far too simplified a view of this issue and that grants may well allow state and local governments to perform more effectively, thereby allowing them to maintain or perhaps even to expand their range of expenditure functions.

There is no quantitative evidence to my knowledge on the Philip hypothesis that federal grants are an intermediate step on the way to a shift of the expenditure function to the central government. I have, however, made one cross-sectional study of state-local finance in the United States that did not reveal the presence of any such tendencies. The study consisted of an examination of the fiscal centralization ratios for each state (that is, state government expenditures as a percent of total state-local spending) for a number of functions for both 1957 and 1967.[28] The idea was to see if there was any relation between the change in the state's share of spending on a particular function during this decade and the level of grants from state to local government in 1957 (measured as a percent of local spending on a particular function over this decade). If Philip's contention were true, one might expect that, in those states where grants for a particular function were quite large, one would find in succeeding years a relatively large increase in the state's share of spending on this function. In a series of regression equations, however, the change in the degree of fiscal centralization was not in any instance significantly related to the percent of local spending in 1957 financed by grant funds. Among the states of the United States over this period, the use of grants would, therefore, not appear to have led to an increased role for the state government in the expenditure function. This evidence is obviously far from conclusive. The period under examination, a decade, is a brief one—perhaps too brief for such tendencies

---

Canadian Tax Foundation (Tax Paper 43), 1966. The figures presented here are from Table 29, pp. 119–20.
[28] More specifically, I used fiscal centralization ratios for total expenditures, general support, public welfare, health, hospitals, highways, and public schools.

to reveal themselves—and the data on expenditure functions are on a higher level of aggregation than is desirable. At any rate the results do not lend support either to the view that grants lead to a greater centralization of public expenditure or, conversely, that by increasing local funds they slow the upward shift of expenditure functions. A broader view of the historical trends in fiscal federalism suggests that intergovernmental grants have been an integral part of a process of growing joint responsibility among levels of government for providing a wide range of public services; as part of this process, grants have provided a means for sharing the costs of these programs.

The future of fiscal federalism

On balance, it does not seem that the evidence supports the contention that multilevel finance is merely a transitory stage in the movement to a system of unitary finance. Both formal analysis and recent historical trends indicate that, for the performance of certain functions, decentralized decision-making in the public sector has compelling advantages over wholly centralized control. This by no means suggests, however, that fiscal federalism is a static structure. Rather, as many political scientists have emphasized, federal systems (particularly in terms of fiscal organization) have changed very significantly over time; federalism has in fact proved to be a highly adaptable form of government.[29] This is true, incidentally, also of those governments that, although not possessing federal constitutions, are federal in the economic sense of placing some reliance on decentralized choice in the provision of public services.

Of particular interest here is the general direction this development of fiscal activities has taken toward an increasingly greater degree of shared responsibility in the provision of public services. The more traditional view of federal institutions is one in which the functions of the public sector are clearly divided among different levels of government that then proceed more or less independently to fulfill their responsi-

[29] See, for example, A. H. Birch, *Federalism, Finance, and Social Legislation* (Oxford, England: Clarendon Press, 1955); and Geoffrey F. Sawer, *Modern Federalism* (London: C. A. Watts, 1969).

bilities. Geoffrey Sawer has characterized this conception, or stage, as one of "co-ordinate federalism," [30] a view advanced elegantly by Lord Bryce, who argued that a federal system was "like a great factory wherein two sets of machinery are at work, their revolving wheels apparently intermixed, their bands crossing one another, yet each doing its own work without touching or hampering the other." [31]

While such complete independence of levels of government has never in fact existed in any federation, one can make a case that this view was perhaps not too far from the truth in the United States in its early history. What is clear, however, is that the historical development of fiscal structures has been away from this form of organization of the public sector and toward one in which different levels of government jointly perform the functions of government. Both Birch and Sawer, for example, suggest that we have moved into a new phase of federalism, one they call "co-operative federalism," in which the typical case is the joint provision of a public service by several cooperating levels of government.[32] This has led Morton Grodzins to characterize the United States federal system as a "marble" rather than a "layer cake." [33] Grodzins cites the example of a county health officer, who is appointed by the state government, paid jointly from state and federal funds, provided an office and assistants by the county, and who performs inspections and enforces regulations for all these levels of government. Similarly, one now finds almost continual cooperative activity among federal, state, and local authorities in the enforcement of criminal laws and the apprehension of criminals. In such an environment it becomes extremely difficult to draw sharp divisions among the responsibilities of different levels of government. As Wheare has observed concerning all federal countries:

> Powers are divided between general and regional governments in such a way that it is difficult to find any useful principle of comparison between the countries or, more bewildering still, to state with precision just where

[30] *Modern Federalism*, p. 64.
[31] *The American Commonwealth*, p. 325.
[32] Birch, *Federalism, Finance, and Social Legislation*, ch. 11; Sawer, *Modern Federalism*, ch. 8.
[33] "The Federal System," in the American Assembly, *Goals for Americans* (Englewood Cliffs, N.J.: Prentice-Hall, 1960), p. 265.

within any federation authority over a given topic may be said to lie.[34]

Economists directly concerned with public policy are well aware of this problem. Selma Mushkin and Robert Adams, for example, have emphasized that the relevant issue is no longer determining which level of government should provide a particular service, but rather seeking the *mix* of government participation that is likely to be the most effective.[35] This issue does, however, appear to raise real difficulties for a theoretical approach to the subject of fiscal federalism. In particular, the theorist is interested in drawing sharp lines between the operations of different levels of government; his theoretical models are likely to approach more closely Sawer's "co-ordinate," rather than the "co-operative," view of federalism.[36] As I mentioned earlier, economic tools of analysis are not (at least not yet) well suited for examining the effects of often relatively subtle alternatives in administrative organization.

If, however, the trend in multilevel fiscal activity is toward growing joint provision of public services, this would seem to suggest that economic theory is becoming increasingly irrelevant to the problems of fiscal federalism. A theory that makes sharp distinctions between the activities of different levels of government might appear ill-suited to the study of modern fiscal structures. It seems to me, however, that this is not at all true. Any view or model of a set of institutions and the way in which they function is an abstraction and as such involves simplification in an attempt to focus attention on the essential elements of the structure. Such abstractions, even though they may (and must) deviate to some extent from the actual structure of these institutions, may still be capable of providing valuable insights into the functioning of the system. It may still be the case, as I think it in fact is, that an admittedly rarified and highly simplified view of fiscal federalism has

[34] *Federal Government*, p. 126.
[35] "Emerging Patterns of Federalism," *National Tax Journal*, vol. 19 (Sept., 1966), pp. 225–47.
[36] The major exception to this proposition is the theorist's interest in intergovernmental grants, since grants might appear to be an institution more consistent with the "co-operative" concept of federalism. However, even here, grants are not viewed as a means of joint decision-making; rather, they serve to provide incentives for decentralized levels of government, which typically are assumed to act independently of one another and solely on behalf of their respective constituencies.

much to contribute to our understanding of the problems of the public sector.

The simplistic view of public redistributive activity advanced in earlier chapters is a case in point. A more involved examination of redistributive programs across different countries and over time would reveal a bewildering complexity of administrative and fiscal organization among levels of government—and it is not at all certain that such a detailed description would have added lessons for us. A more abstract and deliberately simplified approach to this issue does suggest in a very direct way some principles that are useful, I think, both in understanding to some extent the broad lines of historical development of transfer programs and in providing some guidelines for policy formulation in this area. In particular, the analysis suggests the difficulties inherent in undertaking substantial redistributive programs on the level of local finance; this both explains in part, for example, the current fiscal crisis of many large cities in the United States and points up the need for a greater role for federal government support of these types of programs. The analysis does not, however, have much to say about the most effective administrative structure. It may still be best, for example, that local authorities administer such programs even though they are financed primarily by the federal government. My point here is that the fact that the organization of multilevel finance is becoming more complex does not mean that simple, abstract approaches to the subject, involving sharper distinctions than one is likely to find in the real world, are less useful; on the contrary, the more complicated such systems become, the more important it is that we have models that allow us to see through some of the complexities.

In conclusion, the pattern of evolution of fiscal federalism toward a greater interdependence of levels of government does not point with any clarity to the eventual extinction of local finance; the prospect is that federal forms of finance with considerable reliance on decentralized fiscal decisions are likely to continue to be with us for the foreseeable future. There will probably be increased centralization in a number of areas; in particular, the analysis presented here points to a continued trend toward greater centralization of essentially redistributive programs. However, decentralized finance continues to promise important benefits in the provision of a substantial number of public services, and, for this reason (and because of the powerful vested interests in subcentral governments), decentralized levels of government should maintain an important role in the public sector. As Daniel Elazar puts it:

> In any federal system, it is likely that there will be continued tension between the federal government and the constituent polities over the years and that different "balances" between them will develop at different times. The existence of this tension is an integral part of the federal relationship, and its character does much to determine the future of federalism in each system.[37]

[37] "Federalism," *International Encyclopedia of the Social Sciences*, vol. 5 (New York: Macmillan, 1968), p. 360.

Data appendix

This appendix lists the sources of the data used in the cross-sectional, multiple-regression study in Chapter Five and for the regression equation reported in footnote 4 of Chapter Six. In addition, since many of the data come from sources to which some may not have ready access, I have provided a listing of the fifty-eight countries included in the study and the actual data for each of them.

The selection of the sample was itself dictated primarily by the availability of data. In particular, for figures on fiscal operations I have drawn heavily on the *World Tables*, a rich source of information that is assembled by the research staff of the Economic Program Department of the International Bank for Reconstruction and Development (IBRD). The IBRD has used both published United Nations data and figures provided through its own sources to compile the *World Tables*. Those who have worked with National Income and Product data from different countries, particularly many of the less developed nations, know of the often serious imperfections in these estimates. The only answer is that they are all that we have at the present time.

For sociological and political variables, I have relied mainly on Arthur S. Banks and Robert B. Textor, *A Cross-Polity Survey* (Cambridge, Mass.: M.I.T. Press, 1963). The authors classify a great many nations into an enormous number of historical, sociological, and political categories. While such classifications obviously involve some extremely difficult judgments (and the decisions in some cases would no doubt be quite controversial), the Banks-Textor printouts do provide information on a number of important variables in a form suitable for use with standard techniques of statistical analysis. For this reason it did seem worthwhile to try to incorporate this information into an econometric study of federalism.

TABLE A-1
Economic-fiscal variables

DESCRIPTION AND SOURCE

C = Central government share in general government current revenues expressed as a percentage (International Bank for Reconstruction and Development, *World Tables* [Dec., 1968], no. 6, col. 13, for 1964 or 1965 and, in a few instances, for 1960)

CE = Central government share in general government current expenditure expressed as a percentage (IBRD, *World Tables* [Dec., 1968], no. 6, col. 14, for 1964 or 1965 and, in a few instances, for 1960)

CC = Central government share in general government consumption expenditure expressed as a percentage (computed from data for 1965 in United Nations, *Yearbook of National Accounts Statistics* [1968], Table 8, line 8 and Table 9, line 9)

CV = Central government share in general government nondefense (civil) consumption expenditure expressed as a percentage (computed from data for 1965 in United Nations, *Yearbook of National Accounts Statistics,* [1968], Table 8, line 8A and Table 9, line 9A)

Z = Contributions to social security programs expressed as a percentage of general government current revenue (IBRD, *World Tables* [Dec., 1968], no. 6, col. 2, for 1964 or 1965)

G = Tax revenues as a percentage of national income (IBRD, *World Tables* [Dec., 1968], no. 3, col. 12, for 1964 or 1965)

TR = Transfers to households and nonprofit institutions as a percentage of general government current expenditures (IBRD, *World Tables* [Dec., 1968], no. 6, col. 10, for 1964 or 1965)

Y = Gross domestic product per capita in U.S. dollars for 1965 (United Nations, *Yearbook of National Accounts Statistics* [1967], Table 7B)

DATA

COUNTRY	C	CE	CC	CV	Z	G	TR	Y
1. Algeria	85.5	85.3	—*	—	8.2	23.1	12.8	218
2. Argentina	55.9	—	—	—	0	8.5	3.9	778
3. Australia	78.6	69.9	49.0	26.7	0	28.2	29.4	1,843
4. Austria	52.5	45.8	47.1	41.9	21.4	46.4	43.0	1,102
5. Belgium	64.2	61.3	78.2	71.8	28.7	36.6	41.4	1,583
6. Bolivia	71.3	68.2	77.5	72.7	16.2	14.5	18.6	154
7. Botswana	85.5	92.0	91.2	91.2	0	10.6	9.2	89
8. Brazil	55.1	37.7	—	—	14.2	32.7	32.1	230
9. Cameroon	73.4	61.5	—	—	0	—	—	126
10. Canada	51.3	43.7	38.7	20.5	6.0	36.3	32.7	2,155
11. Chile	72.3	—	—	—	31.7	28.0	38.4	493
12. Colombia	64.5	—	65.2	—	7.3	13.8	14.8	315
13. Denmark	72.1	41.6	—	—	6.1	37.4	32.4	2,070
14. Dominican Rep.	87.9	—	—	—	0	13.6	7.5	231
15. Ecuador	86.1	—	—	—	13.0	19.1	20.9	200
16. El Salvador	92.4	—	—	—	0	12.3	23.6	249
17. Finland	65.3	53.5	44.2	37.1	10.7	37.3	27.2	1,568
18. France	58.6	49.2	75.5	—	36.2	50.8	50.1	1,626
19. W. Germany	37.9	26.6	32.9	9.5	27.0	44.9	43.6	1,659
20. Greece	60.9	58.9	78.3	68.1	23.5	25.0	33.8	595
21. Guatemala	81.0	84.2	86.0	—	0	11.2	10.6	277
22. Honduras	83.7	—	91.5	—	0	12.5	1.5	209
23. Iceland	67.5	55.3	—	—	7.8	40.4	35.0	2,109
24. India	65.6	52.7	—	—	0	14.1	11.7	97
25. Ireland	80.4	65.2	58.3	53.4	6.0	31.3	25.0	815
26. Italy	56.7	43.8	68.8	62.0	31.8	36.7	43.1	974
27. Jamaica	95.8	86.4	84.8	—	0	20.2	14.7	465
28. Japan	71.3	60.7	41.5	35.0	16.1	24.6	29.7	803
29. Korea	81.9	67.7	65.7	43.6	0	10.0	9.0	107
30. Luxembourg	56.1	45.5	69.1	64.9	29.3	38.7	44.8	1,586
31. Malagasy Rep.	71.6	—	—	—	0	16.4	—	98
32. Malaysia	90.8	84.7	83.3	78.7	11.2	24.3	5.2	272
33. Mauritius	96.2	91.4	92.8	—	1.0	22.9	17.8	228
34. Mexico	66.2	—	—	—	0	7.1	37.0	441
35. Netherlands	62.8	29.0	41.5	23.3	30.7	45.8	41.9	1,394
36. New Zealand	90.9	82.2	73.8	69.1	0	30.5	27.1	1,867
37. Nicaragua	78.7	—	—	—	0	12.0	7.3	323
38. Nigeria	44.2	37.5	40.5	36.9	0	12.7	14.2	61
39. Norway	72.8	69.6	49.2	34.8	17.9	45.6	30.8	1,712
40. Pakistan	76.4	58.5	—	—	0	8.7	—	101
41. Panama	77.6	78.2	88.3	88.3	18.7	17.3	15.0	479
42. Paraguay	79.4	—	—	—	0	10.6	13.1	207

COUNTRY	C	CE	CC	CV	Z	G	TR	Y
43. Peru	86.7	—	—	—	9.0	18.8	22.6	253
44. Philippines	78.8	79.2	75.8	—	0	12.8	8.5	246
45. Portugal	70.4	77.4	89.4	78.0	20.1	21.9	20.0	371
46. Sierra Leone	90.5	90.8	86.4	—	0	14.1	23.5	142
47. So. Africa†	70.2	60.5	55.6	—	1.8	19.6	14.0	522
48. So. Rhodesia	86.6	77.2	87.4	85.4	0.6	15.5	17.8	232
49. Sweden	59.1	43.3	49.0	32.1	13.8	44.9	31.8	2,248
50. Switzerland	32.7	22.3	27.7	10.1	19.1	25.5	34.4	2,162
51. Thailand	93.7	97.2	—	—	0	14.9	15.7	117
52. Tunisia	84.9	84.5	90.4	89.4	7.3	27.9	13.3	187
53. United Kingdom	72.3	57.5	63.7	44.4	14.7	37.2	25.8	1,579
54. United States	59.3	57.1	53.6	21.5	15.7	33.4	20.8	3,240
55. Uruguay	56.7	—	—	—	49.0	31.0	39.8	559
56. Venezuela	91.1	—	—	—	0	20.0	7.9	917
57. Vietnam	91.0	91.8	93.5	81.8	0	12.2	2.8	119
58. Zambia	96.9	92.1	100.0	100.0	0	40.0	11.2	207

NOTE: In the few instances where social security contributions were not reported, I have assigned this variable a value of zero on the assumption that any such receipts were probably included in the revenues of the central government. Where social security contributions are reported, UN and IBRD accounting conventions exclude them from the revenues of the central government.

* Data not available.

† Includes South West Africa.

TABLE A-2
Demographic, sociological, and political variables

DESCRIPTION AND SOURCE

P = Populations in thousands in 1965 (United Nations, *Demographic Yearbook* [1967], Table 4)

A = Geographical size in thousands of square kilometers in 1965 (United Nations, *Demographic Yearbook* [1967], Table 2)

L = Dummy variable for degree of lingual homogeneity: 1 = lingual homogeneity, 0 = weak or strong lingual heterogeneity (Banks and Textor, *A Cross-Polity Survey*, printout 68)

R = Dummy variable for racial differences: 1 = racial homogeneity, 0 = racial heterogeneity (Banks and Textor, *A Cross-Polity Survey*, printout 67)

T = Dummy variable for differences in religion: 1 = religious homogeneity, 0 = religious heterogeneity (Banks and Textor, *A Cross-Polity Survey*, printout 66)

H = Dummy variable for differences in culture: 1 = cultural homogeneity (that is, if L, R, and T all equal unity), 0 = cultural heterogeneity (that is, if L, R, or T equals zero)

S = Dummy variable for strength of sectional or regional interests: 1 = strong sectional interests, 0 = moderate or negligible sectional interests (Banks and Textor, *A Cross-Polity Survey*, printout 113)

F = Dummy variable for federal form of government: 1 = federal government, 0 = nonfederal government (based on list of federal governments provided by Daniel J. Elazar in "Federalism," *International Encyclopedia of the Social Sciences,* vol. 5 [New York: Macmillan, 1968], p. 365)

COUNTRY	P	A	L	R	T	H	S	F
1. Algeria	11,923	2,382	0	1	1	0	0	0
2. Argentina	22,352	2,777	1	1	1	1	—*	1
3. Australia	11,333	7,687	1	1	0	0	0	1
4. Austria	7,255	84	1	1	1	1	0	1
5. Belgium	9,464	31	0	1	1	0	1	0
6. Bolivia	3,697	1,099	0	0	0	0	0	0
7. Botswana	559	600	0	1	0	0	—	0
8. Brazil	80,766	8,512	1	0	1	0	1	1
9. Cameroon	5,229	475	0	1	0	0	0	1
10. Canada	19,604	9,976	0	1	0	0	1	1
11. Chile	8,584	757	1	—	1	—	0	0
12. Colombia	18,020	1,139	1	0	1	0	1	0
13. Denmark	4,758	43	1	1	1	1	0	0
14. Dominican Rep.	3,624	49	1	0	1	0	0	0
15. Ecuador	5,150	284	0	0	0	0	1	0
16. El Salvador	2,928	21	1	0	1	0	0	0
17. Finland	4,612	337	0	1	1	0	0	0
18. France	48,919	547	1	1	1	1	0	0
19. W. Germany	56,839	248	1	1	0	0	0	1
20. Greece	8,551	132	1	1	1	1	0	0
21. Guatemala	4,438	109	0	0	0	0	0	0
22. Honduras	2,284	112	1	0	1	0	0	0
23. Iceland	192	103	1	1	1	1	0	0
24. India	486,811	3,268	0	1	1	0	1	1
25. Ireland	2,876	70	1	1	1	1	0	0
26. Italy	51,576	301	1	1	1	1	0	0
27. Jamaica	1,791	11	1	0	0	0	0	0
28. Japan	97,960	370	1	1	0	0	0	0
29. Korea	28,377	98	1	1	—	—	0	0
30. Luxembourg	331	3	1	1	1	1	0	0
31. Malagasy Rep.	6,200	587	1	—	0	0	1	0
32. Malaysia	8,039	131	0	0	0	0	0	1
33. Mauritius	741	2	0	0	0	0	—	0
34. Mexico	42,689	1,973	1	0	1	0	—	1
35. Netherlands	12,292	34	1	1	0	0	0	0
36. New Zealand	2,640	269	1	1	0	0	0	0
37. Nicaragua	1,655	130	1	0	1	0	—	0
38. Nigeria	58,000	924	0	1	0	0	1	1
39. Norway	3,723	324	1	1	1	1	0	0
40. Pakistan	102,876	947	0	1	1	0	1	0
41. Panama	1,246	76	0	0	1	0	0	0
42. Paraguay	2,030	407	1	—	1	—	0	0

COUNTRY	P	A	L	R	T	H	S	F
43. Peru	11,650	1,285	0	0	0	0	0	0
44. Philippines	32,345	300	0	1	1	0	0	0
45. Portugal	9,234	92	1	1	1	1	0	0
46. Sierra Leone	2,367	72	0	1	0	0	0	0
47. So. Africa†	18,441	2,045	0	0	0	0	0	0
48. So. Rhodesia	4,260	389	0	0	0	0	—	0
49. Sweden	7,734	450	1	1	1	1	0	0
50. Switzerland	5,945	41	0	1	0	0	1	1
51. Thailand	30,744	514	0	1	1	0	0	0
52. Tunisia	4,360	164	1	1	1	1	0	0
53. United Kingdom	54,436	244	1	1	0	0	1	0
54. United States	194,592	9,363	1	0	0	0	0	1
55. Uruguay	2,715	187	1	1	1	1	—	0
56. Venezuela	8,722	912	1	0	1	0	0	0
57. Vietnam	16,124	171	0	1	—	0	0	0
58. Zambia	3,714	753	0	1	0	0	—	0

NOTE: The Banks and Textor survey did not include Botswana, Mauritius, So. Rhodesia, or Zambia. Where possible, I used other sources to determine the appropriate values for L, R, T, H, and S.

* Data not available or not classified by Banks and Textor.
† Includes South West Africa.

Index

Adams, Robert, 239

Advisory Commission on Intergovernmental Relations, 87n, 91

Ahiram, E., 202n

Arnold, David, 177n

Auld, D. A. L., 189

Australia
  centralization trends in, 230, 232
  geographical size and centralization of, 182n
  stabilization policy for income and employment in, 188–90
  use of intergovernmental grants in, 86, 151, 224n, 234–35

Banks, Arthur, 202, 203n, 205, 206n, 207, 243

Barzel, Yoram, 36n, 42n, 54, 54n, 59n, 201

Baumol, William, 25n, 44n, 70n, 162n, 233

Beck, Morris, 168n

Bickerdike, C. F., 165

Birch, A. H., 194n, 213n, 237n, 238

Bishop, George, 91n, 191n

Black, Duncan, 110n

Boyle, Lawrence, 194n

Bradford, David, 105n, 162n, 233n, 234n

Brainard, William, 103n

Break, George, 89n, 223, 233

Breton, Albert, 34n

Brown, E. Cary, 184n

Bryce, Lord, 222n, 238

Bryce's Law, 221

Buchanan, James, 5n, 8n, 47n, 51, 52n, 68n, 70, 70n, 82, 83n, 84, 84n, 85, 96n, 103n, 117n, 123, 123n

Cameron, Burgess, 190n

Canada
  centralization trends in, 230, 232
  formation of federal system in, 182
  incidence of taxes in, 192–93
  stabilization policy for income and output, 187–89
  use of intergovernmental grants in, 86, 151, 224n, 235

Capital budgets, 160

Centralization of government
  changes over time, 221–41
  econometric study of, 195–219
  economic advantages of, 4–11
  economic disadvantages of, 11–13
  future trends in, 237–41
  measurement of, 19n, 196–99
  political considerations of, 15n
  and size of public sector, 209–12

251

Millhouse, A. M., 160n
Miner, Jerry, 91n
Moose, A. Milton, 235n
Mundell, Robert, 30n
Musgrave, Richard, 9n, 14n, 73n,
  82, 82n, 84, 84n, 90, 90n,
  119, 119n, 125n, 132n, 137n,
  146, 153n, 154n, 158, 185n,
  191n, 196
Mushkin, Selma, 87, 239

Netzer, Dick, 14n, 162n
Nolting, Orin, 177n

Oates, Wallace, 14n, 21n, 22n,
  27n, 30n, 41n, 92n, 105n,
  129n, 137n, 157n, 161n,
  189n, 233n, 234n
Okun, Arthur, 186n
Olson, Mancur, 9, 35n, 47n, 101
Orr, Larry, 137n
Osman, Jack, 91n
Ostrom, Vincent, 35n, 45n
Ott, David, 158n

Peacock, Alan, 225–26, 231, 233,
  235
Pennock, J. Roland, 36n
Penny, W., 194n
Perloff, Harvey, 5, 14n, 44n, 90n,
  150, 184–85
Perry, J. Harvey, 235n
Philip, Kjeld, 195n, 226–27, 229,
  236
Pigou, A. C., 66
Pogue, Thomas, 161n
Preston, Maurice, 25n
Pryor, Frederic, 192, 197, 200n,
  204n, 230, 230n, 231
Public goods
  and optimal-sized jurisdiction.
  See Jurisdictions

and perfect correspondence,
  33–38
provision of, by central governments, 8–10, 31–32
provision of, by decentralized
  governments, 8–13
provision versus production of,
  45

Quandt, Richard, 134n

Rafuse, Robert, 184–85
Ratchford, B. U., 230
Redistribution of income
  in Canada, 192–93
  centralization of, 190–95
  by negative income-tax, 6–7
  role of central governments in,
    6–8, 31–33
  role of decentralized govern-
    ments in, 6–8
  in the United States, 191–92
Renshaw, Edward, 91n
Revenue sharing
  as equivalent to federal tax-
    cuts to individuals, 111–12
  and reduction of decentralized
    taxation, 149–53
Ridker, Ronald, 173n
Robinson, T. R., 189

Sacks, Seymour, 91n
Samuelson, Paul, 8n, 34n
Sawer, Geoffrey, 16n, 237n, 238,
  239
Schaller, Howard, 88
Scott, Anthony, 83n, 84, 84n
Shoup, Carl, 42n
Sills, David L., 15n
Simon, Herbert, 164n
Stabilization of income and em-
  ployment

Weisbrod, Burton, 46, 88, 223
Wheare, Kenneth, 15, 15n, 16, 16n, 65, 90n, 204–05, 226, 233, 238
Whinston, Andrew, 102n
Wildavsky, Aaron, 182n
Wilde, James, 75n, 77n, 89n

Williams, Alan, 103n
Wingo, Lowdon, 14n, 44n
Wiseman, Jack, 225–26, 231, 233, 235

Zeckhauser, Richard, 9, 101

A 2
B 3
C 4
D 5
E 6
F 7
G 8
H 9
I 0
J 1